D0393763

LONDONISTAN

LONDONISTAN

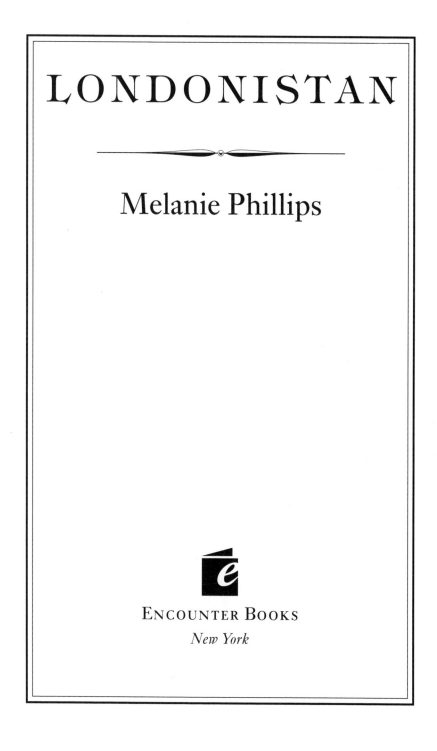

Melanie Phillips

ENCOUNTER BOOKS

New York

First edition published in 2006 by Encounter Books, an activity of Encounter for Culture and Education, Inc., a nonprofit, tax exempt corporation.

Encounter Books website address: www.encounterbooks.com

Manufactured in the United States and printed on acid-free paper. The paper used in this publication meets the minimum requirements of ANSI/NISO Z39.48-1992 (R 1997)(*Permanence of Paper*).

FIRST EDITION

LIBRARY OF CONGRESS CATALOGING-IN-PUBLICATION DATA
Phillips, Melanie
    Londonistan/Melanie Phillips
        p.   cm.
    ISBN 1-59403-144-4
    1.Terrorism—Great Britain 2.Terrorism—Government policy—Great Britain
3. Muslims—Great Britain 4.Terrorism—Religious aspects—Islam 5. London
Terrorist Bombings, London, England, 2005
HV6433.G7 P55 2006
363.3250941 22

                                                        2006007865

10 9 8 7 6 5 4 3 2 1

CONTENTS

———◈◈◈———

INTRODUCTION

It was what Britain had dreaded ever since 9/11. At shortly before
nine in the morning on July 7, 2005, bombs went off almost simultaneously in three London Underground trains deep below the
streets of the capital. Soon afterwards, a fourth bomb blew a red London bus to bits as it trundled through a leafy Bloomsbury square.

The carnage was horrific, particularly in the Tube trains underground. As the gruesome task began of collecting the body parts from
the wrecked trains and bus, and as the wounded emerged dazed and
weeping from the underground tunnels, a shocked Britain had to
confront the terrible fact that the appalling phenomenon of suicide
bombing had arrived on British soil.

Two weeks later, an almost identical attempt was made to blow up
commuters on the Tube and buses. This time—incredibly—all four
bombs failed to detonate. Now, though, the British public was even
more traumatized. It seemed that Britain was in for a campaign of mass
murder targeted at the public transit system, and that the security
that commuters had hitherto taken for granted had now, for the fore-
seeable future, disappeared.

From the moment the bombs went off, however, Britain sought
to deny their full implications. For it quickly became clear that the
bombers were all British. The realization that British boys would want
to murder their fellow citizens was bad enough. But the thought that
they would do so by using their own bodies as human bombs was a horror that people had assumed was confined to the mystifying passions

of the Middle East. So, for some time afterwards, Britain told itself these had not been suicide bombings. Eventually, it was proved beyond doubt that they had been. A shocking videotape surfaced in which the bombers' young leader, clad in an anorak and an Arab keffiyeh, calmly declared that suicide bombing was the only way to make Britain acknowledge Muslim grievances—all in a broad Yorkshire accent. There was now no getting away from the fact that British Muslims had turned themselves into human bombs to murder as many of their fellow citizens as possible.

It was only then that Britain belatedly acknowledged the lethal and many-headed hydra it had allowed to grow inside its own society. The attacks had been carried out by home-grown Muslim terrorists, sub-urban boys who had been educated at British schools and had degrees, jobs and comfortable families. Yet these British boys, who loved cricket and helped disabled children, had somehow been so radicalized within the British society that had nurtured them that they were prepared to murder their fellow citizens in huge numbers and to turn themselves into human bombs to do so.

3.3%

An appalling vista thus opened up for Britain, which houses around two million Muslim citizens out of a population of some sixty million. How many more Muslim youths, people wondered, might similarly be planning mass murder against their fellow Britons? For although no one thinks that the vast majority of British Muslims are anything other than peaceful and law-abiding, the evidence suggests that the numbers who do support either the aims or the tactics of the jihad are terrifying. According to British officials, up to sixteen thousand British Muslims either are actively engaged in or support terrorist activity, while up to three thousand are estimated to have passed through al-Qaeda training camps, with several hundred thought to be primed to attack the United Kingdom.[1]

These figures are staggering, and their implications go beyond any immediate concern for security. They suggest that something has gone very wrong with British society. For none of the usual explanations for suicide bombers is remotely applicable here. These British terrorists and their sympathizers were not radicalized by their experience in refugee camps in faraway lands, or by living under despotic regimes,

or by coming from countries whose national project was hatred of the
West. They were born and brought up in one of the freest, most pros-
perous and most humane countries in the world. Yet these British boys,
the product of British schools and universities and the British welfare
state, behaved in a way that repudiated not just British values but the
elementary codes of humanity. Nor were they oddball loners. What
had caused them to go onto the Tube with their backpacks and blow
themselves and their fellow Britons to bits was an ideology that had
taken hold like a cancer, not just in the madrassas of Pakistan but in
the streets of Leeds and Bradford, Oldham and Leicester, Glasgow and
Luton. And this had happened while Britain was studiously looking
the other way.

European convulsions over Islam—such as the murder of the
Dutch filmmaker Theo van Gogh in 2004 or the French riots in 2005
—have provoked critical discussion of the profound cultural changes
across mainland Europe in response to large-scale Muslim immigration, as in recent books by authors such as Bruce Bawer and Claire
Berlinski.[2]

Great Britain, however, is America's most important ally. The
"special relationship" between the two countries is no less critical
today than when they stood shoulder to shoulder against Nazi Germany. The United States may provide the muscle to defend the free
world against Islamic fascism, but Britain—the originator of the values
that America defends—provides the backbone. The unwavering support for the war in Iraq displayed by Prime Minister Tony Blair has
been as crucial for the moral authority it has lent the United States as
for any military or intelligence contribution. Britain is a champion of
America to the world, using its own moral capital as a guarantor of
America's good faith. And in Tony Blair the American people see the
embodiment of British staunchness and resolve, along with an elo-
quence in putting the case for the defense of freedom and democracy
which has turned him into a hero of the cause.

But what if things in Britain are not as they seem to America? What
if Mr. Blair is an aberration within his own country? What if Britain,
rather than being the front line of defense against the threat of radical
Islam, has become a quisling state that actually threatens to undermine

that defense? What if, instead of holding the line for Western culture against the Islamic jihad, Britain is sleepwalking into the arms of the enemy?

When the London bombings occurred, America felt the shock almost as keenly as did Britain. It was not just that the synchronized attacks in the heart of Britain's capital painfully reminded Americans of September 11, 2001. The bombings alarmingly demonstrated how easy it was to get under the defenses of America's most powerful and dependable ally. If radical Islamists could live as ordinary UK citizens for years while operating as terrorist sleeper cells under the radar of the British authorities, this could easily happen to America too.

There was also something shockingly totemic about these attacks upon Britain. This was, after all, the country that was a byword for bloody-minded independence and a refusal ever to knuckle under to tyranny. This was the bulldog breed that in the 1940s had endured the horrors of the Blitz and had vowed never to surrender. The London bombings were therefore an attack on the historic core of Western liberty. There was admiration in America for the apparently stoical reaction by the British. And there was redoubled respect for Prime Minister Blair, whose subsequent addresses to the nation were felt to be gratifyingly blunt in naming the problem correctly as an evil ideology that had hijacked a religion, and which had to be extirpated along with the terrorists committing mass murder in its name.[3] At last, thought Americans, a leader was prepared to spell out the truth without equivocation.

But the transatlantic telescope furnishes too rosy a perspective. The London bombings revealed a terrible truth about Britain, something even more alarming and dangerous to America's long-term future than the fact that foreign terrorists had been able to carry out the 9/11 attacks on U.S. soil in 2001. They finally lifted the veil on Britain's dirty secret in the war on terrorism—that for more than a decade, London had been the epicenter of Islamic militancy in Europe. Under the noses of successive British governments, Britain's capital had turned into "Londonistan"—a mocking play on the names of such state sponsors of terrorism as Afghanistan—and become the major European center for the promotion, recruitment and financing of Islamic terror and extremism.

Indeed, it could be argued that it was in London that al-Qaeda was first forged from disparate radical groups into a global terrorist phenomenon. During the 1980s and 1990s, despite repeated protests from other countries around the world, Londonistan flourished virtually without public comment at home—and, most remarkably of all, with no attempt at all to combat it by the governmental and intelligence agencies that were all too aware of what was happening.

Incredibly, London had become the hub of the European terror networks. Its large and fluid Muslim and Arab population fostered the growth of myriad radical Islamist publications spitting hatred of the West, and its banks were used for fund-raising accounts funneling money into extremist and terrorist organizations. Terrorists wanted in other countries were given safe haven in the United Kingdom and left free to foment hatred against the West. Extremist groups such as Hizb ut-Tahrir remained legal, despite being banned in many European and many Muslim countries. Radicals such as Abu Qatada, Omar Bakri Mohammed, Abu Hamza and Mohammed al-Massari were allowed to preach incitement to violence, raise money and recruit members for the jihad. An astonishing procession of UK-based terrorists turned out to have been responsible for attacks upon America, Israel and many other countries.

When Abu Hamza was finally jailed in February 2006 for soliciting murder and inciting racial hatred, an astounded British public suddenly discovered that for years he had been allowed to operate from his London mosque as a key figure in the global terrorist movement while the British authorities sat on their hands. Not only had he openly incited murder and racial hatred, but he had amassed inside his mosque a huge arsenal of weapons to be used in terrorist training camps in Britain. Worse still, through his preaching of jihad he had radicalized an unquantifiable number of British Muslims, including three of the London bombers.[4]

Only after the court case was it revealed that the police had made two previous attempts to prosecute him but had been rebuffed by the

Crown Prosecution Service, which defended itself by claiming that there had not been enough evidence to bring a case. It was also revealed that, seven years previously, the British authorities had gathered wire-tap evidence apparently linking Abu Hamza to terrorist offenses abroad.[5] There were suspicions that the only reason he had eventually been prosecuted at all was that America had requested his extradition, and the British had put him on trial solely to avoid his possible incarceration in Guantanamo Bay, whose procedures were regarded by the British government with deep disapproval.[6]

But why had he not been prosecuted earlier if the British authorities knew about his activities? The former home secretary David Blunkett claimed that the police, the security service MI5 and prosecuting authorities had all told him that he was exaggerating the threat posed by Abu Hamza when Blunkett had pressed for him to be dealt with. "There was a deep reluctance to act on the information coming out of Abu Hamza's own mouth and some people did not want to believe how serious it all was," he said.[7]

Why, though, were the British authorities so reluctant? More astonishingly still, Londonistan continued to flourish unhindered even *after* the "wake-up call" of 9/11. Despite the fact that a number of Islamist terror plots against Britain had previously been thwarted, the London bombings in 2005 still caught MI5 with its trousers down. It had no idea that an attack was imminent, and it had never imagined that the foreign radicals whom it had all but ignored might be having a lethal effect on impressionable young Muslims in British cities. How could Britain have slept on its watch like this?

Among ordinary Britons, there has been widespread alarm and incomprehension about such official laxity. America should be even more concerned about what this tells it about its principal ally. For this was no simple lapse; MI5 itself was guilty of a combination of flawed analysis and cynicism. Distracted by the Cold War on the one hand and Irish terrorism on the other, it never understood the power of the Islamic nation—or *ummah*—over its scattered members and for a variety of reasons believed that it was not in Britain's interests to act against Islamist radicals. The security service was content instead to watch as Londonistan took shape, apparently either oblivious or indifferent to the carnage that its proponents might be inflicting overseas.

Shocking as this may be, the intelligence debacle is only the tip of the iceberg. Among Britain's governing class—its intelligentsia, its media, its politicians, its judiciary, its church and even its police—a broader and deeper cultural pathology has allowed and even encouraged Londonistan to develop, one which persists to this day.

Early in 2006, the world was suddenly convulsed by a wave of Muslim violence and demonstrations over the publication in Denmark of a batch of cartoons linking the Prophet Mohammed with violence, which had been published the previous September in the Danish newspaper *Jyllands-Posten*. Despite some local Muslim protests in Denmark at the time, the drawings initially caused no wider problems. Indeed, they were republished in October 2005 on the front page of an Egyptian newspaper, *Al-Fagr*, without incident.

Feelings were inflamed among Muslims, however, by a group of Danish imams who circulated the cartoons throughout the Muslim world, along with others of an obscene nature that had not been published by *Jyllands-Posten* and appeared to have been included purely to stir up passions.[8] As the controversy grew, newspapers in France, Germany, Italy, the Netherlands and Spain republished the Danish cartoons in a gesture of solidarity and to show that the core Western value of freedom of expression would not be cowed by clerical fascism.

The growing disquiet was cynically exploited by other Islamist radicals, along with countries such as Iran and Syria that seized the opportunity to manipulate the global agenda to their advantage.[9] The result was Islamist violence and intimidation across the globe. Denmark was threatened with human-bomb attacks. Death threats were issued against the cartoonists and editors, with Danes, Norwegians and other Europeans being hunted for kidnap. Thousands took part in marches and demonstrations, with calls to behead Westerners and rallying cries for "holy war" by Islam against Europe.[10] In Afghanistan, Libya and Nigeria, people died in mass protests.[11]

Such an attempt at international censorship could hardly have furnished a more graphic example of the assault by one civilization upon another in an explicit attempt to subordinate to Islam a cardinal value of the Western world. Yet the governments of both Britain and America[12] responded by apologizing for "causing offense" to Muslims, while their intelligentsia earnestly debated whether it was wrong to insult someone else's religion—for all the world as if this were a university ethics seminar rather than a world war being waged by clerical fascism against free societies.

Of course it is wrong gratuitously to insult a religion. But the Danish cartoons were not an attack on Islam. They were commissioned as a comment on the fact that a Danish children's author, who was writing an inoffensive book about Islam, could not find an illustrator. This was because, after the murder of the filmmaker Theo van Gogh in the Netherlands for his perceived insult to the religion, Danish illustrators were too frightened to undertake even this commission.

The cartoons were therefore not intended as an attack on Islam, but rather as a political comment on the intimidation being practiced by extremists in its name. Their publication was an attempt to test out the degree of self-censorship that this has caused in Denmark. Far from an attack upon another faith, they were an attempt to *defend* a society from an attack upon its own values by religious fanaticism. They were therefore an expression of high moral purpose and needed to be defended with the utmost vigor.

Nevertheless, Britain did not see it that way. Its foreign secretary, Jack Straw, initially ignored the violence and condemned instead those European newspapers that had republished the cartoons. "There is freedom of speech, we all respect that, but there is not any obligation to insult or to be gratuitously inflammatory," he said. "I believe that the republication of these cartoons has been unnecessary, it has been insensitive, it has been disrespectful and it has been wrong."[13]

Yet while declaring that free speech should be limited to avoid being insulting or gratuitously inflammatory, Britain appeared to believe that it should be unlimited when Muslims incited mass murder. In February 2006, Muslims demonstrating outside the Danish embassy in London's exclusive Knightsbridge area were allowed to call for bombings and decapitations while the police looked on. "Bomb bomb Denmark" and "Nuke nuke Denmark," shouted the demonstrators, while their placards read: "Exterminate those who slander Islam," "Behead those who insult Islam," "Europe you'll come crawling when mujahideen come roaring," "As Muslims unite we are prepared to fight," "Europe you will pay, fantastic four are on their way" (a presumed reference to the London suicide bombers the previous year). And one demonstrator was even dressed in the garb of a suicide bomber.

Not only was such open incitement to murder and terrorism allowed to go on, but the only action taken by the police was actually directed against those passersby who objected to such displays. People who tried to snatch away the placards were held back. Several members of the public tackled senior police officers guarding the protesters, demanding to know why they allowed banners that praised the "magnificent 19"—the 9/11 terrorists—and others threatening further attacks on London. The officers said that their role was to ensure public order and safety.[14] And those who tried to photograph the man dressed as a suicide bomber were threatened with arrest.

The result was public outrage. Realizing that a public relations disaster was in the offing, British Muslim community leaders themselves criticized the police for allowing the demonstrators to threaten violence on British streets. With such calls from the very people they were bending over backwards not to offend, the police and government abruptly changed their tune. Mr. Straw condemned the violence around the world, while the police said they would consider arresting some of the demonstrators.[15]

In stark contrast to their European counterparts, not one British newspaper republished the cartoons. The foreign secretary praised their self-restraint—but the more likely explanation was that they were practicing self-censorship through fear. Far from standing up to intimidation, Britain was caving in. Such weakness merely encouraged yet further demands that Muslim values take precedence over British ones. A gathering of three hundred Muslim religious leaders in the Midlands city of Birmingham demanded that the law should be changed to prohibit the publication of any images of the Prophet Mohammed.[16] This demand for special treatment was backed up by two further large demonstrations in London. The jihad was brazenly beating the loudest and most martial of drums in the capital city of the country that was supposed to be playing a pivotal role in the fight to defend the values of the West—but instead was apologizing for those values and seeking to appease those who were threatening to usurp them.

The British public was increasingly appalled by the feebleness of its rulers in the face of this onslaught. Yet over the past few years, it has failed to sound the alarm at the steady encroachment of radical Islamism into British public life. The Labour mayor of London, Ken Livingstone, has embraced and defended Sheikh Yusuf al-Qaradawi, the prominent Islamist cleric who says it is a duty for Muslims to turn themselves into human bombs in Israel and Iraq. Meanwhile George Galloway, the supporter of Saddam Hussein, was elected to the British Parliament as the leader of a new political party that brings together the far left and radical Islamism—the first such party in Europe. Yet there has been no groundswell to get rid of the popular Livingstone as London's mayor, nor has the Labour party disowned him; while Galloway is regarded as, at worst, a minor irritant or pantomime villain.

The alarming fact is that, far from continuing to embody the bull-dog spirit that enabled it to fight off fascism in the twentieth century, Britain remains in a widespread state of denial. It understands well enough that it faces a mortal threat from radical Islamists. But by and large, it does not understand why it faces this threat. Instead of laying the blame firmly upon the Islamist ideology where it belongs, Britain has itself adopted some of the tropes of that very ideology—in partic-ular, hatred of America and Israel, whose policies it blames as the cause of Muslim rage.

The view is widely shared, for example, that the London bombings were caused by Britain's support for the war in Iraq. Clearly this can-not be so, since Islamist terror not only preceded that war but has been directed against countries that either had nothing to do with it, such as Indonesia, or actively opposed it, such as France.

Equally clearly, however, the war in Iraq—along with Afghanistan and other conflicts—*has* been used to whip up further animus against the West. The distorted and hostile media coverage of Iraq, which has presented regime change as an indefensible conspiracy against the public interest to serve the interests of Israel and the Jewish lobby in America, has undoubtedly helped this process. Instead of challenging the lies that feed Muslim paranoia and rage, it has stoked them up and reinforced the deep prejudices that fuel them.

No less troubling, it has helped spread those prejudices among the wider British society, which, being constitutionally incapable of understanding religious fanaticism and always seeking instead a rational explanation for irrational acts, has developed an ugly climate of rampant anti-Americanism and prejudice against Israel, the legitimacy of whose very existence is now openly questioned. This in turn echoes the romantic attachment to Arab culture long harbored by the British establishment and represented most conspicuously by the heir to the throne, Prince Charles, who has spoken warmly of Islam and expressed dismay at the animosity being displayed towards it in the concern over global terror.[17] So at the very same time that Britons fear the threat from radical Islamism, the warped analysis of foreign policy that lies at its heart is now being echoed in the mainstream British conclusion: that the Iraq war was not a defense against Muslim aggression but its cause, that America is a superpower out of control, and that the origin of Muslim rage against the West lies in Israel's "oppression" of the Palestinians.

Instead of gaining a clear-eyed understanding of the ideology that so threatens it, Britain has thus been subverted by it. Instead of fighting this ideology with all the power at its command, Britain makes excuses for it, seeks to appease it—and even turns the blame that should be heaped on it upon itself instead. After the London bombings, the main concern of the media and intelligentsia was to avoid "Islamophobia," the thought-crime that seeks to suppress legitimate criticism of Islam and demonize those who would tell the truth about Islamist aggression. Consequently, Muslim denial of any religious responsibility for the bombings was echoed and reinforced by government ministers and commentators, who sought to explain the Islamist terror in their midst by blaming, on the one hand, a few "unrepresentative" extremist preachers and, on the other, Muslim poverty and discrimination— even though the bombers came from middle-class homes and had been to university. Even Tony Blair, who had explicitly identified the ideology as the wellspring of terror, has not matched his words with deeds.

His government has sought not to defeat that ideology but to appease it.

In other words, Londonistan is—among other things—a state of mind that has spread well beyond the capital and, even after the London bombings, still has British society firmly in its grip. It is not a transient phenomenon but has deep roots inside British culture, and has been created by the confluence of two lethal developments.

The first was the arrival in Britain of large numbers of Muslims, first from Asia and then from Arab countries, where Islam had been systematically radicalized by a political agenda promoting the conquest and Islamization of the West. The second development, which was critical, was that British society presented a moral and philosophical vacuum that was ripe for colonization by predatory Islamism.

Britain has become a decadent society, weakened by alarming tendencies towards social and cultural suicide. Turning upon itself, it has progressively attacked or undermined the values, laws and traditions that make it a nation, creating a space that in turn has been exploited by radical Islamism. It has thus absorbed much of the inverted and irrational thinking that is subverting not only its own society and the values that underpin freedom and democracy, but also the alliance with America and the struggle to defend the free world.

This book is an attempt to piece together this complex cultural jigsaw, and to show how the deadly fusion of an aggressive ideology and a society that has lost its way has led to the emergence of Londonistan. In doing so, it is not drawing any conclusions about whether Islam is intrinsically a religion of violent conquest or whether it has been hijacked by a revisionist ideology. That issue, the subject of much controversy between scholars learned in the religion, lies beyond this book's scope. Nor is it saying that all Muslims support jihadi terrorism or its aim of conquering the West and subjugating free societies to the tenets of Islam. On the contrary, Muslims are the most numerous victims of this clerical fascism. The premise upon which this book is based is rather that jihadi Islamism, whatever its historical or theological antecedents, has become today the dominant strain within the Islamic world, that its aims if not its methods are supported by an alarming number of Muslims in Britain, and that, to date, no Muslim representative institutions have arisen to challenge it.

In Britain, hundreds of thousands of Muslims lead law-abiding lives and merely want to prosper and raise their families in peace. Nevertheless, moderation among the majority appears to be a highly relative concept considering their widespread hostility towards Israel and the Jews, for example, or the way in which the very concept of Islamic terrorism or other wrongdoing is automatically denied. More fundamentally still, many do not accept the terms on which minorities must relate to the majority culture in a liberal democracy. Instead of acknowledging that Muslim values must give way wherever they conflict with the majority culture, they believe that the majority should instead defer to Islamic values and allow Muslims effectively autonomous development.

The attempt to establish this separate Muslim identity is growing more and more intense, with persistent pressure for official recognition of Islamic family law, the rise of a de facto parallel Islamic legal system not recognized by the state, demands for highly politicized Islamic dress codes, prayer meetings or halal food to be provided by schools and other institutions, and so on. No other minority attempts to impose its values on the host society like this. Behind it lies the premise that Islamic values trump British ones, and that Muslims in Britain are necessarily hostile to the values of the society of which they are citizens—a premise with which many British Muslims themselves would not agree.

Since even "moderate" Muslim representative institutions in Britain convey such a message, it is therefore hardly surprising that so many young Muslims are easy prey for radical Islamism and the call to violent jihad from the internet, or the Wahhabi or Muslim Brotherhood imams who have infiltrated many Muslim institutions and leadership positions in Britain.

And there is little to counter such influence because of a fundamental loss of national self-belief throughout the institutions of British society. Driven by postcolonial guilt and, with the loss of empire, the collapse of a world role, Britain's elites have come to believe that the country's identity and values are by definition racist, nationalistic and discriminatory. Far from transmitting or celebrating the country's fundamental values, therefore, they have tried to transform a national culture into a multicultural society, both in terms of the composition of the country and the values it embodies.

Mass immigration has been encouraged on the twin premises that economic dynamism depends on immigrants and that a monoculture is a bad thing. In some places, the concentration of Muslim immigrant communities has changed the face of British cities. It is, however, considered racist to say so in "multicultural" Britain, where a majoritarian culture is viewed as illegitimate and the nation as a source of shame. Instead, all minorities are deemed to have equal status with the majority and any attempt to impose majoritarian values is held to be discriminatory. Schools have ceased to transmit to successive generations either the values or the story of the nation, delivering instead the message that truth is an illusion and that the nation and its values are whatever anyone wants them to be. In the multicultural classroom, every culture appears to be taught except Britain's indigenous one. Concern not to offend minority sensibilities has reached the risible point where piggy banks have been banished from British banks in case Muslims might be offended.[18]

Britain has become a largely post-Christian society, where traditional morality has been systematically undermined and replaced by an "anything goes" culture in which autonomous decisions about codes of behavior have become unchallengeable rights. With everyone's lifestyle now said to be of equal value, the very idea of moral norms is frowned upon as a vehicle for discrimination and prejudice. Judaism and Christianity, the creeds that formed the bedrock of Western civilization, have been pushed aside and their place filled by a plethora of paranormal activities and cults. So prisoners are now allowed to practice paganism in their cells, using both wine and wands; and a Royal Navy sailor was given the legal right to carry out Satanic rituals and worship the devil aboard the frigate HMS *Cumberland*.[19]

The outcome has been the creation of a debauched and disorderly culture of instant gratification, with disintegrating families, feral children and violence, squalor and vulgarity on the streets. At an abstract level, such moral relativism destroyed the notion of objectivity, so that truth and lies were stood on their heads. This opened the way for the moral inversion of "victim culture," which holds that since minorities are oppressed by the majority they cannot be held responsible for what happens to them. As a result, a climate of intimidation developed in which minorities could demand special treatment and denounce anyone who objected as a bigot. Minority wrongdoing was thus excused and the blame shifted instead onto the majority. This allowed British Muslims, who consider themselves to be preeminently victims of Western culture, to turn reason and justice on their heads by blaming any wrongdoing by Muslims on others.

This communal state of denial continued even after the London bombings. Muslim leaders condemned these attacks—but also said that since they were "un-Islamic," the bombers could not have been real Muslims. In addition, since Muslims regard Western values as an assault on Islamic principles, they routinely present their own aggression as legitimate self-defense. This moral inversion has been internalized so completely that the more Islamic terrorism there is, the more hysterically British Muslims insist that they are under attack by "Islamophobes" and a hostile West. Any attempt by British society to defend itself or its values, either through antiterrorist laws or the reaffirmation of the supremacy of Western values, is therefore denounced as Islamophobia. Even use of the term "Islamic terrorism" is regarded as "Islamophobic."

Such deception and intimidation have worked. So profound is the fear of being branded a racist among British liberals, so completely do they subscribe to the multicultural victim culture, that the obvious examples of illogicality, untruths and paranoia in much Muslim discourse have never been challenged. Instead of attacking Islamic extremism, British liberals attacked Islamophobia. Instead of defending Britain against its attackers, they turned their rhetorical guns upon their own nation. Whenever suicide bombers struck, whether in Iraq, Israel or on the London Tube, the reaction of many in Britain's morally compromised culture—where one man's terrorist is another man's freedom fighter—was to blame not the fanatical ideology that spawned such inhuman acts, but invasion, oppression or discrimination against Muslims by America, Israel or Britain.

These trends are far from unknown in the United States. Indeed, much of the ideology of radical individualism was imported into

Britain from America during the decades after World War II. The kind of feminism that hated men and marriage, educational doctrines that destroyed teaching and knowledge in favor of "child-centered" autonomy, the ideology of racism which laid down that prejudice was confined to people with power—all these destructive ideas and more originated in the United States. Today, the culture wars rage unabated in America, where such thinking has become the orthodoxy in the universities and the media just as it has in Britain. But in the U.S. there has, at least, been a counteroffensive. The grip of the left-wing intelligentsia has been loosened by the growth of conservative think tanks and publishing houses, talk radio and now the internet bloggers. In Britain, by contrast, there has been no equivalent institutional challenge to the hegemony of the left and its stranglehold on the universities, media, civil service and other key institutions. In the United States, at least there are wars over culture; in Britain, there has been a rout.

As a result, virtually the entire British establishment has succumbed to multiculturalism and victim culture, and the attack on British values that these encapsulate. In America, the churches have been in the forefront of the defense of Western values. In Britain, by contrast, the Church of England has been in the forefront of the *retreat* from the Judeo-Christian heritage. At every stage it has sought to appease the forces of secularism, accommodating itself to family breakdown, seeking to be nonjudgmental and embracing multiculturalism. The result has been a shift in Britain's center of moral and political gravity as the Judeo-Christian foundations of British society have come under sustained assault.

Muslims in Britain are as incredulous as they are disgusted at the rout of moral values that has taken place. Indeed, when they speak of Western moral decadence, many in the West would agree with them. In Britain, this decadence not only fuels the rage of Muslims at the moral squalor that so affronts them, it also provides an opportunity to fill with an Islamist perspective the space that has been vacated by the collapse of Judeo-Christian moral authority. Since no fault in that perspective can be admitted, no wrongdoing in imposing it can be acknowledged either. Playing on the pathological fear of prejudice created by victim culture, Muslims refuse to accept responsibility for

Islamist violence, blame the British government instead for siding with America over Afghanistan and Iraq, and denounce any resistance to the imposition of an Islamic perspective as "Islamophobia."

Britain has been unable to counter such intimidation because it has already sold the pass to other "victim" groups. It has effectively allowed itself to be taken hostage by militant gays, feminists or "anti-racists" who used weapons such as public vilification, moral blackmail and threats to people's livelihoods to force the majority to give in to their demands. And those demands were identical to those made by the Islamists: not merely to tolerate their values as minority rights but to replace normative values altogether and subordinate the values of the majority to the minority, because majority values set up a hierarchy that is deemed to be innately discriminatory. So when Muslims refused to accept minority status and insisted instead that their values must trump those of the majority, Britain had no answer.

This in turn is part of a wider movement that has become the orthodoxy amongst the progressive intelligentsia of Britain and Europe. As religion has retreated and morality becomes privatized, individual conscience has become universalized. The nation and its values are despised; moral legitimacy resides instead in a vision of universal progressivism, expressed through human rights law and such supranational institutions as the European Union, the United Nations or the International Criminal Court, and revolving around multiculturalism and minority rights.

This has produced the extraordinary phenomenon of radical Islam—which denies female equality and preaches death to gays—marching under the banner of human rights. The self-styled progressives on the British left, for whom human rights have replaced Christianity as the religion for a godless society, have formed a jaw-dropping axis with militant, fundamentalist Islamism. These two revolutionary camps have put their very sizeable differences to one side so that each can use the other to advance their goal, which is the destruction of Western society and its foundation values.

The effect on Britain of Islamist-chic has gone far beyond left-wing circles. Because of the grip exercised by such circles on British institutions and popular culture, the Muslim/Arab take on America and events in the Middle East has been adopted by the media and other shapers of public opinion, most influentially by the BBC and Christian nongovernmental organizations.

This has had a far-reaching effect on Britain. It has fueled hostility towards America and the Iraq war, which has in turn distorted British political debate and now threatens to undermine Britain's continuing role in the defense against terror. The issues of Iraq, America and Israel are now conflated in the British public mind in a poisonous stew of irrationality, prejudice, ignorance and fear.

Britons believe that the only reason they are currently threatened by Islamist terror is the UK's support for America in Iraq. They do not believe Saddam Hussein was ever a threat to Britain or the West; they believe they were lied to over his weapons of mass destruction. They think the main reason for Muslim rage is the behavior of Israel towards the Palestinians, and that America made itself a target simply because of its support for Israel. And now, after London was bombed, they think the reason for that was Britain's role in Iraq.

The outcome is that—unlike the vast mass of Americans in the more conservative "red states," who may be aghast at the continuing war in Iraq but never doubted that their nation was threatened by clerical fascism—"middle Britain" thinks that America is the fount of all evil, that George W. Bush is a greater war criminal than Saddam Hussein ever was, and that Israel poses the greatest threat to world peace.

The resulting antiwar movement has provided a vast platform for Islamic extremism. It has turned what would otherwise have been dismissed as far-left, inflammatory and deeply unpatriotic statements in time of war into acceptable mainstream opinion. The impact of the daily invective against Jews, Israelis and evil Americans upon young Muslims who were already inflamed against the West has almost certainly turned up the temperature to boiling point. The relentless demonization of America and Israel by the British media, along with the demagoguery of George Galloway and Ken Livingstone, have acted as powerful recruiting sergeants for the jihad and have entrenched Londonistan in Britain's national psyche.

Faced with this potentially lethal cultural meltdown, what is Tony Blair doing to combat it? For Americans who take British support for granted in the defense against terror, the signs are unfortunately ominous. Instead of fighting these prejudices, the British government has decided to take the path of least resistance.

Despite Tony Blair's brave stand on Iraq and his stern words against Islamic fanaticism, the fact is that the Labour party he leads does not follow him. Despite ministers' awareness of the extent of Islamist extremism in Britain, the government's response has been to appease it in the belief that by doing so it will draw the poison and transform Muslims into a model minority. If ministers are pusillanimous, their officials are worse. Throughout the British civil service, there is a refusal to identify fanatical Islamism as the problem. In thrall to a combination of victim culture and pragmatic cynicism, the establishment is salami-slicing its cultural inheritance and being drawn inexorably into the balkanization of Britain.

This book is an attempt to explain how Britain has walked into this situation with eyes firmly shut. It describes a society that has progressively torn up its cultural maps and as a result has become so badly confused that even now it cannot properly grasp the danger that it is in. The effect on America if its principal ally continues down this perilous road will be profound. The consequences for the West, for which Britain remains a cultural beacon, would be incalculable. That is why this book is a warning—to America, to Britain and to all who care for freedom.

London, February 2006

CHAPTER ONE

THE GROWTH OF LONDONISTAN

———◦———

London, Britain's capital city, has become the human entrepôt of the world. Walk its streets, travel on its buses or Underground trains or sit in a hospital casualty department and you will hear dozens of languages being spoken, testimony to the waves of immigration that have transformed the face of London and much of the southeast of England as people from around the world have arrived in search of work. But you will also notice something else. The urban landscape is punctuated by women wearing not just the hijab, the Islamic head-scarf, but burkas and niqabs, garments that cover their entire bodies from head to toe—with the exception, in the case of the niqab, of a slit for the eyes—in conformity with strict Islamic codes of female modesty. In general, religious dress, even of an outlandish kind, makes a welcome contribution to the variety of the nation. But in this case, one wonders whether such attire really is a religious require-ment commanding respect, or a political statement of antagonism towards the British state. The effect is to create a niggling sense of insecurity and unease, as the open nature of London's society is viti-ated by such public acts of deliberate concealment, with faces and expressions—not to mention the rest of the body—hidden from sight. In the wake of the London bombings in July 2005, such con-cealment appears to be a security issue too.

Moreover, as you travel across London you notice that district after district seems to have become a distinctive Muslim neighborhood. Nor is this particular to London. Travel further afield, to run-down northern cities such as Bradford, Burnley or Oldham: in some districts the concentration of mosques, Islamic bookshops and other Muslim-run stores, the Islamic dress on the streets, the voices talking not in English but in the dialects of the Indian subcontinent make you feel that you have stepped into a village in the Punjab that has somehow been transported into the gray, drizzly setting of an English mill town. What becomes even clearer here than it is in London is that these Muslim enclaves are just that: areas of separate development which are not integrated with the rest of the town or city.[1] More than that, this separatism is a cause of communal tension that all too frequently simmers just below the surface in a low-level susurration of aggression between Muslims and their neighbors—and which occasionally explodes in rioting and violence. Except that, in Britain, people don't refer to them as Muslim areas; they are "Asian" areas, and the cause of such communal tension is said to be racism or discrimination. The issue of religion is carefully avoided.

Yet one of the most striking features of Britain today is the significant and increasing role being played by religion—not Christianity, the established religion of the British state, but Islam. It is Islam that is Britain's fastest-growing religion. With the Muslim minority officially estimated to number 1.6 million people out of a population of 60 million—although the true figure, as a result of illegal immigration, is likely to be significantly higher—Muslims are now Britain's second-largest community of faith after Christianity. More people go to the mosque each week than now attend an Anglican church. Over the past two decades, London has become the most important center for Islamic thought outside the Middle East. It is home to some of the most influential Muslim and Arab research institutions, lobby groups and doctrinal groups—Sunni, Shia, Ismaili and Ahmadi—and is a world center for the Arab press, home to the newspapers *Al-Hayat* and *Al-Quds al-Arabi*, the Middle East Broadcasting Company (MBC) and a long list of specialist Islamic publications.[2]

Probe a bit deeper, however, and the situation becomes rather more troubling. Go into one of these bookshops and you may well turn up a copy of *Mein Kampf* or the tsarist anti-Jewish forgery, *The Protocols of the Elders of Zion*, which are openly on sale. Many specialist Islamic publications contain diatribes of hatred against Israel or glorify some of the ideologues of Islamist terrorism. *Filisteen al-Muslima* (Muslim Palestine), the journal of the Palestinian terrorist organization Hamas, is published and distributed from the north London district of Cricklewood. *Al-Sunnah*, the Islamist magazine that calls repeatedly for human-bomb terror operations against the United States, is published from London, as is *Risalat al-Ikhwan* (Message of the Brotherhood), which states: "Active resistance (*muqawamah*) to the occupation and the use of any available means to resist it are a religious Moslem duty, a national duty and a natural right anchored in both international law and the United Nations Charter."[3]

These publications are merely the tip of an iceberg. For London has become a major global center of Islamist extremism—the economic and spiritual European hub of a production and distribution network for the most radicalized form of Islamic thinking, which not only pumps out an unremitting ideology of hatred for the West but actively recruits soldiers and raises funds for the worldwide terrorist jihad.

London is home to the largest collection of Islamist activists since the terrorist production line was established in Afghanistan. Indeed, one could say that it was in Britain that al-Qaeda was actually formed as a movement. It was in Britain that disparate radical and subversive agendas, which until then had largely been focused upon individual countries, became forged into the global Islamist movement that was al-Qaeda. Many of Osama bin Laden's fatwas were first published in London. In the late 1980s and early 1990s, a series of important conferences took place in Britain bringing together radical Islamists from all over the world, ranging from violent groups such as Hamas or Hezbollah to nonviolent groups running for parliament in Jordan or Malaysia. These conferences were where the global Islamist project came together.[4]

Yet the bizarre fact is that the British authorities allowed all this extremist activity to continue with impunity for more than a decade—even after the ostensible "wake-up call" of 9/11. Moreover, although the London bombings in 2005 revealed the devastating fact that

British-born Muslims had somehow been radicalized so that they were prepared to turn themselves into human bombs to murder as many of their fellow citizens as possible, Britain is even now display-ing an extreme reluctance to identify, let alone confront, the fact that a religious ideology connected these young bombers from the northern mill towns with the astonishing procession of terrorists fanning out from London across the globe. Even to talk in such terms, Britain tells itself, is "Islamophobic." Welcome to the alternative political and intellectual universe of Londonistan.

There are two separate but intimately related strands of extremism in Britain. One has arisen from the influx of foreign radicals from North Africa and the Middle East, who arrived in large numbers dur-ing the 1980s and 1990s. The other—along with some converts to Islam from the wider British community—has developed from the radicalization of Britain's own Muslims, who first started arriving during the 1970s and 1980s from Pakistan, Bangladesh and Kashmir. As a result of these twin developments, London has become, over the past two decades, the world's principal center for Islamism outside the Middle East and Afghanistan.

Islamism is the term given to the extreme form of politicized Islam that has become dominant in much of the Muslim world and is the ideological source of global Islamic terrorism. It derives from a number of radical organizations that were founded in the early part of the last century, which all believe that Islam is in a state of war with both the West and the insufficiently pious Muslims around the world. The first was the Tablighi Jamaat in India/Pakistan, secessionists who believed that Muslims must return to the basics of Islam and separate themselves from non-Muslims. The second was the Muslim Brother-hood, which was founded in Egypt by Hassan al-Banna with Sayed Qutb its leading ideologue. Its creed is known as Salafism and is deeply antisemitic; this is virtually indistinguishable from Saudi Ara-bian Wahhabism. The third was the Jamaat al-Islami, founded by Sayed Abu'l Ala Maududi in India/Pakistan, which had similar ideas to the Muslim Brotherhood, and with Maududi providing a major influence over Qutb.

When the Muslim Brotherhood was thrown out of Egypt, its

leaders fled to Saudi Arabia, which became the world's major exponent of Wahhabism and which in turn contributed to the radicalization of Pakistan. Thus a fateful line of extremism was drawn which in due course would lead from the rural villages of Mirpur and Sylhet straight to Bradford and Dewsbury, Luton and London.

It must be said at the outset that there are hundreds of thousands of British Muslims who have no truck whatsoever with terrorism, nor with extremist ideology. They simply want what everyone else wants: to make a living, bring up their children and live peaceful and law-abiding lives that threaten nobody. They are as horrified by the terrorism that has disfigured their community as is anyone else. Nevertheless, it remains the case that not only is such terrorism being carried out in the name of Islam, but the British Muslim establishment has itself been hijacked by extremist elements funded and promoted by the religious establishment in Saudi Arabia, Pakistan and elsewhere. While many imams doubtless promote only messages of peace, there has been no suppression by British Muslims of the ideology of holy war. This shifting of the center of gravity towards extremism in Islamic discourse in Britain has created the sea in which terrorism can swim.

And the number of terrorists who have come roaring out of these polluted British waters is startling. UK-based terrorists have carried out operations in Pakistan, Afghanistan, Kenya, Tanzania, Saudi Arabia, Iraq, Israel, Morocco, Russia, Spain and the United States. The roll call includes Ahmed Omar Saeed Sheikh, killer of the journalist Daniel Pearl and disaffected, brilliant son of Pakistani immigrants; Dhiren Barot, Nadeem Tarmohammed and Qaisar Shaffi, British citizens and al-Qaeda members who plotted to attack major financial centers in the United States; Mohammad Bilal from Birmingham, who drove a truck loaded with explosives into a police barracks in Kashmir; the "shoe-bomber" Richard Reid, who was converted to Islam at Brixton Mosque in south London; Sajid Badat from Gloucester, a putative second shoe-bomber but who was also caught and is now in jail; and Omar Khan Sharif and Asif Mohammed Hanif, the British boys who helped bomb a Tel Aviv bar in 2003 and killed three Israeli civilians.[5] And let's not forget Azahari Husin or the "Demolition Man," the Malaysian engineer who belonged to the al-Qaeda–linked terrorist group Jemaah Islamiyah (JI). He had studied at Reading University in the 1980s, honed his bomb-making skills in Afghanistan in the 1990s, helped mastermind the terrorist attacks in Bali (twice) and finally blew himself up in a gun battle with Indonesian police in November 2005.

Al-Qaeda's first high-profile attack on U.S. targets was partly organized from Britain, and the claim of responsibility for these bombings went out from London.[6] For al-Qaeda, London was a vital nerve center. In 1994, Osama bin Laden established a "media information office" there named the Advisory and Reformation Committee. According to the U.S. Justice Department's indictment of bin Laden, this office was designed both to publicize his statements and to provide a cover for terrorist activity including the recruitment of military trainees, the disbursement of funds and the procurement of necessary equipment such as satellite telephones. In addition, the London office served as a conduit for messages, including reports on military and security matters, from various al-Qaeda cells to its headquarters.[7]

Another al-Qaeda organization based in London was the Committee for Defense of Legitimate Rights (CDLR), which was established by Mohammed al-Massari, a Saudi who had been given indefinite leave to remain in Britain after fleeing Saudi Arabia—according to the Saudis, having been involved in terrorism. In December 2004, al-Massari claimed that CDLR was the "ideological voice" of al-Qaeda.[8] On his website he justified assassinating President George W. Bush and Tony Blair, argued that the death of civilians in terror attacks in Iraq was "collateral damage and a necessity of war," and called for attacks on coalition forces and "apostate" Muslims who helped them in Iraq and Afghanistan.[9]

CDLR's activities went beyond rhetoric into terrorist activity in East Africa, Saudi Arabia and elsewhere. Other terrorist groups—such as the Algerian Armed Islamic Group (GIA), its offshoot, the Salafist Group for Call and Combat, and the Moroccan Islamic Combatant Group—have also used Britain to coordinate attacks against American and European targets. Such groups formed a web of terror with many links to al-Qaeda. The striking feature of all of them was the freedom with which they were able to use London as base camp for their terror activities, providing money, means of communication and bogus travel and identification documents to trainees who had graduated from the terrorist training camps. And all this without any attempt by the British authorities to stop them.

These activities were buttressed by an astonishingly dense network of radical Islamist groups that spread far beyond London, making Britain a key global center for the production and promotion of insurrectionist Islamist ideology of the kind that would be ruthlessly suppressed within the Arab world. The Muslim Brotherhood, for example, operates through a series of interlocking organizations of Palestinian, Syrian, Libyan, Somali, Iraqi and Egyptian origin. These include the Muslim Association of Britain, the Muslim Welfare Trust, Interpal, the Palestine Return Centre, the Institute of Islamic Political Thought, Mashreq Media Services (which publishes the Hamas newspaper *Filisteen al-Muslima*), the English language pro-Hamas paper *Palestine Times*, the Centre for International Policy Studies, and others.[10]

The Ahle Hadith is a smaller Wahhabi movement funded by Saudi Arabia, that runs many extremist madrassas and several terrorist organizations and training camps in Pakistan and Kashmir. It has four dozen centers in England and at least that many madrassas.[11] On its website, it tells readers that their fellow citizens are "Kuffaar," or infidels, and warns them: "Be different from the Jews and Christians. Their ways are based on sick or deviant views concerning their societies."[12]

One of the world's most radical Islamist organizations, Hizb ut-Tahrir, which is banned in many countries where it is considered a major threat, has its headquarters in Britain. HuT promotes the resurrection of the Islamic caliphate, which had been abolished in 1924 on the dissolution of the Ottoman Empire, and holds that Muslims may live only in a Muslim state governed by Sharia law, a goal which takes precedence over all others.

A similar group called al-Muhajiroun—which disbanded but reformed in other guises—is now expanding its influence in other countries. Al-Muntada al-Islami, a Saudi-funded and run foundation in London, specializes in promoting Wahhabi extremism in Africa, where it has two dozen branches. Last year, Nigerian police accused al-Muntada's local representative of transferring millions of dollars to foment religious violence and finance attacks on Christians.[13] In the English Midlands town of Leicester, the Islamic Foundation was set up in 1974 to promote the ideology of the Jamaat al-Islami, which wants to spread the governance of Sharia law to both Muslims and non-Muslims. Professor Kurshid Ahmad, chairman and rector of the Islamic Foundation, is also the vice president of the Jamaat al-Islami opposition party in Pakistan, which aims to turn it into an Islamic state governed by Sharia law.

Scarcely less significant is the European headquarters of the radical proselytizing movement Tablighi Jamaat at Dewsbury in Yorkshire. The Tablighi Jamaat mosque has been flourishing in Dewsbury for almost thirty years. It was built in 1978 with funds from the World Muslim League and has since become the headquarters of the movement, which has become a major recruiter for jihad across the globe. This mosque is of such strategic importance to Islamist radicals that, every autumn, thousands of Muslim pilgrims from across Europe gather there to pray. "The mosque's importance must not be underestimated," one antiterrorist expert said. "Tablighi Jamaat has always adopted an extreme interpretation of Islam, but in the last two decades it has radicalized to the point where it is now a driving force of Islamic extremism." And it was this mosque that has been linked by British intelligence to Mohammed Sidique Khan, the leader of the London bomb plot in July 2005.[14]

So how did this extraordinary network of terrorism and violent revolutionary insurrection with its roots in Arabia and Asia come to develop in Britain, the cradle of Western liberty? How did London, home to the mother of parliaments, turn into Londonistan?

The process started back in the 1970s, when a large influx of immigrants from Pakistan, Bangladesh and India started to arrive in Britain. They came mostly to work in the cotton mills in England's northern industrial towns such as Bradford and Burnley, Oldham and Rotherham. They were brought in as cheap labor because these mills were floundering in the face of competition with the third world. In due course, the mills went out of business anyway and the Asian immigrants found that the land of plenty and promise had turned into the land of unemployment.

Virtually all concerns about this wave of immigration focused upon the alleged racism or discrimination with which the host community in Britain was treating these newcomers. What went almost totally unnoticed was the enormous dislocation between the Muslim immigrants and the host society. These new arrivals came overwhelmingly from desperately poor, rural villages in places like Mirpur in Pakistan and Sylhet in Bangladesh. Many never thought they would stay permanently but expected to make some money and then return after a few years (not that this happened).[15] So they remained umbilically connected to the culture of southern Asia. And what no one had realized was that religious life in Pakistan was in the process of becoming deeply and dangerously radicalized.

When these Muslim immigrants arrived, the highly traditional faith they practiced was largely influenced by introspective, gentle Sufism and was thus passive and quiescent. But in the space of a few years, it became an increasingly activist faith centered on the mosques, which were transmitting a highly radicalized ideology. Groups such as the Jamaat al-Islami were supplying the mosques with imams and setting up research centers like the one in Leicester. As a result, according to Dr. Michael Nazir-Ali, the Pakistani-born bishop of Rochester, a whole generation of Muslim children was indoctrinated with a set of inflammatory ideas about the need for Islam to achieve primacy over the non-Islamic world.[16]

Against this backdrop of steady radicalization, a series of tumultuous developments during the 1980s and 1990s increasingly gave Muslims in Britain a new, highly politicized and deeply confrontational sense of their own religious identity. The first was the Soviet war in Afghanistan during the 1980s, in which the United States and Britain armed and trained Islamic mujahideen to fight and eventually drive out the Soviet invaders. Little did the Americans and the British realize that, in the process, they were helping sow the dragon's teeth from which would spring the killers who would turn so spectacularly upon themselves. For they had armed and trained people who had now found their vocation: holy war. Was not that, these warriors told themselves, precisely what they had waged in Afghanistan, where the forces of Islam had driven out the godless Soviets? The belief that

Islamic warriors had not only won that war but as a result caused an entire superpower to implode became a founding myth of modern Islamism and cemented the concept of the armed jihad as a contemporary pillar of the faith.[17] And as a result of the steady radicalization under way in the Muslim world, the Christian West—which had armed and trained the mujahideen—itself became the next target for the jihad. As secular Afghans from the country's exiled tribal leadership had warned the Americans during the 1980s: "For God's sake, you're financing your own assassins."[18]

If Afghanistan was an inspiration for British Muslims, the Islamic revolution in Iran had produced another electrifying effect. When Ayatollah Khomeini came to power in 1979 and transformed Iran into an Islamic state, Islam became crystallized as a political ideology for people who felt estranged from British secular society and were looking for a cause that would cement their identity and provide something to admire. Within a few years, moreover, the trajectories of both the Iranian revolution and the identity of British Muslims were to fuse in a culturally explosive episode.

In 1989, the novelist and British citizen Salman Rushdie published his novel *The Satanic Verses*. A bitter satire on Islam which understandably gave serious offense, its publication provoked uproar in the Islamic world with protests in the Pakistani capital Islamabad that led to the deaths of five Muslims. Shortly afterwards, in Iran, Ayatollah Khomeini issued a fatwa sentencing Rushdie to death for writing the book, along with "all involved in its publication who were aware of its content."[19] As a result, Rushdie was forced to go into hiding for many years and to live the life of a highly guarded fugitive, with a bounty on his head for anyone who succeeded in murdering him.

This incitement to murder a British subject and his associates in the publishing world set the Muslim community in Britain alight. Literally so—they burned the book in the street, in scenes uncomfortably reminiscent of Nazi Germany. There was a positive feeding frenzy of incitement. Sayed Abdul Quddus, the secretary of the Bradford Council of Mosques, claimed that Rushdie had "tortured Islam" and deserved to pay the penalty by "hanging." Speaking in Bradford, where the first demonstrations against the book took place, he said:

"Muslims here would kill him and I would willingly sacrifice my own life and that of my children to carry out the Ayatollah's wishes should the opportunity arise."[20] Dr. Kalim Siddiqui, director of the Iranian-backed Muslim Institute, shouted at a meeting: "I would like every Muslim to raise his hand in agreement with the death sentence on Salman Rushdie. Let the world see that every Muslim agrees that this man should be put away."[21]

The importance of this episode and the no less significant reaction to it by the British establishment can hardly be overestimated. Such scenes were unprecedented in Britain. The home of freedom of speech was playing host to the burning of books and an openly homicidal witch-hunt. Yet not one person who called for Rushdie to be killed was prosecuted for incitement to murder. The most the government could bring itself to say was that such comments were "totally unacceptable."[22]

On the contrary, they seemed to be not only accepted but even endorsed by certain members of the British establishment. Far from universal condemnation of this murderous expression of religious fanaticism, various people used their public position to jump prematurely upon Rushdie's grave. The eminent historian Lord Dacre said he "would not shed a tear if some British Muslims, deploring Mr. Rushdie's manners, were to waylay him in a dark street and seek to improve them."[23] And in Leicester, the Labour MP Keith Vaz led a three-thousand-strong demonstration intent on burning an effigy of Rushdie, and carried a banner showing Rushdie's head, complete with horns and fangs, superimposed on a dog.[24]

Here in microcosm were all the key features of what would only much later be recognized as a major and systematic threat to the British state and its values. There was the murderous incitement; the flagrant defiance of both the rule of law and the cardinal value of free speech; the religious fanaticism; the emergence of British Muslims as a distinct and hostile political entity; and the supine response by the British establishment. What was also on conspicuous display was the mind-twisting, back-to-front reasoning that is routinely used by many Muslims to turn their own violent aggression into victimhood. Muslim leaders claimed that the refusal by the British government to ban *The*

Satanic Verses showed that Muslims in Britain were under attack, with the political and literary establishment trying to destroy their most cherished values. "They are rapidly coming to the conclusion that they will have to fight to defend Islam in Britain," said Dr. Kalim Siddiqui of his community.[25]

Of course, it was *Britain* that was under attack from an Islamism that required the British state to dump *its* most cherished values in order to placate the Muslim minority. Yet this was promptly inverted to claim that it was Islam that was under attack. Thus Islamist violence was justified, and its victim blamed instead for aggression—the pattern that has come to characterize the Muslim attitude to conflict worldwide.

The Rushdie affair became a rallying cause for Muslim conscious-ness. It was the point at which British Muslims became politicized and hitched their faith to a violent star. According to the writer Kenan Malik, Muslim radicals had until then been on the left, not religious and against the mosque. Now, fired by resentment at the apparent insult by the Rushdie book, they became transformed into religious radicals and formed the pool of discontents for militant Islamic groups like Hizb ut-Tahrir, which began organizing in Britain, partic-ularly on campus, in the late 1980s and early 1990s.[26]

When Khomeini died later in 1989, British Muslims reiterated that the death sentence on Rushdie still stood. A spokesman for the Council of Mosques said: "We are talking about the Islamic revival."[27] It was at that point, therefore, that the promotion of Islam in Britain became fused with an agenda of murder.

Hard on the heels of this seismic episode came two further key developments. The Bosnian war was another major radicalizing factor for British Muslims. They watched the appalling scenes of Bosnian Muslims being massacred by their Christian neighbors. What made this carnage so much worse was that it was taking place in the middle of secular, multicultural Europe. The Muslims being wiped out were pale-skinned and clothed in jeans and track shoes. They looked and behaved like any other Europeans. And yet Britain and Europe were dragging their heels about doing anything to stop the slaughter. So British Muslims believed that it was Islam that was under attack, and that therefore they too were unsafe and threatened in a country that had so conspicuously failed to view the massacre of Muslims with any concern. With their pathological sense of victimization thus accelerating by the day, they started volunteering to fight for the jihad in Bosnia and organizing the "defense" of their own communities in Britain.

At around the same time, Arab Islamist exiles from Libya, Algeria, Egypt and elsewhere started turning up in London in large numbers. Many had fought the Soviet Union in Afghanistan. They had returned to their home countries from where, after instigating violent agitation, they were promptly thrown out. So these trained "Afghan Arab" warriors made their way instead to Britain—attracted, they said, by its "traditions of democracy and justice."[28] But they had now been trained to be killers. They had discovered jihad. And the radical ideology they brought with them found many echoes in the Islamism and seething resentments that by now were entrenched in British Muslim institutions.

Reda Hussaine, an Algerian journalist who supplied information on Algerian radicals in London to both French and British intelligence, says the Algerian connection was particularly crucial. "They came to the UK, the only country that gave asylum and didn't ask a lot of questions," he said. "Thousands and thousands came, wave upon wave, saying they were being repressed in Algeria." Then they started to organize inside Britain against the West. And to provide the religious imprimatur for jihad through the instrument of the fatwa, they recruited Abu Qatada from Afghanistan and sent him to London, where he preached in the Finsbury Park mosque. "From here started the first fatwas calling for the killing of everyone who was against the ideology," said Hussaine. "Then dozens of jihadis started to arrive every week, to raise money, make propaganda."[29]

Abu Qatada was extraordinarily important. He was not only crucial in the development of Algerian terrorism, publishing the newspaper of the Algerian terrorist group the GIA (the French acronym for Armed Islamic Group) in London in the early to mid 1990s. He was also the "spiritual head of the mujahideen in Britain," according to the leading Spanish prosecutor Baltasar Garzón, and "Osama bin Laden's European ambassador" according to French intelligence.[30] Terrorist cells broken up in Germany, Spain, France and Italy were all found to have connections to Abu Qatada. His preaching attracted figures like Zacarias Moussaoui, who helped plan the 9/11 attacks, and videos of his speeches were found in the Hamburg flat of Mohammed Atta, the hijackers' ringleader.[31] Yet for years Britain afforded him the liberty to mastermind al-Qaeda terror.

Many other radicals found a comfortable home in London during this period. Rashid al-Ghannushi, the leader of the Tunisian branch of the Muslim Brotherhood, An Nahda, lived in Britain for about fifteen years after being convicted in Tunisia of bombing an airport—one of the most important Islamic ideologues living in exile, although with a very low public profile. Abu Doha, an Algerian described by intelligence sources as Osama bin Laden's main man in Britain, has been accused of controlling Ahmed Ressam, who plotted to bomb Los Angeles International Airport in 1999, as well as being linked to bomb plots in Strasbourg and Paris. Yasser al-Siri was convicted in Egypt for terrorism after he tried to kill the deputy prime minister and killed a small child instead. And Kamal el-Helbawy, an Egyptian sent to Pakistan as a Muslim Brotherhood point man with Jamaat al-Islami, came to London as the Muslim Brotherhood spokesman in the West and in 1997 established as its British voice the Muslim Association of Britain.

Much of this activity took place below the public radar. But there was also very public evidence of the violent feelings that were being stirred up. One year after the attacks on New York and Washington, a flyer distributed around London by al-Muhajiroun read: "September 11th 2001, a Towering Day in World History," a text illustrated by the Twin Towers. This was followed the next year with a flyer celebrating "The Magnificent 19," with portraits of the suicide attackers involved in the atrocity.

There were also Islamist demagogues who very publicly called for murder and insurrection. The Syrian expatriate Omar Bakri Mohammed, who arrived in Britain after being expelled from Saudi Arabia, founded Hizb ut-Tahrir in Britain in 1986 with another Syrian expatriate, Farid Kassim. He was allowed to call for the murder of the British prime minister with no action taken against him: in 1991, during the first Gulf War, he claimed that Prime Minister John Major was "a legitimate target; if anyone gets the opportunity to assassinate him, I don't think they should save it. It is our Islamic duty and we will celebrate his death,"[32] a point which he later clarified as "a legitimate target if he were to set foot in a Muslim country."

After the 2005 London bombings, the *Sunday Times* conducted an undercover investigation in which it amassed hours of taped evidence and pages of transcripts that showed how Bakri and his acolytes promoted hatred of "nonbelievers" and incited their followers to commit acts of violence, including suicide bombings. His group, the Saviour Sect, preached a racist creed of Muslim supremacy which, in Bakri's words, aimed at "flying the Islamic flag over Downing Street." Followers were told that Islam was constantly under assault in Britain, and that the best form of defense was attack. One speaker claimed that the *kuffar* were trying to "wipe out [Muslims] from the face of the earth" and implored the group "to cover the land with our blood through martyrdom, martyrdom, martyrdom."[33]

And, for all this incitement, the British taxpayer was paying through the nose. Sheikh Bakri acknowledged to the press that he had been living on social benefits of nearly £300 a week in handouts from the British government for himself, his wife and their several children. "Islam allows me to take the benefit the system offers," he explained. "I'm fully eligible. It is very difficult for me to get a job. Anyway, most of the leadership of the Islamic movement is on [state] benefit."[34] Omar Bakri Mohammed continued to foment Islamist insurrection until the government suggested after the July bombings that it might finally take action against such extremists, when he left the country and was promptly barred from returning.

But perhaps most astonishing of all was the history of the institution at the very heart of the British jihad, the Finsbury Park mosque.

The North London Central Mosque in Finsbury Park owed its existence to the Prince of Wales, who persuaded King Fahd of Saudi Arabia to donate well over £1.3 million to construct a new building in the heart of the largely Bangladeshi community in north London. This worthy enterprise, however, was rapidly hijacked in the early 1990s by violent extremists who attacked the mosque's original trustees and others who attempted to resist them. At this stage a mediator appeared in the unlikely form of one Abu Hamza, an Egyptian-born former engineering student and nightclub bouncer, who had lost an eye and an arm in Afghanistan and sported a hook instead of a hand, and who was henceforth allowed to preach in the mosque.[35]

Abu Hamza, however, turned out to be one of the most dangerous men in Britain. In April 2002, the United States listed him as having alleged links to terrorism, accusing him of membership of the Islamic Army of Aden, the group that claimed responsibility for the bombing of the USS *Cole* in Yemen. By his own admission he had "a long association with the Taliban government." During the 1990s, he and his "Supporters of Sharia" were considered to be the propagandists of the Algerian GIA in Europe. At a meeting at the Finsbury Park mosque on June 29, 2001, according to *La Repubblica*, Abu Hamza proposed an ambitious but unlikely plot, "which involved attacks carried out by planes," to kill President Bush at the G8 summit in Genoa. The Italian report concluded: "The belief that Osama bin Laden is plotting an attack is spreading among the radical Islamic groups."[36]

Attempts by the mosque's trustees to evict Abu Hamza were met with violence. In October 1998, the trustees appealed unsuccessfully to the High Court to stop him from preaching. Worshippers then began noticing groups of young men staying overnight at the mosque. These included Richard Reid, the "shoe bomber"; a Tunisian, Nizar Trabelsi, who was told to drive a truck loaded with explosives into the U.S. embassy in Paris; Zacarias Moussaoui, the 9/11 planner; Ahmed Ressam, who was arrested attempting to bomb the Los Angeles airport at the millennium; Anas al-Liby, now on the FBI's most-wanted list and in whose Manchester flat police found al-Qaeda's terror manual in 1998; Abu Doha, wanted in the United States and France for plotting bombings; and others.[37]

Yet Abu Hamza was allowed to preach jihad until police stormed the Finsbury Park mosque in 2003 during an investigation into a suspected plot involving ricin poisoning. The raid involved 150 police officers wearing full body armor with some carrying guns (still unusual in Britain), smashing a battering ram through the front door. Despite this show of lethal force, officers who had sought the advice of Muslim colleagues on "how to behave respectfully" covered their shoes and focused their search on offices, avoiding prayer spaces.[38]

In April 2003, the Home Office finally moved to strip Abu Hamza of his citizenship with a view to deporting him. But although he was banned from preaching inside the Finsbury Park mosque, he held prayers outside the building every Friday until he was eventually put on trial—after some seven years of incitement, and then only after America had applied for his extradition. Hundreds of worshippers filled the street to hear Abu Hamza describe Israel as a criminal state, attack the media as Zionist and denounce Western politicians as corrupt homosexuals—for which the British taxpayers had to fork out yet further hundreds of thousands of pounds, since at least twelve officers had to be on duty outside the mosque when these events took place. The offense of obstructing the public highway was ignored and, in surreal scenes, Hamza sat in an armchair on the pavement after prayers as his followers queued to embrace him and have private conversations.[39]

This astounding standoff by the British authorities produced an even more farcical sequel. After the Abu Hamza debacle, a new board of trustees was appointed to give the mosque a fresh start. But one of these trustees was Mohammed Kassem Sawalha, president of the Muslim Association of Britain. According to U.S. court documents, in the early 1990s Sawalha was a leading militant "in charge of Hamas terrorist operations within the West Bank." Sawalha maintained that he was committed to peace in Britain. Both Muslims and non-Muslims in the British establishment simply looked the other way. Another trustee, Mohammed Sarwar, MP for Glasgow Govan, said he would remain despite being told of Sawalha's links to Hamas, and proclaimed himself happy with the way the mosque was being run. And Barry Norman, the Metropolitan Police chief superintendent who was working closely with the trustees, said: "I am aware of the background, but if I took the view that I'm not working with this or that person I'd end up spending my whole life in my office."[40]

Despite the lethal nature of the activities of Abu Hamza and Omar Bakri Mohammed, Britain persisted in regarding them as little more than pantomime villains. It just did not take them seriously; indeed, until the London bombings in 2005, it paid virtually no attention to the extraordinary network of terrorism and extremist incitement that had developed under its nose. Nor was it taking any notice of those who were warning that British Muslims had become dangerously radicalized. Dr. Michael Nazir-Ali, the bishop of Rochester who had been watching this process with alarm throughout much of this period, says that when he started saying as much to Labour government ministers in the late 1990s he was met with incomprehension. "They would say to me: 'But these are my constituents, they are perfectly nice people.' They just didn't believe me when I told them the kind of things that were being taught in places like the center at Leicester run by the Jamaat al-Islami."[41]

So why were such people allowed to carry out activities in Britain that posed such a threat to the West? Why didn't the British authorities arrest or deport the foreign radicals, shut off their funds and suppress their terrorist infrastructure? Why, indeed, were they allowed into the country in the first place? And why did the authorities allow the growth of a hostile separatism among British Muslims? The answer is as complex as it is troubling. It requires understanding a society that even now is in denial about the threat that it faces, and whose institutions have all been captured by a mindset that poses a lethal danger to the British state by weakening its defenses from within against the threat from without.

CHAPTER TWO

THE HUMAN RIGHTS JIHAD

F or Islamist terrorists and jihadi ideologues, London during the
1980s and 1990s was the place to be. Kicked out of or repressed
within their own countries, they streamed in their thousands to the
British capital because they found it to be more hospitable and tolerant than any other place on the globe.

A more brutal way of putting it, however, is that British entry procedures were the most lax and sloppy in the developed world—a system which asked no questions, required no identity papers and
instead showered newcomers with a galaxy of welfare benefits, free
education and free health care regardless of their behavior, beliefs or
circumstances. To state it more brutally still, during the 1990s Britain
simply lost control of its borders altogether because of the gross
abuse and total breakdown of its asylum system. Of the thousands of
asylum-seekers who arrive every year, most have no legal entitlement
to remain in Britain. Yet only a very small minority are sent home,
and the remainder melt into British society. The reason so many are
attracted is largely because illegal immigrants can simply disappear
with no questions asked.

It was hardly surprising, therefore, that so many Islamist terrorists
and extremists found Britain to be such a delightful and agreeable
destination. As the counterterrorism analyst Robert Leiken has pointed
out, al-Qaeda and its affiliates depend on immigration to get into the

West to carry out their terrorist plots, and to that end they use—or abuse—every immigration category to infiltrate Western countries.[1] According to Imam Abu Baseer, one of the leading religious supporters of al-Qaeda:

> One of the goals of immigration is the revival of the duty of jihad and enforcement of their power over the infidels. Immigration and jihad go together. One is the consequence of the other and dependent upon it. The continuance of the one is dependent upon the continuance of the other.[2]

The asylum shambles thus provided cover for the influx of large numbers of people into Britain who posed a direct threat to the state from without. But the reason why the shambles occurred in the first place is itself intimately related to a threat to the state that had developed from within.

Britain lost control of its borders because it was overwhelmed by a huge increase in the numbers claiming asylum. As Europe played host to a vast migration of peoples from south to north, Britain's lax asylum rules made it a soft touch for those who were not fleeing persecution at all but simply wanted a better life. Ministers and officials in charge of the asylum system, moreover, were among the least likely to possess either the intellectual or the political clout to tackle this problem. This was because, as members of a lowly and disregarded department, they tended to be at the bottom of the political pecking order.

The reason for this, in turn, was that the whole subject of immigration had been absolutely taboo ever since the Conservative politician Enoch Powell made a notorious speech in 1968 when, warning of the consequences of continued unchecked immigration from the Commonwealth, he alluded to a prophecy from Virgil that the river Tiber would "foam with much blood." That speech turned immigration into the topic that dared not speak its name, and racial prejudice became the most neuralgic issue in British politics. So when the asylum system collapsed under the twin strains of multiplying abuses and official incompetence, no one did anything about it for years—until the public started to protest.

When politicians finally did try to tackle the problem, they failed dismally because they refused to address the fundamental reason for the chaos. This was at root an ideology of "human rights" that was nothing less than an assault on the integrity of the nation, along with an obsession with preventing any self-designated "victim groups" from being harmed anywhere in the world. And the topic couldn't even be talked about openly and honestly for fear of accusations of racism. Remarkably, these absurd and dangerous attitudes—the governing creed of the progressive intelligentsia—had become the orthodoxy in the very heart of the British establishment, the judiciary, whose rulings not only reduced the asylum system to a shambles but thwarted all subsequent attempts to restore order.

In 1989, the European Court of Human Rights extended the scope of the provision in the European Convention on Human Rights that prohibits torture or degrading treatment. This ruling made it impossible to deport illegal immigrants—including suspected terrorists—to any place where the judges thought such abuses might be practiced. Although the ruling applied to all signatories to the Convention, the English courts applied it far more zealously than anyone else. At the same time, English judges began to interpret the 1951 United Nations Convention on Refugees much more broadly than other countries, so that the definition of a refugee was expanded from its original meaning of someone persecuted by the state to anyone threatened with harm by any group.

As a result, asylum policy descended into farce. Thanks to its courts, Britain was now obliged to grant asylum to potentially billions of people who could claim to be harmed by any group; and if such immigrants turned out to be themselves harmful to Britain, they could not be thrown out if they claimed that they faced further harm where they were being sent—which many promptly did. This impasse was then deepened by a series of judgments under human rights law—such as the ruling that halting welfare payments to asylum-seekers denied them a right to family life—in which the judges thwarted all government attempts to end the abuse.

The consequence was that human rights doctrine was used to

uphold patently false claims against the British state, with ruinous consequences. Those who were refused asylum simply disappeared into Britain; all they had to do to stop being deported was to claim that they would be ill-treated in their country of origin. As a result, they were not even sent back to the last country of transit, such as France, on the basis that France might in turn deport them to a country that would ill-treat them.

The absolute prohibition of torture is one thing. But to interpret this so that a country is forced to accept people who pose a potential danger to the state, on the grounds that sending them back to a country where torture is practiced is tantamount to practicing torture oneself, is demonstrably absurd. It has stood all notions of justice, logic and elementary prudence on their heads. Thus a Taliban soldier who fought the British and Americans in Afghanistan was granted asylum because he said he feared persecution—from the Western-backed government in Kabul. On the other hand, a group of Afghan hijackers, who diverted a flight to Stansted and then claimed asylum on the grounds that they were fleeing the Taliban, still remain in Britain despite the fact that they had committed a crime, despite the defeat of the Taliban and despite the best efforts of the government to remove them.

The resulting chaos in immigration procedures produced a catastrophic breakdown in British security. According to Home Office figures slipped out quietly just as MPs were departing for their Christmas vacation in December 2005, almost a quarter of all terrorist suspects arrested in Britain since 9/11 have been asylum-seekers.[3] At least two of the men accused of involvement in the failed July 21 attacks on London are alleged to have obtained asylum using bogus passports, names and nationalities.

What's more, the courts refused to extradite terrorist suspects if the countries requesting extradition were themselves suspected of ill-treatment. Case after case was mired for years in legal challenges and court rulings that overturned the government's decision to extradite these extremists. The Algerian Rachid Ramda, for example, was accused by the French government of having financed an attack on Saint-Michel station in Paris in 1995, in which eight people died and 150 were wounded. Britain had granted Ramda asylum in 1992. The

French government requested his extradition in 1995, 1996 and 2001. Ten years after the first request, and after two home secretaries had ordered his extradition, he was finally sent back to France.

In 1995, the home secretary tried to extradite the Saudi extremist Mohammed al-Massari to Yemen after Saudi Arabia, with whom Britain has lucrative and extensive trade dealings, vehemently requested his extradition. When the courts blocked this, a deal was done with the Caribbean island of Dominica, which agreed to take him in exchange for help from Britain with its trade negotiations with the European Union over the export of bananas. The courts blocked this too. As a result, al-Massari has lived for years in north London, posting on his website videos of civilian contractors being beheaded in Iraq—an activity he briefly suspended after the 2005 bombings but then resumed, inciting Muslims to join the global jihad, advocating the beheading of homosexuals and describing 9/11 as the "blessed conquest in New York and Washington."[4]

Why has the judiciary behaved in this way? Britain's judges are independent of political control. Over recent years, however, they have come to see themselves, rather than the democratically elected politicians, as the true guardians of the country's values. In addition, the judges have redefined those values to be in opposition to many British traditional beliefs. For the judiciary and the so-called progressive intelligentsia, human rights law is an article of faith, the legal progenitor of a brave new world in which prejudice, discrimination and oppression are consigned to history. In fact, it has undermined Western society, eviscerated its values and helped create the conditions breeding Islamist extremism and terror in the UK and its export around the world. It lies at the very heart of the hollowing out of British society, which has all but destroyed Britain's internal defenses against the external threat it faces from Islamist aggression.

The rise of judicial activism and human rights culture came from two important developments that changed the way English judges saw themselves. The first was the increasing ambit of European human rights law, with the judges in the European Court at Strasbourg progressively widening their scope as part of the growing ideological belief in universal legal principles that trumped the law of individual countries. Although the Strasbourg court has nothing to do with the European Union, this ideology fitted the accelerating movement towards political union in Europe and the idea of a supranational political entity.

This gave English judges the opportunity to flex their muscles in new directions. During much of the premiership of Margaret Thatcher, the Labour party appeared near to its demise and provided little effective opposition. This encouraged the judges to take upon themselves an opposition role. They saw themselves as the last redoubt of democracy fighting an over-mighty executive. They began to challenge government policy more and more—especially over asylum and immigration cases.

As a result, they came to think of themselves in a much more political way. When the Labour government came to power in 1997, it made a seminal mistake. Instead of putting the judges firmly back in their box, it entrenched judicial activism by incorporating the Human Rights Convention into English law. Bringing human rights law home in this way did much more than repatriate it and make it binding on the English courts. It galvanized special interest groups to make demands on the grounds that these were "rights" enshrined in law, created a burgeoning industry of human rights lawyers and—despite acknowledging the ultimate supremacy of Parliament—effectively transferred much political power from Parliament to the courts.

For New Labour, the issue of human rights was as totemic as state control of the economy had been for its Old Labour predecessors. With the collapse of socialism, Blairite politicians—like left-wingers everywhere—had to find a new radical motif that would enable them to continue their defining mission to transform society and human nature. Human rights provided the perfect vehicle.

The Human Rights Convention was originally conceived in another era altogether. Drafted in the wake of World War II, it was an attempt to lay down a set of principles to ensure that totalitarianism would never deface Europe again. It has now mutated into something very different. Far from protecting European civilization, it has turned into its potential nemesis.

In the shadow of fascism and Stalinism, its original aim was to protect the individual from the state. But in the half-century that has since elapsed, the relationship between the individual and the state has fundamentally changed. The emergence of a culture of hyper-individualism gave rise to a radical egalitarianism of lifestyles and values. Morality was privatized, and all constraints of religion, tradition or cultural taboos came to be seen as an attack on personal autonomy.

Where previously ties of obligation had bound individuals to each other and to the state, the new culture of entitlement imposed instead an obligation on the state to deliver individual demands that were presented as rights. Since radical egalitarianism meant that all lifestyles were of equal value, the very notion of a majority culture or normative rules of behavior became suspect as innately exclusive, prejudiced or oppressive. Moral judgments between different lifestyles or behavior became discrimination; and prejudice, the term for discrimination between lifestyles, became the sin that obviated the moral codes at the heart of Judaism and Christianity, which had formed the bedrock of Western civilization.

All minorities thus became a victim class to be championed. The nation itself became suspect, since it was the embodiment of a majority identity that by definition treated minorities as lower in the cultural hierarchy. So the idea of a nation that represents and protects individual citizens on the basis that they all subscribe equally to an overarching identity and set of values came to be replaced as the key political driver by interest groups defined by race, religion, ethnicity, gender or other existential categories.

The values of the dominant culture thus had to be replaced by the perspectives of the self-designated victim groups. Democracy became effectively redefined from majority rule among equal citizens to power-sharing among ethnic and other interest groups. Multiculturalism became the orthodoxy of the day, along with nonjudgmentalism and lifestyle choice. The only taboo now was the expression of normative majority values such as monogamy, heterosexuality, Christianity or Britishness. Because these were rooted in the particular, they were by definition discriminatory. The only legitimate values were now universal, detached from particulars such as religion, tradition or nation.

So the nation-state itself came to be seen as past its sell-by date, an anachronism responsible for all the ills of the world such as racism, prejudice and war. The remedy was what has been termed "transnational progressivism,"[5] the idea that what we must all sign up to transcends national boundaries. Laws based on the values, traditions and histories of particular nation-states must be replaced by laws and delivery mechanisms that are universal. So international law trumps the political decisions of sovereign states, and human rights law trumps their values.

These supranational laws and values are imposed by supranational institutions such as the European Court of Human Rights, the European Union, the United Nations or the European Court of Justice, which increasingly are becoming the sole sources of legitimacy. Indeed, law itself now trumps other forms of human interaction such as, at one end of the spectrum, informal relationships based on custom or convention and, at the other end, defending liberty through war. Instead, the view took hold that the application of law would settle all the world's problems and conflicts. It was law that by regulating behavior and attitudes would bring about a new and uplifted universal psyche. Codifying principles to which all civilized people could sign up would, it was thought, eradicate hatred, impose global order and remove any occasion for war. Indeed, law would now trump war. To paraphrase Winston Churchill, it seems that law-law is always better than war-war.

This legal supremacism has now developed into an industry that threatens to usurp the democratic process itself. Instead of being governed by the rule of law, we increasingly have rule by lawyers. Instead of being the vehicle to convey a nation's values, law has increasingly become a moral end in itself.

Accordingly, English common law is being steadily eroded by the encroachment of European law, on the basis that these distinctions no longer matter because we are all now bound by universal legal principles that brook no opposition. But they *do* matter. European law is deeply foreign to the tradition of English common law, which is founded on the premise that everything is permitted unless it is expressly forbidden. This is the very basis of English liberty. But European law, which is now taking precedence, presupposes instead that whatever is acceptable has to be expressly codified and permitted. The result is that, far from enhancing liberty, human rights law is a key mechanism for those who want to force people to conform to highly subjective notions of how to behave.

These developments are based on the elevation of law to a doctrine of legal infallibility. The law itself has become a kind of secular religion, with lawyers acting as the new priesthood. As a result, governments and other public authorities now look to lawyers to bestow or withhold their blessing on their deeds.

But rule by lawyers is based on assumptions as flawed as they are dangerous. International law, for example, is of dubious authority since it is not rooted in any democratic jurisdiction. It is merely an expression of prevalent political or ideological views, which are subject to disagreement. Some of the judges in supranational courts have not been judges in their own countries, or are not even lawyers but diplomats; and their deliberations are inseparable from political maneuvering. The legal tail is now wagging the national dog. The widespread opposition to the Iraq war in the British legal world seemed to be motivated by a fundamental outrage that it took place despite the absence of consent by international lawyers, which in itself made it an illegitimate exercise. But the idea that no prime minister can take the action he considers necessary to defend his country unless international lawyers give him permission is preposterous.

Judicial universalism supersedes the nation and represents a direct attack on democracy, on the ability of individual nations to express their own traditions and cultural preferences through their own laws. The argument is that no one could possibly object to the values conferred by human rights law because they are universal; that the judiciary are the custodians of these universal values; and so if politicians take actions to which the judiciary object on the grounds that they conflict with these universal laws, such politicians are acting in a tyrannical and despotic manner.

Thus one of Britain's most important judges, Lord Bingham, a senior law lord, said it was a "complete misunderstanding" for people to suggest "that the judges in some way seek to impede or frustrate the conduct of government." The judges were simply "auditors of legality," who quashed government decisions from time to time because they were contrary to law, not because the judges happened to disagree with them.[6]

But law is not, as Lord Bingham implied, immutable. Laws depend on interpretation by the courts. Far from providing certainty, law is a battleground of contestable viewpoints where victory may depend on highly subjective judgments. And nowhere are these judgments more subjective and contestable than under human rights law. Unlike national laws, which require the courts to interpret the intentions of the parliaments that passed them, human rights law requires the courts to arbitrate between the competing principles of the Human Rights Convention, in which the vast majority of rights are balanced by their exception. So by definition, these "rights" are not universal at all. On the contrary, they are highly contingent, dependent on the opinion, prejudices or whims of the judges who are called upon to arbitrate between them. And these are deeply divisive issues—which means the judges inevitably stray into territory that is properly the province of politicians, elected by and responsive to public opinion.

An example of this was provided by Lady Hale, who upon becoming Britain's first female law lord—equivalent to a justice of the U.S. Supreme Court—gave a press conference. She was in favor, she said, of gay adoption, legally recognized gay partnerships and improved legal rights for heterosexual cohabitants, and she wanted to see the concept of fault removed from divorce law. These issues, which are among the most divisive in our society, are all political topics. They are the subject of heated debate in Parliament and among the general public. The notion that one of England's most senior judges, supposedly the acme of impartiality, should have proclaimed her views like this suggested that any cases she heard on these topics would be prejudged by an ideological agenda.

That agenda, moreover, far from embodying universal values, represents a direct and deadly attack on the normative values of family life that underpin British society. It is, nevertheless, the agenda of a significant section of England's judiciary. These are judges who either are terrified of being thought "out of touch" with modern life or, having never grown out of the sixties counterculture when they came to maturity, have whole-heartedly embraced the obnoxious "victim culture" that gives unchallenged preference to minorities, however they behave, at the expense of the majority, who are deemed to "oppress" them.

This was explicitly justified by Lord Bingham when he said that the Human Rights Convention, which existed to protect vulnerable minorities who were sometimes disliked, resented or despised, was an "intrinsically counter-majoritarian" instrument. It should come as no surprise, he added, that decisions vindicating their rights "should provoke howls of criticism by politicians and the mass media. They generally reflect majority opinion."[7]

So majority opinion, it seems, is essentially illegitimate, and the role of the judiciary is to use human rights law to override it. This unashamed justification of judicial supremacism is as antidemocratic, subversive and unjust as it is arrogant. It does not allow for wrongdoing by any "disliked, resented or despised" minority, but presupposes that it is in the right simply by virtue of being such a minority.

This view is based on the doctrine of moral equivalence, which has redefined equality as "identicality" in a secular universe of—in the pungent phrase of the writer David Selbourne—"dutiless rights."[8] It is duty and obligation that forge a community; rights detached from obligations fragment a society into competing interest groups fighting each other for supremacy. The only duties recognized by the rights agenda are the obligations on the state to deliver group rights. The individual claimant is liberated from obligations to the state, to convention or to other individuals in the cause of his own unchallengeable autonomy.

Human rights doctrine is thus the principal cultural weapon to undermine the fundamental values of Western society—with an activist judiciary turned into culture warriors, marching behind the banner of militant secularism. As the human rights activist Francesca Klug boasted in her book *Values for a Godless Age*, "Human rights are now probably as significant as the Bible has been in shaping modern western values."[9] The result of this judicial activism is an increasing breakdown of social, legal and moral conventions by unelected, unaccountable judges. In some cases, they have unilaterally challenged moral norms without public opinion even being consulted, and have undermined concepts such as family life, truth, social order, citizenship and law itself.

Three examples:

• In 1999, the law lords ruled that gay tenants should have the same rights under the Rent Acts as married couples and blood relatives. This in turn followed remarks by the leading family judge Dame Elizabeth Butler-Sloss that it was acceptable for gay couples to adopt children. Asked about such judicial liberalism, the then Lord Chief Justice Bingham said it was important for the law to "keep in touch with changing social attitudes."

Yet his assumption that the judges were simply reflecting cultural change was wrong. Tolerance of homosexuality and sympathy for a gay man who has faithfully cared for his sick partner are one thing. The law lords' decision, though, went much further than that and effectively redefined the family. According to Lord Slynn, the leading judge in the case, "family" need not mean either marriage or blood relationship. If "family" is defined, as he suggested, merely by love, care and attachment, it would appear that two devoted elderly spinsters would also be defined as "family." Is this really the judiciary merely "auditing legality"—or using the law to reshape society?

• The Court of Appeal ruled that gypsy families who had moved onto land they bought in Chichester, West Sussex, in open defiance of the planning laws should be allowed to stay because human rights law gave them "the right to family life." The ruling effectively gave the green light for illegal gypsy camps the length and breadth of the land to become legally untouchable, in flagrant breach of the planning laws. It thus legitimized widespread lawbreaking.

How can unlawful behavior suddenly be deemed lawful, even though the law that prohibits it is still on the statute book? The answer is that the Human Rights Act has become the law that subverts the rule of law itself. When Parliament incorporated the European Convention on Human Rights into English law, the public were reassured that the courts would not be able to strike down acts of Parliament if these were judged to be in conflict with human rights law. But this case showed that the Human Rights Act can trump other legislation. So the courts can simply push aside laws such as planning controls as if they didn't exist.

Although a subsequent ruling by the Law Lords in 2006 upheld the eviction of a gypsy family on the grounds that they had not established sufficient links with the place for it to be considered their home,[10] the earlier Chichester ruling destroyed the compact at the very heart of citizenship—the guarantee that there is equality for all under the law. Instead, the judges decided that for certain favored groups, they may waive the legal requirements that apply to the rest of us. All citizens have rights—but minorities, it appears, have more rights than others.

• The Gender Recognition Act was passed to conform with a ruling by the European Court of Human Rights. This ruling laid down that a transsexual had the right to claim that his or her gender at birth was whatever he or she now deemed it to be, as agreed by a panel of experts.

The act accordingly gave transsexuals the right to a birth certificate that does not record the actual gender into which they were born, but states instead that they were born in the gender that they now choose to be. While the plight of transsexual identity obviously deserves sympathy, this means that their birth certificate—the most basic guarantee that we are who we say we are—will be a lie. It means that someone who was born a man, married as a man and fathered children as a man will have a birth certificate, if he so chooses, that says he was born a female.

Worse still, a wide variety of people will be prosecuted if they make known the truth. Suppose a fitness club advertises for a personal trainer and takes up a reference at another gym for an applicant named Barbara. If that gym's owner employed this person as Barry, it will be a criminal offense for him to say so. So he may be forced to tell misleading half-truths about "Barbara's" performance. If a woman becomes a man, "he" nevertheless remains the mother of his (her?) children. Similarly, a man remains the father of his children and is therefore still liable for child support—even though his birth certificate might say he was born female. Such are the absurd and unjust contortions that result from a legislated lie—a lie brought into being as a direct result of judge–made human rights law.

Such law is also turning social order on its head along with the concepts of right and wrong. Two more examples:

• In 2002 an elderly street preacher, Harry Hammond, was fined £300 for displaying a placard that said: "Stop immorality. Stop homo sexuality. Stop lesbianism." He had been surrounded by a group of thirty to forty people who had thrown dirt at him and poured water over his head. Despite the fact that he had been assaulted, *he* was the one who was prosecuted. His conviction was upheld by Appeal Court judges who said his behavior "went beyond legitimate protest" because it had provoked disorder. So causing offense, it seems, is now a crime while assault is not—because the anti-majoritarian position is deemed inviolable and beyond criticism. Was this "auditing legality"—or redefining it?

• The government's drive against yob culture includes the imposition of antisocial behavior regulations, which may impose nighttime curfews for young people or order them to stop wearing hooded tops that obscure their faces from CCTV cameras. The High Court ruled in one case that forcibly removing a youth from a curfew zone breached his human rights; apparently the police could only *ask* him to leave. And in another case, it ruled that the ban on a boy's hooded top was illegal after his lawyers argued that it was "a breach of his right to personal development." "Auditing legality"—or defying common sense?

Armed with this doctrine, the English judiciary appears over and over again to have placed itself on the wrong side of the country's battle against terror and extremism. When it comes to Islamism, its human rights mindset seems to render it quite unable to grasp just who needs to be protected from what. In March 2005, the Court of Appeal ruled that a sixteen-year-old schoolgirl, Shabina Begum, should be allowed to wear a full-length jilbab, and that the decision of her school that she should wear school uniform instead—which already included shalwar kameez and an approved headscarf for the 80 percent of its girls who were Muslim—had denied her the right to manifest her religion in public under the Human Rights Convention.

This was despite the fact that her headmistress warned that permitting her to wear the jilbab would leave other Muslim girls defenseless against targeting and intimidation by fundamentalists; despite the fact that the affair was clearly a political stunt, with the girl claiming that the school's ban on the jilbab was a result of the "vilification" of Islam after 9/11; and despite the fact that she was backed by Hizb ut-Tahrir, the group that wants to see Sharia law in Britain and the restoration of the global Islamic caliphate, and which has been banned in countries around the world.

It seems that the judges are so blinded by their obsession with minority rights and their belief in the morally unchallengeable logic of human rights law that they cannot grasp that it might be used to *imperil* members of a minority at the hands of its own extremists. As a result Dr. Ghayasuddin Siddiqui, chairman of the Muslim Institute, rebuked them when he said: "This may be a victory for human rights but it is also a victory for fundamentalism."[11]

Still worse was to come, however, when the law lords delivered a seminal ruling over the detention of foreign terrorism suspects without trial. Blocked by the courts from deporting such extremists, the government locked up the ones it considered most dangerous in Belmarsh prison pending their eventual deportation. But in 2004, the law lords struck down the provisions that allowed for the detention without trial of suspected foreign terrorists on the grounds that they were discriminatory and disproportionate under human rights law.

Their reasoning was deeply flawed and illogical. They argued that locking up foreign Islamic terror suspects without trial was discriminatory, because there were also Muslim UK nationals who were terror suspects and who were not being locked up without trial. They compared foreign nationals and British nationals and decided that, as the former were not being treated the same as the latter, this was unlawful discrimination.

But this was not to compare like with like. Foreign nationals do not have the rights or responsibilities of British citizens. Most pertinently,

British nationals cannot be deported, nor once arrested are they free to move to another country. The foreign terror suspects in question were always free to leave prison at any time if another country would take them. They were only being held pending deportation. To say that it was discrimination to treat suspects being held pending deportation differently from suspects who cannot be deported and cannot freely leave the country once in custody amounted to the belief in "identicality" that is such a feature of human rights law, and which claims that only identical treatment is fair even if the circumstances are different. This produces in fact not fairness but gross injustice—and in the case of the terrorist threat to this country, a possibly lethal outcome.

Yet the reaction of some of these judges to holding foreign terror suspects without trial in circumstances where they were actually free to leave was little short of hysterical. Lord Scott said this situation was "associated whether accurately or inaccurately with France before and during the Revolution, with Soviet Russia in the Stalinist era and now associated, as a result of section 23 of the 2001 Act, with the United Kingdom."[12]

Another of the judges, Lord Hoffmann, declared that Muslim extremism did not threaten the life of the British nation. He said: "The real threat to the life of the nation, in the sense of a people living in accordance with its traditional laws and political values, comes not from terrorism but from laws such as these."[13]

So the real danger was not a terrorist movement whose aim was to defeat Western democracy and reinstitute a seventh-century Islamic empire that stretched halfway across the globe, but the measures that a free society had devised to protect itself from such a threat.

The Belmarsh judgment did not merely suggest that the highest judges in the land had been suborned by the moral bankruptcy of victim culture. It also illustrated how the English judiciary was now using human rights law to tear up the very definition of citizenship, the compact with the state that gives citizens different rights and duties from noncitizens. It was but the most striking example to date of a judiciary that, assuming the mantle of legal infallibility and universal authority, was now not only threatening the democratic process but undermining the security and integrity of the nation along with its values.

At any time this would be disturbing enough; but in the present circumstances it is potentially lethal. For Britain, along with the rest of the free world, faces a threat to its security and values from without. A nation can fight to defend itself only if it knows what it is fighting for, if it is secure in its own identity and values. Yet these are being steadily undermined from within by the legal universalism of human rights doctrine, which, in weakening Britain's physical security while hollowing out its values on the grounds that minority rights must take precedence, is inadvertently providing a legal battering ram for the Islamic jihad.

CHAPTER THREE

THE SECURITY DEBACLE

66"The terrorists have come home," said a senior intelligence official based in Europe who often works with British officials. "It is payback time for a policy that was, in my opinion, an irresponsible policy of the British government to allow these networks to flourish inside Britain."[1]

The London bombings in July 2005 provoked a certain amount of grim schadenfreude among security officials in countries that for years had been watching the relentless development of "Londonistan" with incredulity and exasperation. They could not understand why successive British governments had allowed so many extremists and terrorist godfathers to enter Britain, take up residence and be left undisturbed to organize, recruit for, fund and disseminate the jihad against the West, often being paid generous welfare benefits to do so—and in a country that was always likely to be on the target list for such activities. So how could Britain, America's principal ally in the defense of the West, apparently have been asleep on its watch?

The July bombings were said to have caught the British security establishment unawares. It simply never saw them coming. In the United States, 9/11 had taken the authorities by surprise but only insofar as the details of the actual plot were concerned; they had been uncomfortably aware that an attack was an imminent possibility. But the British appeared not to have had a clue that the threat about which they had been issuing warnings ever since 9/11 was now imminent. Indeed, the threat assessment by the government's own Joint Terrorist Analysis Centre, finished just a month before the bombings, was actually taken *down* a notch, declaring that "there was no group with current intent and the capability" of mounting terrorist strikes in the UK of the kind that would shortly occur. To the extent that there was terrorist-related activity in the UK, it said, this was the direct result of events in Iraq.[2]

What also shook the security establishment was that the bombings revealed all too starkly just how little it knew about the radicalization of British Muslim boys. Apparently it had absolutely no idea of the extent to which religious fanaticism had taken hold of a segment of the British Muslim community. If it suspected so, it certainly wasn't on top of it. Even after the famous "wake-up call" of 9/11, the British still had enormous gaps in essential intelligence.

Government ministers were appalled by how little the security service knew. According to a senior Whitehall source present at meetings of COBRA, the government's crisis command group convened to react to the London bombings, there was general shock at the absence of information coming from the intelligence community about who was behind the bombings. He said: "We were all waiting for some answers. We lived in hope that the security service would provide a thread, or a sliver, but no. That was a shock to the system." The official said there was a question whether MI5 had "ever really engaged with the possibility that terrorists would be home-grown, British, English-speakers." "There was a real understanding," he said, "that this was our 9/11, but at least in the US reports had come in about concerns over the hijackers. Here there was nothing."[3]

Subsequently, there were unconfirmed reports that Britain's counterterrorism officials had missed several chances over a four-year period to identify as an Islamist terrorist Mohammed Sidique Khan, the Briton who was thought to have masterminded the July 7 attack. The al-Qaeda expert Rohan Gunaratna told the BBC that Khan was reported to have been associating with people identified as terrorist suspects by Western security services prior to the attacks on Britain, and even had links to an al-Qaeda fixer. It was also alleged that Khan was caught on film and recorded by the security services meeting a British-based terrorism suspect.[4]

We don't know whether this is true. But what is clear is that after 9/11, at least some British officials understood that Britain was also a target. Shortly after the American atrocities, the Prime Minister's Office published an analysis that said:

> Al Qaeda retains the capability and the will to make further attacks on the US and its allies, including the United Kingdom. . . . There is a continuing threat. Based on our experience of the way the network has operated in the past, other cells, like those that carried out the terrorist attacks on 11 September, must be assumed to exist. . . . Al Qaeda functions both on its own and through a network of other terrorist organizations. These include Egyptian Islamic Jihad and other north African Islamic extremist terrorist groups, and a number of other jihadi groups in other countries including the Sudan, Yemen, Somalia, Pakistan and India. Al Qaeda also maintains cells and personnel in a number of other countries to facilitate its activities. . . .[5]

The British clearly knew, therefore, that al-Qaeda was a many-headed hydra consisting of extensive and complex global networks of apparently disparate groups all connected by a particular overarching ideology. Yet even after 9/11, they still took no action against the Islamist extremists embedded in London. Moreover, they had also known since at least the late 1990s that British Muslims were becoming radicalized and recruited for the jihad—with British targets included in their sights.

In December 1998, eight young British Muslims from Birmingham, London and Luton were arrested and eventually convicted in the Yemeni capital Aden of plotting terrorist attacks against British targets in Yemen and abducting a group of tourists. Subsequently, security officials confessed they had no idea the youths had been recruited from mosques around England and were being trained at special "terrorist camps" sponsored by Osama bin Laden. "It was a complete shock to us, and it was a shock that chilled us to the bone," the source said.[6]

British security officials seem to specialize in being "shocked" time and again by such developments—but then doing nothing about them. What made this attitude even more astounding was that according to the prosecution, Abu Hamza had been the linchpin of the conspiracy, masterminding the terror from the mosque in Finsbury Park. Although he denied being thus involved, he admitted that one of the British terrorists was his son and another his godson, and that he had been phoned by one of them just after he had abducted the tourists.[7] Yet, despite being urged by the Yemenis to do something about Abu Hamza, the British did nothing.

The following year, a newspaper reported that every year some two thousand British Muslims were attending clandestine terrorist training camps around Britain to learn about holy war. The camps were run by al-Muhajiroun, a group based in London that advocated replacing Western governments with Islamic rule. The camps were being held most weekends in Birmingham and London and trained recruits in hand-to-hand combat and survival skills, telling them they should seek real military instruction in countries such as Yemen and Afghanistan.[8] Yet the British authorities seemed to regard such camps with indifference.

If by some chance the security service had been struck by a fit of absent-mindedness over the Yemen plot, a string of subsequent events would have reminded them that British Muslims were turning into jihadis. In December 2001, Richard Reid, an al-Qaeda sympathizer, tried to carry out a suicide attack by detonating a bomb in his shoe on a Paris-to-Miami airliner. In 2002, Ahmed Omar Saeed Sheikh masterminded the kidnap and murder of U.S. journalist Daniel Pearl in Pakistan. And in 2003, two more British boys, Mohammed Hanif and Omar Khan Sharif, helped carry out the suicide bomb attack on the Mike's Place beachfront bar in Tel Aviv.

Given the inescapable fact that British Muslim boys were indeed being recruited as suicide bombers, why therefore were the British authorities apparently so unprepared for the prospect of such British boys blowing up Britain?

The foiled millennium plots of 1999 and 2000, when al-Qaeda planned a series of attacks in Europe, the United States and the Middle

East, all led back to London. From these, say intelligence analysts, it became clear at that time that, although Hamburg, Milan and other cities were all important terrorist hubs, London represented a kind of headquarters on both a political and a strategic level. From October 2001, it was known that Abu Qatada was leading the Spanish, Milan and German al-Qaeda cells from his base in London. And the Mike's Place bombers had been indoctrinated by Omar Bakri Mohammed, known to be the ideologue who preached attack on the West and the Islamization of the United Kingdom.[9]

If British security officials didn't make the connection between such activities and the extremists promulgating the jihad from London, there was no shortage of foreign governments trying to enlighten them. Over the years, the governments of India, Saudi Arabia, Turkey, Israel, France, Algeria, Peru, Yemen and Russia, among others, lodged formal or informal protests about the presence in Britain of terrorist organizations or their sympathizers.[10] The French were passing information about Algerian radicals to the British but were mortified by their failure to act on it. They were particularly furious that Abu Qatada—later described by a British judge as being at the center of terrorist activities associated with al-Qaeda in the UK—was at one time allowed to "disappear" from London for a period.[11] After Abu Hamza welcomed the massacre of fifty-eight European tourists at Luxor in October 1997, Egypt denounced Britain as a hotbed for radicals. The Egyptian State Information Service posted a "Call to Combat Terrorism" on its official website. Of its fourteen most-wanted terrorists, seven were based in Britain, among them Yasser al-Siri, sentenced to death in absentia for plotting the failed assassination of an Egyptian prime minister, and in charge of the Islamic Observation Centre in London, a mouthpiece for Egyptian rebels.[12]

Many countries asked Britain to extradite radicals back to the countries they were threatening but were turned down, often by the courts. Morocco was reported to have sought the extradition of one man who they said planned the May 2003 attacks in Casablanca which killed forty-five people. He was identified as a founder of the Moroccan Islamic Combatant Group, cited by the United Nations as a terrorist network connected to al-Qaeda and said to have had sleeper cells prepared to mount synchronized bombings in Britain, France, Italy, Belgium and Canada. The British refused. Baltasar Garzón, a Spanish investigating magistrate, requested the extradition of Abu Qatada. Britain refused. For ten years, France fought for the extradition of Rachid Ramda over his suspected role in a bombing in Paris in 1995 staged by Algeria's militant Armed Islamic Group. The British courts refused,[13] finally allowing his extradition in December 2005.

After the British courts refused to extradite to Saudi Arabia Dr. Mohammed al-Massari, who was suspected of terrorist acts there and who helped set up al-Qaeda's office in London, the former Saudi ambassador to London, Prince Turki al-Faisal, described Saudi frustration: "When you call somebody, he says it is the other guy. If you talk to the security people, they say it is the politicians' fault. If you talk to the politicians, they say it is the Crown Prosecution Service. If you call the Crown Prosecution Service, they say, no it is MI5. So we have been in this run-around for the last two and a half years."[14]

One former senior U.S. intelligence official was reported as saying of the British: "They have a really hard time understanding that people like Massari and Abu Qatada are real goddamn problems. It took a long, long time before they began taking those threats seriously. . . . There is a certain amount of reluctance on the part of the British to move quickly. What they never seem to realise is that by the time they know they have a problem it is too late."[15]

So why has Britain been so singularly reluctant to act against the Islamist extremists in its midst? The reasons, as always when questions are asked about the behavior of the secret state, are inevitably murky. But through the self-serving excuses, evasions and obfuscations that such an inquiry tends to throw up, a picture emerges that raises some urgent questions about Britain's ability even now to defend itself and the rest of the free world against Islamist terror.

The first explanation is that, during the 1990s, both the British and the Americans failed to grasp the threat to the West that was developing in the Islamic world. The British, moreover, were gazing firmly in the wrong direction. Instead of studying the Middle East as a cause for concern, they were staring across the Irish Sea at Northern Ireland, where a terrorist insurrection against the UK had been in progress since the 1970s. The mindset, on both sides of the Atlantic, was that terrorism was tied to discrete grievances against individual states. And with the end of the Cold War, the notion of a global threat rooted in ideology was assumed to be dead and buried.

James Woolsey, who between 1993 and 1995 ran the Central Intelligence Agency, says that both American and British intelligence made the same mistake. Communist ideology had actually died a long time before communism itself imploded. Western intelligence agencies therefore no longer had the analysts who could recognize and decipher an ideology. So they never understood that with the resurgence of the Salafi/Wahhabi form of Islam, they were facing a set of ideas that had gripped the minds of believers so deeply they would march against the free world under its banner. Instead, the agencies tended to discount what such people were saying because it all sounded so crazy. "When they talked about the worldwide rule of the caliphate, we dismissed it," Woolsey said.[16]

Britain, moreover, believed that it had no Middle East interests that might present a problem. It was America that was principally embroiled in the Israel/Arab impasse. France, which had been facing Islamic terrorism on the streets from the early 1990s, was thought to be suffering the after-effects of its entanglement with Algeria. Britain had no such issues in the Middle East. It furthermore never occurred to the establishment that Britain's Muslims might be touched by Middle East radicalism since they had come overwhelmingly from the Indian sub-continent. So after the Cold War, MI5 decided to focus its attention upon Northern Ireland, the drugs trade and economic espionage. That was what the government asked it to do. The intelligence world did not deliver the goods on what was going on in the Middle East because its customers in the political world didn't commission it to do so.

In 1994, MI5 disbanded G7, the unit it ran jointly with the foreign intelligence service MI6 to monitor Islamist terrorism. When it reorganized its coverage again in late 1996 in response to the growing phenomenon of Islamist violence, vital continuity and expertise had been lost from the service. "People just disappeared from view," a source was reported as saying. "We more or less had to start again."[17] Perhaps just as crucially, in 1992 it also disbanded its anti-subversion unit, which had been engaged in studying communism and, to a lesser extent, neo-Nazi ideology.[18] With the disappearance of this unit there vanished not only irreplaceable expertise in spotting subversion and analyzing the way it worked within societies, but the very notion that subversion remained a problem to be addressed. Indeed, to this day the suggestion that radical Islamism poses a subversive threat to Britain and the West tends to be dismissed with incomprehension by those responsible for directing British counterterror strategy.

Nevertheless, the explanation for official indifference does not lie wholly in the dismal ignorance, among the political and intelligence class, of the intellectual earthquake taking place in the Muslim world. For there *were* people in Britain who tried to alert the rest of the establishment to what was happening.

Oliver Revell was head of counterintelligence for the FBI from 1980 to 1991 and then headed the FBI in Texas for a further three years. He had much to do with the British intelligence community in the 1990s. During that period, he says, there was certainly an awareness within that community of the development of Wahhabi Islamism and the potential threat this posed to the West. But the politicians weren't listening.[19]

The former archbishop of Canterbury, Lord Carey, recalls that he was so concerned in the early 1990s about the Islamist extremists pouring into London that he told Prime Minister John Major about his anxieties, but was fobbed off with a meeting with the head of MI5, who agreed that "we needed identification cards."[20]

A senior Conservative politician, the Marquess of Salisbury, says that during the 1980s and 1990s he tried to warn the governments of both Margaret Thatcher and her successor, John Major, about the growing threat to Britain and the West from Islamist extremists, but was brushed aside. "There were people then who saw very clearly what was happening," he said. "Alastair Crooke [a former MI6 officer] wrote a brilliant paper about the nature of fundamentalist Islam when he was station chief in Islamabad, in which he warned of the danger it posed to the West. I read it. But no one listened. It was like appeasement before the Second World War. If you have a set of prejudices, it's inconvenient to question them."[21]

Another intelligence source said that during the 1990s, opinion within British intelligence circles was divided. "There was a lot of talk about extremist activity but it was said to be better to let them let off steam than bottle it up," he said. "They thought that if the Muslim community was targeted, the fallout would be greater. It could affect British interests around the world and project Britain as a less than democratic society. There were some who said there was no threat at all, and some who said there was a threat—but it could be dealt with in a different way. There were substantial constituencies on both sides of this argument."[22]

David Blunkett was Britain's home secretary from 2001 to 2005. He believes that the British security and political establishment did not—and still does not—fully understand the dimensions of the monster it is fighting. The security world, he said, was not generally given direct instructions from politicians but was instead sensitive to the general zeitgeist. "It all got mixed up with people's perceptions of what was going on in Israel and the Middle East," he said. "People were saying, if only there was justice across the world these demands would be negotiable. Politicians were looking for political solutions to issues such as Palestine; this was what was in the air at the time, and the intelligence world would take its cue from that."[23]

Reda Hussaine is an Algerian journalist who started inquiring into Algerian radicals in London after his Paris office, where he was trying to start up an independent Algerian newspaper, was ransacked in 1993. The French police told him that the attack had been organized from London, that the group responsible was sending money to terrorists in Algeria, and that Abu Qatada was behind it.

Hussaine came to London and met supporters of the GIA, the Algerian terrorist group. "I went to the mosques and picked up leaflets claiming killings and assassinations," he said. "Scotland Yard was approaching these groups to find out what was going on but it was being told lies that they were doing nothing. But they started talking about launching attacks in Europe against France. They killed a French diplomat in Algeria, hijacked a plane and planned to bomb the Paris Metro. All these claims were coming from London.

"I went to French intelligence and started to understand from them that the British wouldn't listen. The French thought the British didn't care about what was going on outside the UK. The British thought it was an Algerian and French problem."

Hussaine made contact with Scotland Yard. "I told them these people were going to Afghanistan to train. They said they couldn't arrest them because they were free to come and go on their papers. I told them these were false papers but they said it was difficult to inter-fere. I told them: 'They are being trained to kill you, not Algerians'; but they said they couldn't interfere. They didn't believe me."[24]

A few months later, Hussaine was put in touch with MI5. With the Algerians and the French, he had dealt with senior people. But MI5 sent him only junior officials to talk to, a sign of the lack of seriousness with which his intelligence was being treated. He gave them informa-tion, he says, between 1999 and 2000 before he finally gave up because they were ignoring what he was giving them.

"I watched young Muslims at the Finsbury Park mosque in Lon-don in the late 1990s being prepared for journeys to military camps," he said. "Money was raised for their air fares by selling books and films in stalls at the mosques. Those who were chosen to go were the most fanatical—and also the most obedient. I saw Richard Reid, the shoe bomber, at the mosque and many others like him before they went abroad to learn their skills as mujahideen."[25]

So why were such warnings brushed aside? According to Hussaine, his MI5 handlers told him the reason.

"My contacts there said to me, we are giving these people a roof over their heads, food, free health care—and the security of Britain will be very safe. We don't care what is going on outside this country. They told me this face to face. The British had a problem under-standing the culture of the Arabs. I told them, you don't understand this kind of threat. One day they may attack you as unbelievers. They said, we don't think they will do it here. This is a special place. I told them Britons were going to fight, but they never thought they would fight their own country. But when these people go to the mosque they are told that their country is paradise and they swear allegiance not to their country but to God."[26]

British officials privately admit that such a bargain did indeed

form part of their calculations. The Islamists were being left undisturbed to conduct their activities on the assumption that they would
not then attack Britain. As a former British Special Branch security
officer was reported to say, "There was a deal with these guys. We told
them if you don't cause us any problems, then we won't bother you."[27]

The Islamists understood very well what a gift they were being
handed by the British state. In 1998, Omar Bakri Mohammed was
asked why the Islamist groups never attacked Britain. He replied: "I
work here in accordance with the covenant of peace which I made with
the British government when I got [political] asylum. . . . We respect
the terms of this bond as Allah orders us to do."[28] Once Britain started
defending the West against them in Afghanistan and then in Iraq,
however, the Islamists declared that this covenant was destroyed. But
the fact is that Britain had always been a target of the war upon the
West. It simply had failed to understand this until it was too late.

This bargain, or "covenant of security," had been the dirty little
secret at the heart of the British government's blind-eye policy. It had
allowed Islamist radicals free rein in London and elsewhere in Britain
in a kind of unspoken "gentlemen's agreement" that if the British
authorities left them alone, they would not turn on the country that
was so generously nurturing them. The British didn't care what they
were up to in other countries. Abroad wasn't their concern. As long as
there was no threat to Britain, the government and security establishment just didn't want to know. They kept a weather eye on the radicals,
but only to make sure that English law wasn't being broken.

Such tunnel vision was accompanied by attitudes straight out of the
colonial handbook. To the higher mandarinate of Whitehall, Islamist
extremism was merely an arcane dispute between different kinds of
unpleasant, swarthy people who were always doing terrible things to
each other in far-flung places. There was certainly no cause for
Britain to take sides.

Accordingly, the Islamist exiles in London were seen as being but
the latest of all the dissidents and radicals to whom Britain had traditionally given refuge for centuries. At a dinner one evening, the bishop
of Rochester was startled to hear the Algerian foreign minister com-
plain that when the Algerians had tried to warn the British government

about the terrorists in London, the British replied dismissively that they were "freedom fighters."[29] In a country that had so catastrophically lost its role in the world, the sacred principle of freedom of speech now came to define its claim to global virtue. It trumped all other considerations. Moral judgment, along with common sense, was therefore suspended for the duration.

It was also inextricably mixed up with the delicate issue of Britain's traditionally close if ambiguous ties with the Arab world. Not for nothing was the British Foreign Office known jovially as "the camel corps." Britain's interests had long been associated with Arab countries to such an extent that a mindset composed of both unprincipled groveling and postcolonial contempt towards the Arabs, possibly in equal measure, had come to suffuse much of the British establishment.

"The intelligence world did take the view that we should soft-pedal on these radicals in London because of our interests in the Arab world," said the former home secretary David Blunkett. In particular, Britain had extensive commercial interests with Saudi Arabia. But Saudi Arabia was impaled on its own huge internal contradiction. It was the principal exporter of Wahhabism to the world, and yet it was also a principal target of the Wahhabis of al-Qaeda. So while it was trying to buy off those radicals who it thought posed a threat to its own security, it was doing nothing to shut down the conveyor belt of fanaticism it had set in motion. "Our people just didn't understand the nature of this threat at a time when it could have made the difference," said Blunkett.[30]

Saudi Arabia's internal contradictions were reflected in Britain's deeply ambiguous relationship with the oil-soaked kingdom. After all, wasn't Britain doing huge business with the Saudis? And yet, it also said to itself while holding its collective nose, were they not a despotic regime that flagrantly abused human rights?

Lord Salisbury recounts how, when parliamentarians like himself visited Saudi Arabia during the 1980s, the Foreign Office would brief them on how to respond when the Saudis inevitably complained that Saudi radicals had been allowed into London. "The answer was that we had freedom of speech, that Saudi was a repressive regime and although it was important to us there was a limit to what we would do for our allies. It was the attitude of the 'camel corps' that this was a fight between people of an alien faith and it was nothing to do with us. We were prepared to sell them almost anything. But we shouldn't be seen to have part of our domestic policy dictated by Saudi. We were all 'white men' and we had a tradition of refugees. It was hugely self-indulgent."[31]

It was also congruent with the example being given from the top. For during this period the British government was dealing with terrorists all the time—such as the Irish Republican Army or Yasser Arafat—under the most transparent of fig leaves. Indeed, British governments have always been prepared to negotiate with terrorists, as they once showed in Kenya, Malaya, Aden and elsewhere. Even when the IRA were engaged in blowing up bits of the United Kingdom, the government was still talking to them. This is because the official British mind always goes for the short-term solution. Some call this pragmatism. Others call it a national instinct for appeasement. In the case of Londonistan, it was a policy of gross irresponsibility. In cynically promoting the narrowest interpretation possible of the national interest, the British acted as midwife to the monster of global jihad.

But there was another part of the British mindset that was more troubling even than its cynical short-termism or postcolonial arrogance. This was its profound unwillingness—shared with the United States—to acknowledge that what the country was being confronted with was religious fanaticism, an unwillingness that continues to this day.

The former FBI officer Oliver Revell says that both the U.S. and the UK have serious problems in dealing with radicalism rooted in religion. "The extremists have found the soft underbelly of Western civilization, the sanctuary provided in its very heart by the commitment to freedom of speech," he said. "In both the U.S. and the UK, there was and still is a great reluctance to investigate any religious activity unless there is clear evidence that a crime has been committed. It's a fastidious reluctance to enter into the sphere of religion, which is felt to be a legitimate private activity in which the state has no right to interfere. So there has been no support for collecting intelligence on a religion, and we are also reluctant to intervene in fundraising by terrorist groups because they often shelter behind religious social welfare activities."[32]

To understand the depth of this reluctance and incomprehension in Britain, however, it is necessary first to bear in mind one of the most deeply rooted of all aspects of the British character. This is its belief in the rational, the everyday and what is demonstrably evident, and its corresponding suspicion of the abstract, the theoretical and the obscurantist.

Wars of religion, when different kinds of Christian burned each other at the stake in post-Reformation England, are seared into the British historical memory but belong to a premodern period of savagery upon which the country has long resolutely turned its back. The liberal settlement that followed the Enlightenment in Britain put religion very firmly back into its box and elevated reason to pole position as the supreme national virtue. This sturdy empiricism lies at the very core of the British love of liberty, and has bequeathed to them their deep skepticism of all forms of extremism. Presented with a ranting ideologue, the British are less likely to succumb than to scoff.

But the downside of this robustly down-to-earth approach is that the British now find it very hard to deal with religious fanaticism. They no longer recognize it—or want to recognize it. Presented with patently ludicrous ideological ranting, they refuse to believe that anyone can take it seriously. So when Islamist clerics such as the hook-clawed Abu Hamza or Omar Bakri Mohammed were loudly trumpeting their hatred of the West and their calls to holy war against it, MI5 regarded them as little more than pantomime clowns, shooting their mouths off in the open where everyone could hear them and laugh them to scorn. Except, of course, a number of impressionable young Muslims did not laugh at all. Such ranting incited them instead to enlist in that holy war against the West which Britain refused to accept was an actual and lethal reality.

As one foreign intelligence source put it: "During the 1990s, many attempts were made to enlighten the British about what was happening. But they refused to see this problem as having a religious character. If this was a religious problem, it became a religious confrontation—and the specter of a religious war was too horrendous. A religious war is different from any other war because you are dealing with absolute beliefs and the room for compromise is very limited. Religious wars are very protracted and bloody, and often end up with a very high toll of lives.

"So the British turned a blind eye to the fact that freedom of religion for Muslims means the freedom to propagate their religion in every possible way. There was almost a conscious psychological suppression of this subject. Politicians didn't want to think about it at all. The official class wanted to think about it in as narrow a way as possible by dealing with individual incidents as they occurred, but no more than that. They were very concerned about social unrest among Asians in cities like Bradford, but they treated it more as a criminal matter. There was a conscious and subconscious effort to deracialize and de-politicize it and distance themselves from its religious aspects. After 9/11, they woke up in principle but not in practice. They still thought that the UK wasn't in the front line, and if they continued with their policy of 'benevolence' the same thing wouldn't happen to them."[33]

That is surely why—at least in part—the British authorities were so shocked by the emergence in July 2005 of Muslim Britons who turned themselves into human bombs against other Britons. They knew well enough—how could they not have known?—that some young British Muslims were being recruited for the jihad. But they clung nevertheless to the last vestige of their self-delusion, that such British jihadis might go and blow up places abroad but they would not turn on Britain because they would not bite the hand that had so generously fed them. It was the same assumption of the covenant of security that had allowed so many jihadi ideologues to remain at liberty in Britain. It was cynical, opportunistic—and lethally wrong. Yet the very same mistakes are being made even now. There are still people in the political and security establishment who believe that Britain is not an ideological target of the jihad and that the only reason terrorism has erupted on its shores is because of Britain's support for America's "war on terrorism." The bitter national divisions over the war in Iraq and the anti-Americanism that has swept the country ever since 9/11 are reflected within not just political circles but the intelligence world, too.

David Blunkett candidly admits that it has taken him a long time to comprehend the real nature of the threat. "We just didn't understand that they [the Islamists] were not just anti-Western but on a different plane altogether and this is still not widely understood in the UK," he said. "We can be as nice as pie to them but that's not the issue. They are on a mission that has taken them outside anything we can say, a mission to destroy completely our way of life." Even now, he said, the British authorities were failing to ask themselves what had so captured the minds of young men from Yorkshire that they would turn themselves into human bombs. "Because they think it's 'just a few extremists,' they are continuing to track the threat of big spectacular attacks, looking for example at transfers of materials for bombs, whereas what they should be looking at is what's going on inside people's heads."[34]

The extreme difficulty that Britain is having in dealing with the religious dimension of Islamist terrorism is illustrated by the behavior of the police. True, they have raised their game ever since 9/11 shocked them into realizing the threat facing Britain—notwithstanding the grievous error made after the London bombings, when the Metropolitan Police shot dead an innocent Brazilian wrongly suspected of being a suicide bomber—and have reportedly had a number of successes in thwarting terrorist plots. But the challenge posed by Islamist terrorism has placed them in a dilemma they have been unable to resolve.

The first line of defense against terrorist attack is the police. But the British police have become a symbol of a society that has lost its way. Britain has been progressively crippled by a "victim culture," in which minority groups effectively use moral blackmail against the majority on the grounds of its alleged oppressive behavior. Ever since a watershed case in the 1990s, when the police were branded "institutionally racist" following the bungled investigation into the murder of a black student in south London, they have been paralyzed by the fear of giving offense to any minority group and being tarred with the lethal charge of prejudice.

The anathema that was pronounced upon them of "institutional racism" delivered a near-terminal blow to an institution that was already on the ropes. A succession of corruption scandals and miscarriage-of-justice cases back in the 1970s and 1980s had profoundly undermined police self-confidence; and this was exacerbated by the reaction of successive governments, which tied them up in red tape and official directives. As a result, police professionalism took a dive and one high-profile criminal investigation after another became mired in incompetence.

In this lowered state, the charge of racism had a shattering effect. From being the thin blue line against disorder, the police now transformed themselves into the coercive arm of state-enforced virtue. Instead of preventing offenses being committed, they now gave priority to preventing offense being given. Displaying an obsession with minority rights, they devoted disproportionate time and resources to prioritizing the agendas of the fullest possible range of self-designated victim groups such as gays, lesbians, bisexuals, transgender people, disabled people, Gypsies, women and of course ethnic minorities, and training themselves to do nothing that could conceivably give offense to any such group.

A proper concern to be respectful to cultural differences thus turned into the wholesale adoption by the police of victim-culture mentality, the pursuit of radical grievances against the majority population. So great was the grip of this mindset that officers' freedom of maneuver was often hampered by the fear that if they inadvertently offended a victim group, they would find themselves on a disciplinary charge accused of discrimination.

This was dramatically illustrated when Britain's leading police officer, the Metropolitan Police commissioner Sir Ian Blair, was himself rebuked by an employment tribunal for "hanging his own officers out to dry" to prove his antiracist credentials. The tribunal found that he had racially discriminated against three white officers who were disciplined after alleged racist remarks at a training day, in which one of them had referred to Muslim headwear as "tea cozies," mispronounced Shi'ites as "shitties" and said he felt sorry for Muslims who fasted during Ramadan. The disciplining of the officers had been grossly disproportionate. Yet Sir Ian responded to this finding against himself by declaring that he was "unrepentant," repeating that the remarks were "Islamophobic" and declaring that the Met had to "embrace diversity."[35]

As this case indicated, Muslim sensitivities were uppermost in police minds. The charge of "Islamophobia" was one that the police would go to almost any lengths to avoid. This near-pathological sensitivity was heightened still further by the government's instruction, first after 9/11 and then again after the London bombings of 2005, to avoid doing anything to alienate Britain's Muslims, in accordance with government strategy to bring the bulk of them on board. But since Muslims tend to be alienated by any action that suggests there is anything wrong with their community or their religion, this meant the police had to deny the nature of Islamist terrorism altogether.

This was why, on the day that four Islamist suicide bombers blew themselves and more than fifty London commuters to bits, the Met's deputy assistant commissioner, Brian Paddick, stood before the television cameras and made the noteworthy comment: "As far as I am concerned, Islam and terrorists are two words that do not go together."[36]

He amplified this by saying that while the bombers may have been Muslim the crime was not Islamic because Islam forbade the taking of innocent life. That may well be so; but across the world, hundreds of thousands of innocent lives have been ended by terrorists who are doing so under the banner of Islam, find justification in Islam for their deeds and are told by Islamic religious authorities that such actions are a religious duty. At a stroke, therefore, this senior British policeman had denied not only the nature of the atrocity on British soil but the whole basis of the war against the West.

This was not a rogue comment. For the British police say they do not use the phrase "Islamic terrorism" or even "Islamist terrorism." They use other phrases instead, such as "international terrorism." They say that it is as misleading to talk about Islamic terrorists as it would be to refer to the IRA as Catholic terrorists. But this comparison reveals a major category confusion. True, the IRA were Catholics and their adversaries were Protestants. But their cause was not Catholicism. It was a united Ireland. They did not want to impose the authority of the Pope upon Britain. They wanted their own authority over Ireland. There is simply no comparison to the agenda of the Islamists who want to defeat the West in the name of Islam, impose Sharia law and re-establish the medieval caliphate throughout the world. That is a religious war, a jihad transposed from the seventh century to today. And that is what the police and much of the British establishment are desperate to deny.

Six months before the London bombs, the Metropolitan Police commissioner, Sir Ian Blair, said: "There is nothing wrong with being an Islamic fundamentalist." When the journalist interviewing him suggested that the family of Theo van Gogh, the Dutch filmmaker who was killed for questioning Islamic attitudes to women, might beg to differ on that one, Sir Ian replied, "There were lots of fundamentalist Muslims who didn't shoot him. . . . Look at Jerry Springer [the stage show *Jerry Springer: The Opera*]. Christian fundamentalists objected very strongly but they didn't shoot the producer. And nor do 99.9 percent of Muslims want the sort of extremism that leads to violence. They know the consequences of terrorists claiming to be Muslim, so our job is to help. Bridges will be built."[37]

Here was another major confusion. Certainly, not all religious fundamentalists are terrorists. But it all depends what the "fundamental" truths of the religion are. The New Testament does not advocate the killing of the unfaithful. The Koran does. This does not mean that all Muslims—or, indeed, all "fundamentalist" Muslims—believe that they must do so. Plenty of them find enough succor from the peace-promoting, spiritual content of their religious texts. But it does mean that others can and do find a religious authority in those texts for holy war. Sir Ian's argument is a bit like saying that since not all smokers develop cancer, it follows that cancer cannot be caused by smoking. What bedevils this subject is the equally illogical belief that talking about Islamist terrorism implies that all Muslims support terror. Clearly, they do not. But some do; the interpretation of the religious authority they cite may be a matter for theological dispute but its roots in the religion are real, and it is dangerously deluded to pretend otherwise.

The key to Sir Ian's attitude almost certainly lies in his declaration: "Bridges will be built." The strategy is to win over the majority of British Muslims; so the police are bending over backwards to show sympathy for them and respect for their religion. In Nottingham, the police handed out green ribbons after the London bombings to express solidarity with Muslims, who, according to the chief constable, were on the receiving end of Islamophobic attacks.[38] And guidelines for the Bedfordshire force say that when officers raid Muslim homes they should remove their shoes, not use dogs and not mount predawn raids because at that hour people might be "spiritually busy."[39]

The belief is that the police can defeat the terrorists only if the community that harbors them takes the side of the police instead. But if that community is itself in deep denial and refuses to accept that the terrorism is rooted in its own religious ideology, the police will not only fail to get the cooperation they need but will also neuter their own efforts.

So it has proved. Opposition by the police forced the government to abandon part of the antiterrorism policy it brought forward after the London bombings. Senior officers claimed that the proposed power to close down extremist mosques could send the "wrong message" to Muslims and lead to the police missing out on vital intelligence. They also opposed the proposal to outlaw the extremist group Hizb ut-Tahrir on the grounds that since it was "against violence," driving it underground was wrong.[40] Once again, the police displayed a dismaying failure to grasp the particular nature of Islamist terrorism and the way it derives its energy—and recruits—from indoctrination along a continuum of religious extremism.

Worse still, this conceptual failure to understand the link between ideology and terrorism drove the police to seek assistance from the people of whom they should be most wary. They regularly met the Islamic Human Rights Commission to discuss safety in Muslim communities, even though its official adviser was the key al-Qaeda fixer Mohammed al-Massari.[41] At various conferences to discuss the terrorist threat, senior police officers declared their respect for the Muslim Brotherhood and its mouthpiece in Britain, the Muslim Association of Britain, despite its extremist views and support for terrorism in Iraq and Israel. This enraged secular Muslims who were present, who protested that by cozying up to such extremists the police were betraying the Muslim community.[42] And a government adviser revealed that the Metropolitan Police Muslim Contact Unit had commented favorably on Sheikh Yusuf al-Qaradawi because, it said, he had "a positive community impact in the fight against al-Qaeda propaganda in the UK."[43] This was the same Sheikh Qaradawi who called suicide bombing in Israel and Iraq a religious duty and who, in a speech to an Islamic conference in Ohio in 1995, had said: "We will conquer Europe, we will conquer America, not through the sword but through dawah [proselytism]."[44]

In response to all of which, the British security establishment has its eyes firmly shut as it sleepwalks into collusion with the enemy it should be fighting.

· CHAPTER FOUR ·

THE MULTICULTURAL PARALYSIS

Dewsbury is a small town in the West Riding of Yorkshire, one of the many northern English mill towns that saw an influx of Asians to work in the textile mills in the latter decades of the last century. In 1987, it became the site of a bitter battle when the parents of twenty-six white children refused to send them to an overwhelmingly Muslim state-run primary school, and taught them instead in a room above a public house.

The parents did this because they wanted their children to be given Christian education, to be taught to a high standard especially in English, and to avoid what they saw as prejudice by teachers who were thought to be privileging Asian and Muslim culture. The school to which their children were being directed pursued instead the "multifaith" approach in accordance with government policy laid down a couple of years earlier, that schools should educate children in the values shared between cultures and to appreciate cultural diversity.[1]

Contrary to assurances from local officials who said they were committed to equality for all cultures, the parents discovered that local education policy aimed to counter a "Eurocentric" syllabus on the grounds that this was racist. They also discovered that ostensibly Christian acts of worship at the school were actually a multifaith mishmash, since priority was being given to "building bridges" between the Muslim and Christian communities. To this end, the chairman of the school's governors (who was a parish priest) seemed to be saying that Christianity and the Bible were "divisive and anti-social."[2] Needless to say, the parents were denounced by progressive opinion as "racists."

Eighteen years later, Dewsbury woke up to the fact that it had been the home town for a while of Mohammed Sidique Khan, the apparent leader of the July 7 suicide bombers. The Tablighi Jamaat mosque in Dewsbury was said to be a driving force for Islamist extremism. As reporters crawled over the town, they discovered that Mufti Zubair Dudha, who taught children, teenagers and young adults at the local Tarbiyah Academy and who had condemned suicide bombings, never-theless was revealed to have written in support of physical jihad against the West, and to have taught his students that "the enemies of Allah" had schemed "to poison the thinking and minds of [Muslim] youth and to plant the spirit of unsteadiness and moral depravity in their lives."[3]

These snapshots over time of one British town illustrate a trend that has transformed the whole of British life during the past four decades—one which has drastically weakened it from within to the threat from without. That trend is multiculturalism, the doctrine that is now the orthodoxy throughout all the institutions of British public life. Put at its simplest, it holds that Britain is now made up of many cultures that are all equal and therefore have to be treated in an identical fashion, and that any attempt to impose the majority culture over those of minorities is by definition racist.

This doctrine was a complete break from the earlier tradition of assimilating immigrants, which itself arose from Britain's once robust sense of and pride in its national culture and history. The break occurred because a series of developments shattered Britain's confidence in its own integrity and, deeper still, its very sense of what the nation was.

Britain's demographic profile is radically changing. Since 2001, the number of Britons who are emigrating has shot up from 50,000 to 120,000 per year. Under the triple pressures of a continuing inflow from the Indian subcontinent, the loss of control over asylum and an undiscussed government decision to encourage immigration on the grounds that it is good for the economy, Britain now has a net inflow of approximately 220,000 immigrants per year—four times the rate between 1985 and 1995. The government puts the net immigration figure rather lower, at 145,000 per year. On the basis even of this more modest statistic, Britain's population of about sixty million will rise over the next three decades by some six or seven million—and 83 percent of that new growth will come from immigration, most of that probably from the third world.[4] If these trends persist, therefore, by the end of this century Britain's population make-up will be unrecognizable.

Until about forty years ago, British society had been relatively homogeneous. True, the nation had originally been forged from waves of invasion by Romans, Angles, Saxons, Vikings and Normans; but for around one thousand years, its demographic profile remained remarkably stable. Such immigrations that occurred during that time, such as by the Irish, the Huguenots or the Jews from eastern Europe, were on a very small scale. During that period, British national identity centered upon a set of traditions, laws and customs arising out of its Christian heritage. This strong majoritarian culture meant that minorities were expected to fit in. They were treated with varying degrees of tolerance —and sometimes rank intolerance—but the rules of the modern settlement were clearly understood by both majority and minorities. The minorities were free to practice their religion, customs and culture in private, but where these conflicted with the law of the land or its fundamental traditions, the majoritarian culture would hold sway.

From the late 1960s onwards, however, Britain started to take in many more immigrants, first from Afro-Caribbean countries and then in much larger numbers from Asia and Africa. These waves brought in people from very different cultural and religious backgrounds, particularly those from the Asian subcontinent who, unlike the Christian Afro-Caribbeans, were Muslims, Hindus, Sikhs and other cultures foreign to the Judeo-Christian Western heritage.

Many of these newcomers, like earlier immigrants, very much wanted to identify with a nation whose own culture, values and history they admired and within which their separate ethnic identities could flourish under the umbrella of a shared sense of national identity. But they found that Britain was no longer willing to assimilate them to a national identity because it no longer had any belief in it, and certainly did not admire it—or even necessarily know any longer what it was.

This collapse of national self-confidence arose from a combination of things: postwar exhaustion, the collapse of the British Empire and therefore of national purpose, postcolonial flagellatory guilt of the kind that white liberals have made their specialty, and the Suez debacle in 1956, which brutally revealed to the humiliated British their own powerlessness in the world. This left the British establishment particularly vulnerable to the revolutionary ideology of the left, which took deepest hold during the 1960s and 1970s in the Western world, at the core of which lay a hatred of the mores of Western society. As a consequence, the British elite decided not only that the British nation was an embarrassment but also that the very idea of the nation was a damaging anachronism responsible for all the ills of the world, from racism through colonialism to war.

Britain in particular, and the nation in general, therefore had to be unraveled and a new world order constructed from principles untainted by the exclusive particulars of national culture. Thus Britain became enmeshed in the European Union, subscribed to the doctrine of universalism expressed through human rights law, and placed its faith in transnational institutions such as the United Nations, the International Criminal Court or the European Court of Justice as the major sources of legitimacy. Only the universal and the nation-busting could be innocent of prejudice. Only by being dismantled could the nation become legitimate again.

The expression of British majority values therefore became synonymous with racism. Multiculturalism and antiracism were now the weapons with which minorities were equipped to beat the majority. Not all minorities, mind you—Jews were not considered to be a minority because of the prevalent Marxist analysis that racism necessarily involved power, and since Jews were seen to be powerful, they were part of the majority and so could never be victims. Anyone from the third world, however, was suitably powerless and therefore their values had to trump those of the majority. And anyone who resisted this was pronounced guilty of racism or xenophobia. This was the new "tolerant" society.

In 2000, a widely remarked report by the multiethnic campaign group the Runnymede Trust[5] said that there should not be "a fixed conception of national identity and culture," declared that "British-ness has systematic, largely unspoken, racial connotations," and suggested that the nation was an artificial construct. It recommended that government should declare Britain to be a multicultural society, that candidates for senior police ranks should undergo training on racial equality and cultural diversity issues, that contracts and franchises should be awarded only after the production of plans to increase black and Asian staff at all levels, and so on.[6]

All this has duly come about. Multiculturalism has become the driving force of British life, ruthlessly policed by a state-financed army of local and national bureaucrats enforcing a doctrine of state-mandated virtue to promote racial, ethnic and cultural difference and stamp out majority values. Institutions have been instructed to teach themselves that they are intrinsically racist and to reprogram their minds in nonjudgmentalism. Government departments, local councils, the police and other bodies now give preferential treatment to ethnic minority candidates and projects and discriminate against white Western applicants.

The BBC has its own Asian network providing news and features inside the UK in Urdu, Bengali, Punjabi and Gujarati. There are now more than 140 housing associations in England catering to ethnic minorities; one of them, the Aashyana in Bristol, provides special apartments for Muslims with the toilets facing away from Mecca. The Lake District National Authority wanted to drop its guided walks organized by volunteer rangers because the participants were "too white and middle-class." Almost 10 percent of bodies subsidized by the Arts Council describe themselves as black or ethnic minority organizations. "British culture is not a single entity; we should rightly speak of British cultures," the Arts Council said.[7]

The ever-multiplying examples of British society trying to denude itself of its identity range from the invidious to the idiotic. Novelty pig calendars and toys were banned from a council office in case they offended Muslim staff.[8] Ice creams were withdrawn from the Burger King chain after complaints from Muslims that a whorl design on the lid looked like the word "Allah."[9] Various councils banned the concept of Christmas, on the grounds that it was "too Christian" and therefore "offensive" to peoples of other faiths, replacing it with references to winter festivals.[10] Some London education authorities tried to prevent ethnic minority children from watching the Queen Mother's funeral on television, with the argument that it would not mean anything to them.[11] A performance of Christopher Marlowe's sixteenth-century play *Tamburlaine the Great* at London's Barbican was censored for fear of upsetting Muslims; the scenes where Tamburlaine burns the Koran and criticizes the Prophet Mohammed were cut out.[12] These decisions were taken even though many provoked protests from Muslims and other minorities at their absurdity and inappropriateness.

Since the London bombings, there has been some anxious discussion about the possible ill-effects of the multicultural obsession. The chairman of the Commission for Racial Equality, Trevor Phillips, attacked the way in which it had divided the country and harmed social cohesion. He warned that the country was "sleepwalking towards segregation" along lines of ethnicity and religion, and warned that parts of some cities would soon be "black holes into which no one goes without fear."[13]

Phillips's main concerns were about separate development. But while this is indeed a troubling consequence, there is an even more significant point. Multiculturalism is said to promote equal treatment for all cultures. But this is not true. There is one culture that it does not treat equally at all, and that is the indigenous British culture. What purports to be an agenda of equality actually promotes the radical deconstruction of majority culture, the idea of the nation itself and the values of Western democracy—in particular, its understanding of morality and truth. Separatism is not the worst of it. This is a cultural scorched-earth policy: year zero for the secular, universal world order, in a Britain whose consequent moral, cultural and spiritual vacuum is rightly scorned as decadence by radical Islamists who are seizing the opportunity to fill it.

Nowhere has this attack on the nation been more pronounced, and with more devastating consequences, than in the schools. The British

education system simply ceased transmitting either the values or the
story of the nation to successive generations, delivering instead
the message that truth was an illusion and that the nation and its values
were whatever anyone wanted them to be. The country's history and
English teachers, the custodians of the core of national identity,
decided that Britain's national story and culture were racist and colo-
nialist and should therefore be traded in for a new, multicultural model.

One teacher argued that transmitting a sense of national identity
through education was "the new fundamentalism" associated automatically with the "superiority of the British Empire." Teaching
British history was to promote "notions of national supremacy which
equate the achievements of western society with the achievements of
humanity in general."[14] An education lecturer approvingly quoted
writers who questioned whether there could be any shared values at all.[15]
Two other education lecturers decided that "Englishness" not only
was monolithic, anachronistic and pernicious, but it funneled teachers
into such imperialistic programs as teaching children to read rather
than promoting socially desirable antiracist initiatives.[16] A head teacher
wrote: "The common culture of pre-1940 England, based on the
canon of English literature, the Whig interpretation of history and
the liturgy of the Church of England, has died. . . . Life and language
have outgrown the confines of English belief, history and ethnicity."[17]

The consequence of such cultural obsequies was that neither
indigenous nor minority British children were taught the history, culture or even the language of their country. The landmark achievements
of Western civilization were barely touched upon. Non-Western societies were portrayed as heroic and good. Western societies were portrayed as oppressive and brutal. Pupils were left radically disconnected
from both the past and the future. Indigenous children were left in
ignorance of anything in their heritage that they could connect with
or take pride in. Minority children were effectively confined to the
culture of the ghetto. Disenfranchised through ignorance, they were
left unattached to the society they inhabited and unequipped to take
their place in it as equal citizens.

Anyone who tried to uphold the transmission of British identity
was denounced as a racist, vilified and had his job placed in jeopardy.

In the early 1980s, Ray Honeyford, a Bradford headmaster at a school where languages such as Urdu, Gujurati and Hindi predominated over English, protested Bradford council's policy of educating ethnic minority children according to their own culture, predicting that the move would create divisions between white and Asian communities. Concerned that "we were getting nine-year-olds who had never sat in the same class as a white child," Honeyford wanted to teach English as a first language and teach the history, culture and customs of this country, so that children of all cultures and creeds could identify with and participate in the society of which they were part. He was accused of racial prejudice and hounded out of education, retiring early to save his family from further harassment. He wrote later that he was told he had been forced out because his attitudes were "racist" and his insistence on integrating Asian children was "dangerous and damaging."[18]

At a deeper level still, the underlying message in the classroom was that there was no historical truth at all, and whatever had happened in the past was merely a matter of opinion. Objectivity was bunk and so truth went out the window—and with it went the ability to weed out lies. The education system had been turned from the repository of disinterested knowledge to a vehicle for "antiracist" and other propaganda. Instead of being taught how to think, children were now told what to think. The result was that, over a generation, Britain became less and less able to think at all.

At the heart of this unpicking of national identity lies a repudiation of Christianity, the founding faith of the nation and the fundamental source of its values, including its sturdy individualism and profound love of liberty. The majority of Britons still profess to be Christian. Protestantism is the established faith through the Church of England, British institutions are suffused with it and British public life is punctuated and defined by Christian language, symbols and traditions.

Yet Britain's Christian identity is fast becoming notional. Few go to church; even fewer send their children to Sunday school. For the secular elite, Britain is now a "post-Christian" society; and insofar as this is not yet the case, this elite is determined to make it so. Under the rubric of multiculturalism and promoting "diversity," local authorities and government bodies are systematically bullying Christianity out of existence. Christian voluntary groups fall afoul of such bodies on the grounds that to be Christian suggests these groups are not committed to "diversity." So they are treated with suspicion even where they have a proven track record of success.

The Christian outreach group FaithWorks provides some examples. Highfields Happy Hens in Derbyshire, a free-range poultry farm, has been transformed into a vocational training center for young offenders and pupils excluded from school. Run with a clear Christian ethos, its program has one of the smallest reoffending rates of any young offenders' program in the county. Yet discussions with local and central government about replicating it stalled because the councils wanted to do so without the Christian ethos—which was responsible for its success.

Romford YMCA in Essex looks after hundreds of needy young people. But its major funder, the Housing Corporation, objected to the fact that only Christians were board members. As a result, it deemed the YMCA incapable of "diversity"—even though it was open to people of all faiths and none. Then there is Barnabas House in Kings Lynn, Norfolk, which houses homeless young men. Norfolk City Council objected that the inclusion of the word "Christian" in its constitution might deter non-Christians from participating. Under pressure, Barnabas House agreed to alter the requirement for board members to be Christians; instead, they need only be "in sympathy with the Christian ethos of the organization." The council still balked at this, insisting that the word "Christian" be removed altogether, although it later accepted the proposed formula.[19]

In other words, "diversity" is a fig leaf. These voluntary groups all practice diversity in that they cater to all faiths. What is clearly not part of "diversity," however, is to put the Christian faith into practice. The "diversity" agenda is thus a cover for an attack on Christianity, on the illogical premise that it is divisive and exclusive whereas minority faiths are not. At the same time, antireligion is being positively encouraged. Prison inmates are now allowed to practice paganism in their cells, including prayer, chanting and the reading of "religious" texts and rituals. In addition to a hoodless robe, prisoners can keep a flexible twig as a wand, a chalice and rune stones. This followed a decision to give a Royal Navy sailor the right to carry out Satanic rituals and worship the devil aboard the frigate HMS *Cumberland*.[20]

So as Christianity is eased out, all faiths and unfaith are being encouraged to fill the gap. But in Britain, unlike America, Protestantism is established as the state religion. It thus has ostensibly the most powerful protector possible in that the monarch bears the solemn title "Defender of the Faith." So is it being thus defended against the all-out assault mounted by multiculturalism? The Queen takes this role, like her Christian faith itself, very seriously. At the Anglican Synod that took place four months after the London bombings, she pointedly referred to the unique way Christianity spoke to people's needs through the Gospel.[21] This drew a sneering response from an elder of the Labour party and former cabinet minister, Lord Hattersley, who wrote that the established church was an "absurd anachronism" that had "no place in a multicultural society" because it was "Islam that is building new mosques and Sikhs who are converting Methodist chapels into temples."[22]

Al-Qaeda, of course, does not see the established church as an anachronism at all. On the contrary, since—unlike Lord Hattersley—it treats religion with the utmost seriousness, it understands very well the crucial significance of Christianity in the life of the British nation. Dethrone Christianity, and the job of subjugating the West is halfway done. That's why al-Qaeda has specifically targeted the "crusader" Queen for assassination. But it might as well save itself the bother, because the heir to the throne, Charles Prince of Wales, will apparently do the job of dethroning Christianity for it.

Prince Charles has floated the idea that when he becomes King he will no longer be Defender of the Faith but "defender of faith." This subtle but vitally important distinction revealed that he no longer believes that Britain is or should be a Christian country. His remark implied that he believes it is instead a "multicultural" society. This renunciation of the bedrock religious settlement of the British nation amounts to a repudiation of national identity by its future monarch—who has thus implicitly allied himself with those who seek to destroy it.

Moreover, and even more remarkable considering that his nation is under assault by radical Islamism both from within and from without, Prince Charles has spoken many times in support of Islam as a solution to the problems of the spiritual poverty of the West, which he thinks Christianity cannot resolve. He has expressed his displeasure at the way he thinks Islam has been traduced by the criticism of Islamic extremism and terrorism. Indeed, according to some reports, when he and his new wife, the Duchess of Cornwall, visited the United States in November 2005, he intended to lobby President Bush about the merits of Islam because he thought the president had been too intolerant of the religion.[23]

For the Prince of Wales, Islam is a religion of peace, and so extremism and violence are foreign to its nature. In a major address in 1993 given in Oxford, where he is patron of the Centre for Islamic Studies, he said:

> Our judgment of Islam has been grossly distorted by taking the extremes to the norm. . . . For example, people in this country frequently argue that the Sharia law of the Islamic world is cruel, barbaric and unjust. Our newspapers, above all, love to peddle those unthinking prejudices. The truth is, of course, different and always more complex. My own understanding is that extremes, like the cutting off of hands, are rarely practised. The guiding principle and spirit of Islamic law, taken straight from the Koran, should be those of equity and compassion.[24]

Startlingly, he went on to suggest that the Islamic world had just as much respect for women's rights and maybe more than did Europe, "since Islamic countries like Turkey, Egypt and Syria gave women the vote as early as Europe did its women—and much earlier than in Switzerland!" with equal pay and a "full working role."[25]

In the current crisis over British Muslims, there is great anxiety about separate Islamic schools because of fears that such separate education may promote segregation and even hostility to Britain. Yet in a speech at the Foreign Office Conference Centre at Wilton Park in Sussex in 1996, Prince Charles called on Islamic pedagogy and philosophy to help young Britons develop a healthier view of the world. Praising Islamic culture in its traditional form for trying to preserve an "integrated, spiritual view of the world in a way we have not seen fit to do in recent generations in the West," he went on to say:

There is much we can learn from that Islamic world view in this respect. There are many ways in which mutual understanding and appreciation can be built. Perhaps, for instance, we could begin by having more Muslim teachers in British schools, or by encouraging exchanges of teachers. Everywhere in the world people want to learn English. But in the West, in turn, we need to be taught by Islamic teachers how to learn with our hearts, as well as our heads.[26]

Traveling extensively in the Arab world, the heir to the throne is used by the Foreign Office as a point man for British interests. But he has never once visited Israel, Britain's supposed geopolitical ally in the region. The less charitable might also consider that his infatuation with Islam is all the more strange considering the punishments meted out to adulterers under Sharia law.

It was the Prince of Wales who was a prime mover behind the building of the Finsbury Park mosque in north London, which became the clerical epicenter of the jihad in Britain. Flanked by Muslim leaders, the Prince would tour this dilapidated corner of North London in the early 1980s with wealthy businessmen and local councilors in tow, pointing out the ideal nature of the location.[27]

Clearly, he had no idea it was to be hijacked by such extremists. But this was not simply an unfortunate episode of innocent blundering. For the heir to the British throne—who when he becomes King will be the symbol and embodiment of British national identity—has displayed a profound attraction to Islam at the expense of his country's founding faith, so much so that like British Muslims themselves he appears to be unable to acknowledge the great threat throughout the Muslim world of resurgent extremism. And at a time when Britain's fundamental values are under attack, its future monarch is preparing to abandon them with an explicit aim of replacing them by the "spiritually superior" forces of Islam.

The promotion of multiculturalism had another unforeseen effect. The culture of separate groups replaced the universal vision of humanity in which all individuals shared the same national project on equal terms. By making such a fetish of the promotion of minority cultures as proof of Britain's antiracist virtue, it encouraged British Muslims to start campaigning for public recognition of their religious agenda by the state. As the writer Kenan Malik observed, by the late 1980s the focus of antiracist protest in Bradford had shifted from political issues, such as policing and immigration, to religious and cultural issues: a demand for Muslim schools and for separate education for girls, a campaign for halal meat in school, and the confrontation over *The Satanic Verses*. As different groups began asserting their identities ever more fiercely, so the shift from the political to the cultural arena helped create a more tribal city. Secular Muslims were regarded as betraying their culture. This process was strengthened by a new relationship between the local council and the mosques, which were now looked to as the voice of the community. This marginalized secular radicals and allowed religious leaders to reassert their power.[28]

And as multiculturalism thus unwittingly fomented Islamist radicalism in the sacred cause of "diversity," it simultaneously forbade criticism of Muslim practices such as forced marriages or polygamy, or the withdrawal of children from school to be sent for long periods to Pakistan. Even to draw attention to such practices was to be labeled a racist. After all, were not these customs now said to be morally equal to British traditions, such as equal rights for women and the protection of children's educational interests? And so, as British identity was steadily eviscerated by multiculturalism, real human rights abuses on British shores were studiously ignored and its victims left abandoned in its name.

Despite its promotion of multiculturalism, the Labour government has displayed persistent unease about the progressive fragmentation of British society and its weak sense of national identity —without ever acknowledging that the one helped create the other. Accordingly, it has tried to beef up community cohesion by promoting citizenship education and citizenship tests for new immigrants. But these initiatives merely institutionalized the hole at the heart of British national identity. Paying lip service to notions of duty and social responsibility, they subscribe to the doctrines of secular human rights, multiculturalism and antidiscrimination.

Far from being the essence of British citizenship, these doctrines are in fact foreign to British identity, which is founded instead on Christianity, the common law and the history of an island people—of which both newcomers *and* indigenous citizens remain ignorant. The government's Race, Equality, Faith and Cohesion unit in the Home Office says that the idea of citizenship is "founded on an understanding of the responsibilities that citizenship entails, such as tackling racism, sexism and ageism and embracing diversity and cultural differences." [29] But the principal responsibilities of a citizen are to the laws and institutions of the country. The British government has now redefined them to be instead responsibilities to an ideology—and one that threatens to dismember the very meaning of citizenship itself.

Hand in hand with this progressive negation of British identity has come a systematic repudiation of its values. At the heart of multiculturalism is a radical notion of egalitarianism, in which everyone's culture and lifestyle has equal validity and moral stature. This extreme type of individualism, which replaces objective standards by subjective opinions and feelings, has been translated comprehensively into the moral sphere governing personal behavior. Morality has been privatized, so that instead of asking the question "what is right?" the individual now asks "what is right for me?"

After the war, authority was junked in favor of boutique values centered upon self-actualization. Religion—the restraint on behavior —was substantially replaced by therapy, which diagnosed such restraint as unhealthy repression. The slow death of Christianity in Britain meant a transfer of belief from messianic redemption to a secular utopia. Saint Paul yielded to Jean-Jacques Rousseau, and the doctrine of Original Sin was replaced by a doctrine of Original Innocence. Instead of fallen mankind redeemed by a savior on the cross, the goodness of mankind had to be redeemed from the corrupting effects of authority of any kind. Instead of salvation by faith or by good works, the association of free and unfettered spirits would create heaven on earth.

But secular humanism had opened Pandora's Box. Detaching values from religion meant there was no reason to adhere to any frameworks at all. The elevation of the individual and the attack on authority opened the way to an even more fundamental attack on the culture—

the nihilistic doctrines of postmodernism, which reduced everything, including the concepts of truth and objectivity, to meaninglessness.

This offered a perfect opportunity to the left. The fall of communism brought to an end the dream of class war. During the 1960s, the decade in which so many of our current leaders remain firmly stuck, the most influential thinker was the Italian communist Antonio Gramsci. He grasped that the most effective means of overturning Western society was to subvert its culture and morality. Instead of mobilizing the working class to take over the world, the revolution would be achieved through a culture war, in which the moral beliefs of the majority would be replaced by the values of those on the margins of society. And this would be brought about by capturing all of society's institutions—schools, universities, churches, the media, the legal profession, the police, voluntary groups—and making sure that this intellectual elite all sang from the same subversive hymn-sheet.

In Britain, Gramsci's revolutionary aims have been accomplished to the letter. The intellectual class was overwhelmingly captured. The moral codes of society were profoundly subverted and weakened as all the barriers fell. Previously marginalized groups, such as never-married mothers or transsexuals, now became the arbiters of morality, which was defined in their "nonjudgmental" image in order to spare their feelings. Teachers resisted transmitting a belief in marriage or saying that premature sexual activity or drug-taking among their pupils was wrong. Instead they set out the facts and let children decide for themselves.

The British cradle-to-grave welfare state promoted a culture of rights that systematically eroded the notion of social duty and substituted an unshakeable belief in personal entitlement. This combined with the therapy culture to give everyone a reason to have a grievance. Resentment became a weapon of social advantage; bad behavior by those identified as "victim groups" was either ignored or deemed to "prove" their victim status; and more and more interest groups were formed to claim the rewards. State monopoly over British schools and universities meant there was no challenge to these ideas, which all aimed to uncouple citizens from the traditions and established values of the nation. And faced with this rout, the Church of England merely wrung its hands and dutifully followed suit. As a result, the three pillars of national identity—family, education and church—have all crumbled. In their place, victim culture is enforced by a doctrine of "human rights" that ruthlessly enforces a prevailing secular and nihilistic ideology.

The consequence of this moral and cultural relativism is that people are increasingly unable to make moral distinctions based on behavior. Such moral equivalence rapidly mutates into moral inversion, in which those doing wrong are excused if they belong to a "victim" group while those at the receiving end of their behavior are blamed simply because they belong to the "oppressive" majority. This is on repeated display over a wide range of domestic issues such as family breakdown, drug abuse and the various demands of the "victim culture," including the response to examples of Muslim aggression.

Alan Buchan, who owns and edits a newspaper called the *North East Weekly* in Aberdeenshire, published an article opposing a resettlement center for asylum-seekers in his area. As a result, he was charged with inciting racial hatred. But Dr. Yaqub Zaki, deputy leader of the Muslim Parliament of Great Britain, was not charged after he said that he would be "very happy" if there were a terrorist attack on Downing Street and would not mind what happened to the "inmates" of No. 10.[30]

Such a climate of moral inversion has turned Britain and Europe into fertile territory for manipulative propaganda by both terrorists and their ideological bedfellows. There is a tendency to equate and then invert the behavior of the perpetrators of violence and that of their victims, so that self-defense is misrepresented as aggression while the original violence is viewed sympathetically as understandable and even justified. This was on display in Britain immediately after 9/11, when there was a groundswell of feeling that America "had it coming to them." It means that Palestinian or Iraqi suicide bombers are seen as victims because they are "up against" powerful states, which by definition are oppressive. It means that people think one person's terrorist is another person's freedom fighter. And it means that fear of Islamist terrorism takes second place to fear of the fear of Islamist terrorism, or "Islamophobia," the insult hurled at anyone who dares criticize Muslims or Islam.

Obviously, there is prejudice against Muslims in Britain just as there is prejudice against other minorities, and this is to be deplored. However, although there was some rise in anti-Muslim incidents in Britain particularly in the immediate aftermath of the London bombings, there has been no great outbreak of violence against mosques or desecration of Muslim graves, unlike attacks on the Jewish community in Britain. When polled, most Muslims reported no incidents of prejudice against them.[31] Even after the July bombings, 80 percent of Muslims polled said they had experienced no hostility against them as a result.[32]

Nevertheless, the claim of Islamophobia is deployed as a weapon to shut down legitimate and, indeed, crucial debate on the basis that to criticize a minority faith group is by definition an act of prejudice. A report published in 2004 by the Commission on British Muslims and Islamophobia claimed that British society was "institutionally Islamophobic" and thus held Britain responsible for Muslim extremism.[33] In the authors' view, it seemed that every disadvantage associated with the Muslim community—poverty, overcrowding, poor educational achievement, unemployment and so forth—was evidence of institutional Islamophobia. In 1997 the Runnymede Trust, an independent think tank on race relations, had similarly reported that Islamophobic discourse was part of everyday life in Britain and was driving Muslims into the arms of extremists. Examples of such prejudice included claims that Muslim cultures were "monolithic" and "unchanging" and "intolerant of pluralism and dispute"; the perpetuation of stereotypes about Islamic fundamentalism or mistreatment of women; mentioning Islam as a successor to Nazism and communism; claims that Islam's adherents use their faith mainly for political purposes and for strategic and military advantage; linking such a critique to opposition to immigration; dismissing Muslims' contribution to debates about Western liberalism, modernity and secularism; and the acceptance of such anti-Muslim ideas and sentiments as increasingly respectable.[34]

But the alleged false assertions about Muslims in this list are without exception true, at least in part. They characterize attitudes that are politically dominant within the Islamic world and are driving global terror. Of course, not all Muslims subscribe to these attitudes. A small minority in Britain are horrified by them all. But a troubling number of British Muslims subscribe to all of them and the majority subscribe at least to some. To deny such attributes and seek to suppress any discussion of them at a time when Britain faces physical attack from the ideology they represent—which, contrary to the report's claim, is an example of a faith being used "for political purposes and for strategic and military advantage"—displays a spectacular proclivity towards national suicide.

The "antiracist" Asian writer Kenan Malik has suggested that Islamophobia is a myth and is being exaggerated to suit politicians' needs and silence the critics of Islam:

> The more the threat of Islamophobia is exaggerated, the more ordinary Muslims believe that they are under constant attack. It helps create a siege mentality, it stokes up anger and resentment, and it makes Muslims more inward looking and more open to religious extremism. It also creates a climate of censorship in which any criticism of Islam can be dismissed as Islamophobic. The people who suffer most from such censorship are those struggling to defend basic rights within Muslim communities.[35]

In other words, it is not "Islamophobes" who are helping create Muslim extremism and violence. It is, on the contrary, those who conjure up the specter of Islamophobia.

And meanwhile, accounts of what is really going on are systematically being suppressed. This account by an ethnic-minority, Christian primary school teacher paints a frightening picture of a society that is committing national immolation:

> On many occasions I have attended conferences with other colleagues in education from the north of England. According to my colleagues in these multicultural areas, their schools consist

of at least 75%–100% Muslim children. White British children are in the minority and often feel intimidated. The daily grief their staff endure is unbelievable. White, British female teachers are often insulted by their own pupils, suffer sexual harassment from young Muslim males and are intimidated by Muslim fathers (in their own classrooms) who have no respect for women. Parents aggressively handle their own children, undermining school codes and ethos in front of the children. One colleague said she was told by a father [that] if his daughter did not achieve academically, she (the teacher) should tell her that she is stupid, lazy and useless and let him know so that she can be beaten at home! This is a regular occurrence in schools—especially Church of England schools, and teachers have their hands tied as opposition would be branded as religious hatred and racism.

Heads and governors are frightened to step a foot wrong in their own schools, lest they offend the community by upholding Christian values and denying the right for Muslim children to pray during the day. There is so much fear that paralyses and I believe actually prevents clear religious dialogue because Christianity is seen as inferior and submissive to the wishes of Islam. I work in a predominantly white school. I am the only ethnic minority teacher on staff, and there are only a handful of children from ethnic minority groups. Even in this predominantly Christian school, there is fear of being associated with Islamophobia and racism. Many people are afraid to talk about religion these days. Religious discussions are seen as taboo, as they may cause offence.

We actually held a themed "multicultural week" this year, and the person who coordinated it decided not to cover any religious education during the week as it could upset some people. So we looked at the nations of China, India, Pakistan without even a mention of their religious beliefs and festivals! As our area is not very multicultural at all, there weren't even any minority groups who could visit and share their culture. Needless to say, the children were left with a very narrow and

unrealistic view of the places and the cultures they were studying. I know that this is only a brief mention or a snapshot, but
when I think of all the multicultural schools across Manchester, Birmingham, Leicester and London, there must be thousands of children (British Christians and British Muslims) who
are seeing Christianity undermined while Islam forces its way
in. These children, shaped by our example and actions now,
will be Britain tomorrow.[36]

These observations, if made in public, would undoubtedly cost this
teacher her job and cause her to be branded as a racist. Such is the climate of intimidation in Britain, a nation that is paralyzed by a multicultural threat that it cannot even bring itself to name.

· CHAPTER FIVE ·

THE ALIENATION OF
BRITISH MUSLIMS

T wo months after the London bombings in 2005, the British
public was further jolted by a videotape that was suddenly all
over the TV screens. It featured Mohammed Sidique Khan, the apparent leader of the first bomb plot, dressed in an anorak and Arab keffiyeh
and calmly talking the language of homicidal hatred against his own
country, Britain, in a broad Yorkshire accent.

He warned his fellow countrymen to expect more death and
destruction unless the British government ceased to take part in the
oppression of Muslims. "Our words are dead until we give them life
with our blood," he said. "Therefore, we are going to talk to you in a
language you understand. . . . We are at war and I am a soldier. Your
democratically elected governments continuously perpetuate atrocities against my people and your support of them makes you directly
responsible, just as I am directly responsible for protecting and
avenging my Muslim brothers and sisters. Until we feel security, you
will be our target. Until you stop the bombing, gassing, imprison-
ment and torture of my people, we will not stop this fight."[1]

The "you" was Britain, and the "my people" and "we" were Muslims. Thus he drew a lethal line between the two. This Leeds boy had
no allegiance to, nor identification with, the Britain where he was

born and brought up. His allegiance was instead to the worldwide community of Muslims, the *ummah*.

Since the London bombings, both British Muslims and the wider community have systematically downplayed the religious significance of those atrocities and the religious motivation of those who carried them out. The ritualistic nature of the suicide attacks and their continuity with similar attacks around the world, whose one overwhelmingly consistent feature was their inspiration by religious fanaticism, were brushed aside. The radical hostility and disengagement displayed by Mohammed Sidique Khan towards the country of his birth were similarly not ascribed to the ideology of Islamism, at the core of which lies an irrational hatred of the West and a desire to subjugate it to the tenets of Islam. Instead, the British heard the phrase "atrocities against my people" and decided that Britain had been bombed because of its role in the invasion of Iraq. Despite the fact that the bombers had not been poor or marginalized but had been well educated, held down jobs and been to all eyes integrated members of the wider community, the British intelligentsia also decided that the roots of this impulse to mass murder lay in the segregation of Muslims within British cities. And the reason for such segregation was economics, discrimination, racism—anything but religion.

This played well with British Muslims, whose main reaction to the bombings was to disclaim responsibility for what had happened, to maintain that it was utterly "un-Islamic" and the bombers had been not proper Muslims, that the overwhelming majority of British Muslims were wholly opposed to violence and of moderate opinions, and that the main victims of the London bombings were in fact the Muslim community, who were being oppressed and victimized by "Islamophobic" reactions.

In the wake of such atrocities, it is certainly important not to demonize an entire community for the misdeeds of a few. With emotions so heightened, there is a risk of victimizing innocent people who have been besmirched by the activities of a small number doing violence in the name of the religion they all share. Last but not least, across the world it is Muslims who have been victims of Islamist terror in greater number than anyone else.

However, it is unfortunately not so easy to agree that British Muslims are overwhelmingly moderate in their views, and that those holding extremist views are so small in number as to be statistically insignificant. The crucial question is what exactly "moderate" is understood to be.

If "moderation" includes reasonableness, truthfulness and fairness, the reaction by British Muslims to the London bombings was not moderate at all. Yes, they condemned the atrocities. But in the next breath they denied that these had had anything to do with Islam. Thus they not only washed their hands of any communal responsibility but—in denying what was a patently obvious truth that these attacks were carried out by adherents of Islam in the name of Islam— also indicated that they would do nothing to address the roots of the problem so as to prevent such a thing from happening again.

In the immediate aftermath Mohammed Naseem, chairman of the Birmingham Central Mosque, said there was no proof that the London suicide bombers were Muslims. He called Tony Blair a "liar" and an "unreliable witness" and questioned whether CCTV footage of the suspected bombers actually showed the perpetrators. He said that Muslims "all over the world have never heard of an organisation called al Qaeda."[2]

From such nonsense, it was but a short step to saying that those who did point out that the roots of such terrorism lay in Islamist ideology, and therefore expected the Muslim community to do something about it, were guilty of prejudice. Accordingly Sir Iqbal Sacranie, secretary general of the Muslim Council of Britain, was quick to say that "the real victim of these bombings is the Muslim community of the UK."[3] And if the Muslim community was the real victim, then it followed that the British, far from being the targets of terrorism, were actually to blame for causing it by supporting the war in Iraq. This moral inversion was then turned into a threat that unless the British changed their foreign policy they could expect more of the same.

Thus Dr. Azzam Tammimi of the Muslim Association of Britain said: ". . . and God knows what will happen afterwards, our lives are in real danger and it would seem, so long as we are in Iraq and so long as we are contributing to injustices around the world, we will continue to be in real danger. Tony Blair has to come out of his state of denial and listen to what the experts have been saying, that our involvement in Iraq is stupid." The marketing manager for the *Muslim Weekly* newspaper, Shahid Butt, said: "At the end of the day, these things [violent incidents] are going to happen if current British foreign policy continues. There's a lot of rage, there's a lot of anger in the Muslim community. We have got to get out of Iraq, it is the crux of the matter. I believe if Tony Blair and George Bush left Iraq and stopped propping up dictatorial regimes in the Muslim world, the threat rate to Britain would come down to nearly zero."[4]

Other Muslim groups went even further and supported terrorism in countries other than Britain, including by implication the violence against British and American forces in Iraq, by relabeling it "resistance." A joint statement signed by groups including the Association of Muslim Lawyers, the Federation of Student Islamic Societies, the Islamic Human Rights Commission, the Muslim Association of Britain and *Q-News* magazine said: "The Muslim community in Britain has unequivocally denounced acts of terrorism. However, the right of people anywhere in the world to resist invasion and occupation is legitimate." The statement, which also opposed the banning of Hizb ut-Tahrir and any proposal to close "extremist" mosques, went on: "If the government hopes to pander to Zionist pressure by condemning and excluding from this country people who are critical of Israeli apartheid, it is in fact supporting apartheid."[5]

The charge that Israel is an "apartheid" society is of course one of the Big Lies propagated by the Muslim world. And relabeling terrorism as "resistance," if it takes place in connection with one of the iconic conflicts of Islamist demonology, is a sleight of hand to conceal support for the murder of innocents. It was therefore no surprise that the same statement dismissed the word "extremism" as having "no tangible legal meaning or definition" and being "unhelpful and emotive." For such views were indeed extremist. Yet most of these were supposedly mainstream organizations.

Hope of a response by British Muslims that truly reaffirmed moderation rose briefly when the British Muslim Forum issued a fatwa against terrorism. But this was promptly dashed by the text of this fatwa. It unequivocally condemned suicide bombings in London but did not unequivocally condemn them elsewhere, for example in Iraq or Israel:

> Islam strictly, strongly and severely condemns the use of violence and the destruction of innocent lives. There is neither place nor justification in Islam for extremism, fanaticism or terrorism. Suicide bombings, which killed and injured innocent people in London, are *haraam*—vehemently prohibited in Islam—and those who committed these barbaric acts in London are criminals not martyrs. Such acts, as perpetrated in London, are crimes against all of humanity and contrary to the teachings of Islam.

This left wide open the question of whether suicide bombings elsewhere were permitted. And if the religion *did* permit them elsewhere, then obviously it was not true that "there is neither place nor justification in Islam for extremism, fanaticism or terrorism." The fatwa condemned the "destruction of innocent lives" everywhere, but that also left open the question of the meaning of "innocent." This suspicion deepened when it added:

> The Holy Koran declares: "Whoever kills a human being . . . then it is as though he has killed all mankind; and whoever saves a human life, it is as though he had saved all mankind" (Koran, Surah al-Maidah (5), verse 32). Islam's position is clear and unequivocal: Murder of one soul is the murder of the whole of humanity; he who shows no respect for human life is an enemy of humanity.

But it is not unequivocal at all, because the passage that is quoted here contains other phrases, left out in this fatwa, that change the meaning altogether:

> That was why we laid it down for the Israelites that whoever killed a human being *except as punishment for murder or other*

villainy in the land [my emphasis] shall be regarded as having killed all mankind; and that whoever saved a human life shall be regarded as having saved all mankind. Our apostles brought them veritable proofs; yet many among them, even after that, did prodigious evil in the land. *Those that make war against God and His apostle and spread disorder in the land shall be slain or crucified or have their hands and feet cut off on alternate sides, or be banished from the land* [my emphasis].[6]

In other words, where there is "villainy," killing is expressly permitted; and since villainy can mean anything, and since Islamist extremists regard Western or democratic influence as acts of war against Islam, it follows that in such circumstances the slaughter of Western or reformist Muslim innocents is expressly permitted—because they are not regarded as innocent in the first place.[7]

Concern about the extremist character of British Muslims does not rest solely on their responses to the London bombings. Survey evidence suggests that, while the vast majority do not support violence, a frighteningly large number do; and, beyond them, a much larger proportion dislike British values and would like to replace them by the tenets of Islam.

A survey carried out by the Home Office in 2004 provided deeply alarming evidence. It found that no fewer than 26 percent of British Muslims felt no loyalty to Britain, 13 percent defended terrorism and up to 1 percent were "actively engaged" in terrorist activity at home or abroad, or supported such activity. This last number, deemed "extremely small" by the Home Office, added up to at least sixteen thousand terrorists or terrorist supporters among British Muslims.[8] Meanwhile the former Metropolitan Police commissioner Lord Stevens revealed that up to three thousand British-born or British-based people had passed through Osama bin Laden's training camps.[9] Security agencies believed that the number who were actually prepared to commit terrorist attacks might run into hundreds. Polling evidence revealed similar numbers who supported attacks on the United States. In 2001, a BBC poll had found that 15 percent of British Muslims supported the 9/11 attacks on America.[10] In 2004, a

Guardian poll recorded that 13 percent of British Muslims thought that further terrorist attacks on the USA would be justified.[11]

In addition, polling evidence revealed a dismaying amount of anti-British feeling among Britain's Muslim citizens. Following the London bombings, a poll found that the overwhelming majority rejected violence, with nine in ten believing it had no place in a political struggle. Nevertheless, one in ten supported the attacks on July 7, and 5 percent said that more attacks in the UK would be justified, with 4 percent supporting the use of violence for political ends.[12]

The evidence of Muslim alienation from Britain was no less disturbing. Between 8 and 26 percent have said they feel either not very or not at all patriotic.[13] Another poll revealed that while 47 percent said they felt "very loyal" to Britain, nearly one in five—more than one hundred thousand British Muslims—said they felt little or no loyalty at all. And while 56 percent said Muslims should accept Western society, 32 percent believed that "Western society is decadent and immoral and that Muslims should seek to bring it to an end."[14]

These numbers were simply horrifying. While the vast majority were opposed to terrorism, the numbers who supported it were wholly intolerable and almost certainly unique; no other community in Britain contains such an enormous reservoir of potential violence against the state. Moreover, to have almost a third of the community hostile to Western society and wanting to bring that society to an end clearly makes a mockery of the claim that British Muslims are overwhelmingly moderate. That is a huge pool in which terrorism can swim.

Why are so many British Muslims so angry and alienated? After the Muslim riots of 2001 in northern English towns, a clutch of official reports concluded that the essence of the problem lay in the fact that Muslims tended to be segregated from the rest of the community, in terms of both where they lived and how they behaved. But this failed to address the further question of why they were segregated. To some extent, it was because poor, vulnerable communities with very different traditions do tend to stick together for mutual support in a strange culture. But there were two obvious flaws in this argument.

The first was that other minorities, like the Hindus, had no problem integrating at all. The second was that British Muslims drawn into terrorism were not necessarily poor or marginalized. As British officials had noted, they tended to fall into two groups: "*a*) well educated, with degrees or technical/professional qualifications, typically targeted by extremist recruiters and organizations circulating on campuses; *b*) under-achievers with few or no qualifications, and often a non-terrorist criminal background—sometimes drawn to mosques where they may be targeted by extremist preachers and in other cases radicalized or converted whilst in prison."[15]

So it would appear that there is something particular to Islamic culture at this present time that makes it vulnerable to this kind of extremism. Indeed, since a number of terrorists are Muslim converts who have not come from these segregated communities, the reason goes beyond ethnicity or economics. And although many in Britain lean over backwards to deny this, the case that the cause lies in the religious culture itself is overwhelming.

One must acknowledge that the Muslim community in Britain is extremely diverse, consisting of many subcommunities with different geographical and cultural antecedents and views as well as different positions on the religious spectrum. Many British Muslims just want to get on with life and have no leanings towards religious extremism, let alone violence.

But the fact that so many do not succumb to religious extremism does not mean that it doesn't have a profound influence on others. And all the evidence suggests that a doctrinal radicalization that took root in Britain more than twenty-five years ago has fed upon a widespread sense of cultural dislocation, resulting in a disastrous effect upon many Muslim youths.

In recent decades, the Islamic world has succumbed in large measure to an extreme version of the religion that emerged out of the postcolonial ferment and the rise of Arab nationalism in the late nineteenth and early twentieth centuries. This version, which gave rise to the Muslim Brotherhood in Egypt in 1928, was promulgated by hugely influential Islamic thinkers such as Sayed Qutb and in India by Sayed Abu'l Ala Maududi, and later fused with the puritanical Wahhabi doctrine, that was the orthodoxy in Saudi Arabia.

Sayed Qutb laid down that Muslims must answer to God alone and that human government was illegitimate. It was therefore a proper target for jihad, which would be waged by true believers, "destroying the kingdom of man to establish the kingdom of heaven on earth."[16] This approach is the basis of Islamism, whose defining characteristic is the belief that the world should be conquered for Islam. It is a doctrine that forms a continuum of clerical fascism which has at its extremity al-Qaeda—but with many other punctuation points along its route.

In 1973, the Conference of Islamic Cultural Centres in London decided to set up an Islamic Council of Europe to propagate the "true teachings of Islam" throughout Europe. In 1978, the Organization of the Islamic Conference sponsored a seminar in London organized by the Islamic Council of Europe to consider the position of Muslim communities in non–Muslim countries. It said that such communities must establish autonomous institutions with help from Muslim states, and lobby the host country to grant Muslims recognition as a separate religious community, as a step towards eventual political domination:

> Once the community is well organised, its leaders should strive to seek recognition of Muslims as a religious community having its own characteristics by the authorities. Once recognised, the community should continue to request the same rights the other religious communities enjoy in the country. Eventually the community may seek to gain political rights as a constituent community of the nation. Once these rights are obtained then the community should seek to generalise its characteristics to the entire nation.[17]

The Islamic Foundation in Leicester espouses the ideas of the Jamaat al-Islami, whose guiding star was Sayed Maududi. He said: "The truth is that Islam is a revolutionary ideology which seeks to alter the social order of the entire world and rebuild it in conformity with its own tenets and ideals." In 1982, the Leicester foundation said in its declaration that the Islamic movement "is an organised struggle to change the existing society into an Islamic society based on the Koran and the Sunna and make Islam, which is a code for entire life, supreme and dominant, especially in the socio-political spheres."[18] In 2005, the foundation's chairman and rector, Kurshid Ahmad, said that a revolutionary idea that lets people "try to change the world on the basis of values of faith in Allah, justice, service to humanity, peace and solidarity" was nothing to be frightened of.[19]

For more than twenty years, therefore, the Islamic Foundation, a prestigious and influential institution in the Muslim community, has been effectively teaching sedition to British Muslims. In line with prevailing Islamic religious and political authority, it has preached the message that they have a religious duty to change Britain into an Islamic society. While not everyone who passed through its portals will have been thus influenced, a considerable number will have been, along with graduates of many other similarly radicalized Islamic institutions—profoundly altering the way British Muslims see themselves in relation to the wider community.

Dr. Taj Hargey, chairman of the Muslim Education Centre in Oxford, which promotes what he calls "progressive inclusive Islam," has said there is a virtual apartheid in parts of Britain, self-imposed by those Muslims who regard non-Muslims as *kuffar*, or inferior— although they would never say so in public. "We see it from the time you're a child, you're given this idea that those people they are *kuffar*, they're unbelievers. They are not equal to you, they are different to you. You are superior to them because you have the truth, they don't have the truth. You will go to heaven, they will go to hell. So we have this from a very young age."[20]

This deeply alienating message has been amplified by the widespread perception of Western decadence. British Muslims are overwhelmingly horrified and disgusted by the louche and dissolute behavior of a Britain that has torn up the notion of respectability. They observe the alcoholism, drug abuse and pornography, the breakdown of family life and the encouragement of promiscuity, and find themselves therefore in opposition to their host society's guiding values. What they are recoiling from, of course, is the *breakdown* of Western values. After a visit to the United States in 1948, Sayed Qutb wrote: "Humanity today is living in a large brothel!"[21] Similarly, British Muslims have concluded that the society that expects them to identify with it is a moral cesspit. Is it any wonder, therefore, that they reject it?

But for young Muslim men, who are so numerous—more than half of British Muslims are under age twenty-five, compared with only one-third in the rest of the population[22]—Britain's secular corruption has had a very much more ambiguous and often lethal impact. While they despise it—and as a result of the multicultural scorched-earth policy in the schools, they will never have been taught what authentic British values are, let alone been invited to share them—the West's seductive doctrine of personal liberty has nevertheless entered their souls.

As the British prison doctor Theodore Dalrymple has written, many of these young men are not pious and barely set foot inside a mosque. Deeply secularized, they have little religious faith and adopt the habits of other slum-dwellers, including soccer and pop music, drugs, alcohol and casual sex. But rather than integrating, their lives run in parallel with the young white men whose habits they share. In particular, says Dalrymple, they want to exercise dominance over women—who are of course highly emancipated and sexually available. In this fragile and disconnected state of mind, any perceived insult can turn them into terrorists overnight, particularly since British society constantly reinforces their sense of grievance by telling them that discrimination is to blame. The only way some of them can resolve such terrible tensions, Dalrymple concludes, is to become a human bomb, since to die for the faith is the one thing that can expunge the West from their psyche.[23]

Such young men, stranded between the mores of Mirpur village life on the one hand and the degraded nihilism of British "liberal" society on the other, are thus easy prey for the puppet-masters of terror. What makes these fragile egos yet more vulnerable still, moreover, is the pathological inferiority complex that afflicts Muslim society, the exaggerated notions of shame and honor which mean that every slight turns into a major grievance, disadvantage morphs into paranoia, and Islam itself is perceived to be under siege everywhere. This is then held to be a justification for attack, to "defend" Islam against those who are waging this imagined war against it. And so every act of defense against this Islamic aggression is therefore reconceptualized as an attack on Islam. This inversion is a pathological distortion running through the Islamic world from Dohar to Dewsbury.

For instance, in October 2005, the British home secretary Charles Clarke declared that:

> [T]here can be no negotiation about the re-creation of the Caliphate; there can be no negotiation about the imposition of Shariah law; there can be no negotiation about the suppression of equality between the sexes; there can be no negotiation about the ending of free speech. These values are fundamental to our civilisation and are simply not up for negotiation.[24]

This defense of British society against attack was promptly inverted to represent an assault on Islam. Dr. Imran Waheed of Hizb ut-Tahrir Britain said: "These latest comments from Clarke have clearly exposed the reality of this so-called war on terror. . . . These offensive comments about the Shariah and the Caliphate will leave no doubt in the Muslim world that this is a war against Islam and not about individuals or groups committing acts of violence."

It is impossible to overstate the importance, not just to Britain but to the worldwide struggle against Islamist extremism, of properly understanding and publicly challenging this moral, intellectual and philosophical inversion, which translates aggressor into victim and vice versa. For it has unbalanced debate by allowing Muslims to argue—and to a large extent, by accepting their logic—that British foreign policy is unfair, and thus aggressive, towards the Muslim world. In an internal briefing note, government officials wrote:

> It seems that a particularly strong cause of disillusionment amongst Muslims, including young Muslims, is a perceived "double standard" in the foreign policy of Western governments (and often those of Muslim governments), in particular Britain and the US. . . . This seems to have gained a significant prominence in how some Muslims view HMG's [the British

government's] policies towards Muslim countries. Perceived Western bias in Israel's favour over the Israel/Palestinian conflict is a key long-term grievance of the international Muslim community which probably influences British Muslims. This perception seems to have become more acute post-9/11. The perception is that passive "oppression", as demonstrated in British foreign policy, eg non-action on Kashmir and Chechnya, has given way to "active oppression"—the war on terror and in Iraq and Afghanistan are all seen by a section of British Muslims as having been acts against Islam.[25]

This incendiary confusion is being further inflamed by propaganda from Pakistan and the Arab world, beamed into British Muslims' living rooms on satellite TV, about how Hindus are out to massacre them or how Israel is the enemy of the world. And it is further whipped up by religious leaders, even those who are considered utterly mainstream. For example, the imam of the Leeds Grand Mosque—where one of the London bombers, Abdullah Jamal, used to pray—has delivered sermons proclaiming the supremacy of Islam and a conviction that Christians and Jews are plotting to undermine it. "We know the reason behind the United States attack on the Muslim World. . .," he declared; "we have come to see only their plotting to decrease the faith."[26]

After the London bombings, this mosque said that it "unequivocally condemned" the killing of innocent people, and that "such acts of terrorism have no place in Islam."[27] But in March 2004, Sheikh Taher preached a sermon at the mosque that was published on its website, in which he said that preserving the *deen*, or laws of Islam, could justify the taking of life:

> If the forces of evil stop and intervene between the people and them entering this *deen* as Allah, exalted is He, loves for them, it is legislated for those who call, when they face these oppressive forces, to fight jihad in the path of Allah, and it is legislated for them to sacrifice themselves for the sake of this *deen* and for the sake of making the *da'wah* of Islam reach every heart. . . .

The preservation of the *deen* comes before the preservation of life. . . .

He went on to justify the killing of Israelis because Israel had killed the Hamas "spiritual" leader Sheikh Yassin, and then descended into open, theological anti-Jewish hatred:

The assassination of Sheikh Ahmad Yassin reminds you of the treachery of the Jews; their plotting and their scheming. Who tried to kill your Prophet by throwing a rock from the top of the house which the Prophet (*sallalahu 'alaihi wa sallam*) was sitting in, and who is the one who put poison into the lambs' meat which was given to the Prophet (*sallalahu 'alaihi wa sallam*)?[28]

This message preached by such religious leaders, that Britain and America are engaged in a war on Islam rather than a defense of their society against attack, is a potent incitement to terror by whipping up a hysteria that Muslims are under attack from the West. So any attempt by the West to defend itself against terror becomes a recruiting sergeant for that terror. The more atrocities committed against the West, the more the West tries to defend itself; and the more it does so, the more hysteria rises among Muslims that they are under attack, and the more they are thus incited to hatred and to terrorism. The circle is completed by British fellow travelers who promulgate the same morally inverted thinking, and thus help further incite both Muslim extremism and Western defeatism.

The mosques have been widely blamed for preaching this radicalism, particularly through imams brought over from India and Pakistan who are supporters of Saudi Arabian Wahhabism or other similar ideologies. True as this may be, however, they are by no means the only or even the most important conduit for hatred and incitement. Even worse damage is being done over the internet, and within Britain in addition by a silent army of highly influential community interlocutors including youth workers, peripatetic teachers, prison counselors and a host of voluntary organizations moving below the official radar.

Moreover, British universities have been exceptionally important breeding grounds for Islamist radicalism—and almost wholly over-looked. The list of terrorists who have been through the British university system is striking. Ahmed Omar Saeed Sheikh, who masterminded the kidnap and murder of the U.S. journalist Daniel Pearl in Pakistan, attended a British public school before dropping out of the London School of Economics.[29] Among the London bombers, Mohammed Sidique Khan and Shehzad Tanweer had studied at Leeds Metropolitan University. Zacarias Moussaoui, one of the Hamburg cell responsible for 9/11, had completed a master's degree at South Bank University, London. Afzal Munir, who was killed fighting in Afghanistan, had studied at Luton University. And there are many more.

In an internal paper, government officials noted that al-Qaeda was secretly recruiting affluent, middle-class Muslims in British universities and colleges to carry out terrorist attacks in Britain. A network of "extremist recruiters" was circulating on campuses, targeting people with technical and professional qualifications, particularly degrees in engineering and information technology. Most of the al-Qaeda recruits tended to be loners "attracted to university clubs based on ethnicity or religion" because of "disillusionment with their current existence." The officials added: "Students and young professionals from better off backgrounds have also become involved in extremist politics and even terrorism. They provide better recruits, as they may have the capability for wider and more complex proselytising."[30]

In other words, it was not that Islamist radicals happened to be going to British universities. It was that British universities were being used to create Islamist radicals. In an important report published in 2005, the terrorism expert Professor Anthony Glees and Chris Pope documented the extensive jihadist activity on campus and suggested that the time young British Muslims spent at British universities was a "thin red line" that linked them to terrorism. They identified a number of Islamist groups that, although officially banned from campus, were still operating under the mask of cover names and front groups. Hizb ut-Tahrir, for example, which has been banned in many countries and preaches the reincarnation of the caliphate, the extension of Sharia law to Britain and hatred of Jews, was deeply embedded on campus under such camouflage. A BBC TV *Newsnight* program

reported that Kingston University's Islamic Society had been criticized for not reporting the presence of Hizb ut-Tahrir on campus. A
former president of the society replied: "What could we have done,
tell me? You're telling us to go to the *kuffar* against a Muslim, is that
what you are saying we should have done?"[31]

Glees and Pope reported that the police had always been resistant
to proactive surveillance of extremists on campus, not least because
since the early 1990s the security community had no longer targeted
subversion, insisting that it had been superseded by terrorism. But as
Glees and Pope argued, subversion was the production of the ideas
that led to terrorism—and so it was hardly a surprise that the universities, as the laboratories of ideas, therefore provided a crucible for the
ideology of jihad.[32]

The universities had failed to put into place elementary safe-
guards to prevent such recruitment into terrorism. However, when
this report was published they did not jump to do so, nor did they
even express any concern about its findings. Instead, they attempted
to blacken Professor Glees's name and get him sacked from his own
university job.[33] Having unwittingly fueled the flames of jihad in
Britain, the universities—with one or two honorable exceptions—
resolutely refused to face up to what was happening. As with the rest
of the British establishment, denial was the name of the game.

One of the problems that bedevils this issue, however, is just what
is considered to be either "moderate" or acceptable within mainstream debate. A view seems to have taken hold that "moderate"
means anyone who does not actually advocate violence. Thus many
Islamic groups, institutions and publications are deemed to be moderate even though the views they express carry messages of hostility
or hatred towards the West.

For example, *The Muslim* magazine, which describes itself as the
"voice of Muslim students," routinely features articles endorsing
Sayed Qutb and other founding fathers of Islamism, talking about the
mission of Islam to end the division of the world into Muslims and
non-Muslims because "the key to the revival of a degenerate Muslim
society and the emancipation of the non-Muslim society is one and
the same."[34] In one issue, Sheikh Qaradawi wrote that "Islam will

inherit all these civilizations" [the West] and would work to this end among laborers and women as well as students in a battle that was "religious, political, economic, intellectual and ideological."[35] Elsewhere in its pages, the wife of Sheikh Abdullah Azzam, who was said to have been Osama bin Laden's mentor, called on Muslim women to "awake for the jihad" and to "urge Muslim men to make jihad in the cause of Allah, for you will get all that you long for in this life only under the auspices of strong men who hold weapon [sic] and fight the enemies to protect their faith, their land and their honours, who spread fear and respect in the hearth of their enemies and who are prepared to offer one 'shaheed' [martyr] after another."[36]

An even greater problem is presented by Muslim representative institutions. These are considered to be mainstream and therefore moderate, but the views expressed both collectively and by the individuals running them exhibit an alarming degree of support for Islamist extremism and, in particular, an obsessive demonization of Israel and the Jews.

The Muslim Council of Britain, for example, is regarded by the British establishment as the most reliable mainstream voice of the Muslim community, and is constantly used as the principal interlocutor with the community. Yet the MCB boycotted the ceremony commemorating the liberation of Auschwitz in 2005, saying it "excluded ongoing genocide and human rights abuses around the world and in the occupied territories of Palestine."[37] The council offered condolences to the family of the leading Hamas terrorist Abdul Aziz al-Rantissi after he was killed by the Israelis.[38] It has consistently supported Sheikh Qaradawi—the Islamic scholar who has said that suicide bomb attacks in Israel and Iraq are a religious duty for Muslims—as being deeply respected by millions of Muslims around the world.[39]

The MCB's secretary general, Sir Iqbal Sacranie, has branded Israel a "Nazi state" and accused it of "murderous leadership," "Zionist brutality" and the "ethnic cleansing of Palestine."[40] He has compared Hamas suicide bombers to Nelson Mandela and Mahatma Ghandi, saying: "Those who fight oppression, those who fight occupation, cannot be termed as terrorist, they are freedom fighters"; and he has referred to the founder and spiritual leader of Hamas, Sheikh Ahmad Yassin, as "the renowned Islamic scholar."[41] He brands as an "Islamophobe" anyone who even uses the term "Islamic terrorism" and says they should be prosecuted for incitement to religious hatred.[42]

It is not surprising that the MCB should be so extreme since it is influenced by Sayed Maudadi, who created Jamaat al-Islami and preached the need for jihad to bring about the "universal revolution" of Islamic state rule. In August 2005, BBC TV's *Panorama* current affairs show revealed the close connections between the MCB, the Islamic Foundation in Leicester and the Maududi ideology behind them. It also revealed the brazen extremism of many of the MCB's affiliates, which were nevertheless defended by Sir Iqbal Sacranie. The show made a great impact, since it was virtually the first time the facts had been made known about so-called moderate Muslim representative institutions—and much of the damning evidence was provided by other British Muslims, who condemned this extremism and said it did not represent them.

The response to the show was, however, remarkable. The MCB's public affairs officer, Inayat Bunglawala, who had attempted to dismiss his own anti-Jewish remarks as "youthful indiscretions," now wrote: "The Panorama team is more interested in furthering a pro-Israeli agenda than assessing the work of Muslim organisations in the UK. . . . The BBC should not allow itself to be used by the highly placed supporters of Israel in the British media to make political capital out of the July 7 atrocities in London."[43]

There were no such links to Israel; indeed, the director and reporter on this show were not Jews. So much for the Muslim representative organization considered to be "moderate" by the British establishment.

The essence of a "moderate" attitude in a minority is that it is prepared to live as a minority, to subscribe to the overarching values and institutions of the state while practicing its own culture in the private sphere. British Muslims, however, are increasingly pushing for their culture to be highly visible and given parity in the public sphere. Halal meals and separate prayer rooms are now commonplace throughout British institutions. At the University of Newcastle, the Islamic society persuaded the students' union to back their demand for Friday afternoon teaching to be rescheduled around prayer times in accordance with "the right to education without discrimination against religious needs."[44] At the University of Leicester, Muslim students asked for halal food and were told they could have their very own café. Elsewhere in the city, municipal swimming pools provide separate women's sessions and even a separate session for women to swim fully clothed in chadors. When sporting or music activities are planned, some Muslim groups say they don't want men and women to sit or participate in the activity together. Meetings held in public buildings are sometimes divided by screens so that women are separated from men.[45] No other minority group has asked for such privileges. That is because they run counter to the normal relationship between British society and its minority groups. While minorities are free to pursue their own customs, they do not expect public services available to all to be adapted to their requirements, let alone encourage a form of separate development.

In many areas, old churches, public houses or other buildings are being bought by Muslims and converted into mosques, along with brand new mosques that are springing up, backed by the kind of international funds that no other faith groups can command— mosques which sometimes promulgate clearly dubious attitudes.

In June 2004, the New London Muslim Centre opened in east London. With room for ten thousand worshippers, it was said to be one of the largest Islamic cultural centers in Europe. Among those leading Friday prayers at its opening was one Sheikh Abd al-Rahman al-Sudais. This gentleman has distinguished himself in the past by calling for violence against Christians, Hindus and Americans. He has also called the Jews "calf-worshippers, prophet-murderers, prophecy-deniers . . . the scum of the human race whom Allah cursed and turned into apes and pigs. . . . These are the Jews, a continuous lineage of meanness, cunning, obstinacy, tyranny, licentiousness, evil, and corruption."[46] No one in the wider community saw fit to comment on the propriety of inviting such an individual. Virtually no one even knew of his record.

There are now proposals to build a massive mosque beside the

Olympic complex in London for the 2012 Olympic Games. The mosque is planned to hold seventy thousand people, only ten thousand fewer than the Olympic Stadium, and would become the "Muslim quarter" for the Games. The cultural significance and symbolism of a project on this scale are unmistakable. It would make the most powerful statement possible, on the back of the high-visibility Games, about the primacy of Islam in Britain. That is why it is being proposed. "It will be something never seen before in this country. It is a mosque for the future as part of the British landscape," said Abdul Khalique, a senior member of Tablighi Jamaat, which is behind the proposal.[47]

Tablighi Jamaat is often described as a "worldwide Islamic missionary group" and is said to be pacific and apolitical. Two years ago, according to the *New York Times*, a senior FBI antiterrorism official claimed it was a recruiting ground for al-Qaeda. The counterintelligence expert Alex Alexiev characterizes Tablighi Jamaat as a driving force of Islamic extremism and a major recruiting agency for terrorist causes worldwide.

For a majority of young Muslim extremists, he says, joining Tablighi Jamaat is the first step on the road to extremism. Perhaps 80 percent of the Islamist extremists in France come from Tablighi ranks, prompting French intelligence officers to call Tablighi Jamaat the "antechamber of fundamentalism." U.S. counterterrorism officials are increasingly adopting the same attitude. "We have a significant presence of Tablighi Jamaat in the United States," the deputy chief of the FBI's international terrorism section said in 2003, "and we have found that al-Qaeda used them for recruiting now and in the past."[48] Is this really what Britain wants to symbolize its culture at the 2012 Olympics?

But then, Britain is sleepwalking into its relentless transformation. In 1980, the Islamic Council of Europe published a book called *Muslim Communities in Non-Muslim States*, which explained the Islamic Agenda in Europe. When Muslims lived as a minority, it said, they faced theological problems, because classical Islamic teaching always presupposed a context of Islamic dominance. The book told Muslims to organize themselves with the aim of establishing a viable Muslim community, to set up mosques, community centers and

Islamic schools. The ultimate goal of this strategy was that the Muslims should become a majority and the entire nation be governed according to Islam.[49]

By no means all British Muslims would support such a plan. Nevertheless, it was surely an unfortunate oversight that such a conference proclaiming such an intention in London, and with a sizeable Muslim community in Britain, should have been paid no attention whatsoever by the host community. For there is evidence that some of the stages of such a strategy are indeed being implemented, and that a majority of British Muslims want—if not that the "entire nation be governed according to Islam"—at least a parallel legal and cultural system of their own.

A poll conducted by the *Guardian* newspaper found that 61 percent of British Muslims wanted to be governed by Islamic law, operating on Sharia principles—"so long as the penalties did not contravene British law." A clear majority wanted Islamic law introduced into Britain in civil cases relating to their own community. In addition, 88 percent wanted to see British schools and workplaces accommodating Muslim prayer times as part of their normal working day.[50]

The Association of Muslim Lawyers went even further, saying that it wanted formal recognition of a Muslim man's right under Sharia law to have up to four wives. Ahmad Thomson, a member of the AML, said: "Under the Human Rights Act they actually have a right to live and practise as Muslims and part of that is having this principle recognised by the law of the land."[51] Thomson, who has given the Blair government legal advice on official recognition of the Sharia legal system, is now one of the advisers to the British government on dealing with Muslim extremism.

As government officials noted, "There are tentative moves towards developing Islamic jurisprudence for Muslims living in Europe and the Western World."[52] This, however, has drawn no adverse comment from the host community on the grounds that such moves might undermine social cohesion and the common values of British citizenship. Indeed, there has been no discussion of it at all, even though the aims of the Islamic Sharia Council—the Muslim body that is developing claims for such a parallel jurisprudence—could not be plainer. The council says on its website that it wants Parliament "to take into consideration the Islamic point of view in their legislation in at least the field of family law," which it claims is a right enshrined in the Universal Declaration of Human Rights.[53] But no other minority has ever required the host community to adapt its laws to that minority.

Although there is at present no question of English family law being so adapted, there is a slow acceptance of a parallel jurisdiction taking place. After considerable Muslim lobbying, major banks now offer non-interest-based, Sharia-compliant "Islamic mortgages." This is even though the European Council for Fatwa and Research, which recommended that Muslims use Islamic alternatives to forbidden usury, nevertheless also ruled that Muslims *could* buy houses using interest-based mortgages according to the ancient Islamic edict that "it is permissible for Muslims to trade with usury and other invalid contracts in countries other than Islamic countries." The implication, according to the Institute for the Study of Islam and Christianity, is that Sharia-compliant mortgages are a political maneuver to create a separate Islamic space in Britain.[54]

If so, the British authorities are falling over themselves to help this process along. The Inland Revenue revealed that, after representations from Muslims, it was considering recognizing polygamy for tax purposes. Existing rules allow only one wife for inheritance tax purposes. Officials have agreed to consider relaxing this rule to allow a Muslim with up to four wives to divide his estate between them.[55]

And while polygamy is not recognized in English law, Britain is turning a blind eye to the practice. Muslim men are entering into polygamous marriages by going through mosque ceremonies not recognized under English law. This leaves many such "wives" in a parlous state, with no rights to their husband's income, pension, benefits or share of the family home should the relationship break up.

There are British Muslims who are deeply opposed to this and are campaigning to have it stopped. Dr. Ghayasuddin Siddiqui of the Muslim Institute says he wants imams to be prevented from carrying out a marriage service unless they have also seen the certificate from the civil ceremony.[56] But those Muslims who actually want to subscribe to British norms find that the British are busy tearing them up. Resistance to acknowledging polygamy, for example, is being made very much more difficult by the fact that in the wider community having multiple sexual partners, along with having multiple babies by different fathers or mothers, is now commonplace and even regarded as normal. Why, then, should a minority feel expected to toe a cultural line that is fast disappearing?

In February 2006, Dr. Patrick Sookdheo, director of the Institute for the Study of Islam and Christianity, warned that the day was coming when Islamic communities in Britain would form "a state within a state." He said he believed that "in a decade, you will see parts of English cities which are controlled by Muslim clerics and which follow, not the common law, but aspects of Muslim Sharia law. It is already starting to happen—and unless the Government changes the way it treats the so-called leaders of the Islamic community, it will continue. . . . The more fundamentalist clerics think that it is only a matter of time before they will persuade the Government to concede on the issue of Sharia law. Given the Government's record of capitulating, you can see why they believe that."[57]

As in so many areas of contemporary British life, truly moderate Muslims are finding that the host community is cutting the ground from under their feet and delivering them into the hands of the extremists by its refusal to hold the cultural line. According to Dr. Siddiqui, most Muslims have never discussed whether they want Sharia law or not. Often, he says, they don't understand what issues like this are actually about. British Muslims need guidance from the majority, he says, to show them what proper minority status requires of them.[58]

But Britain is not giving them such guidance because it no longer seems to know whether it wants to *be* a majority culture. Indeed, Britain is making it more and more difficult for itself even to study the faith at the core of this particular minority in an objective fashion. In its willingness to tear up its own tenets in the scramble to appease Muslim demands, it is destroying one of the cardinal rules of secular scholarship. When religion is taught at university level, a crucial issue for teachers is to explain how scriptures are situated in their historical context. A number of academics, however, report that this is fast becoming impossible. Because of Muslim sensitivities, they cannot teach historical criticism of the Koran.

According to Professor Alan Billings, who teaches religious studies at Lancaster University, students would normally be made aware of the origins of the sacred texts and the history and development of the faith, the notion that there *is* a history and a development, and that people don't necessarily believe in the same way that they did in earlier centuries. "But with the Koran this is totally avoided," he said. "It is presented instead as if it has immediate and direct relevance, so you read off from that document into your present situation."

In other words, British universities are teaching the Koran not as an objective and detached analysis of a religion, as would be the case with teaching any other religion, but from the perspective of the most obscurantist believer that it is true and not open to challenge. So British universities, the supposed stewards of rationality, have been suborned into becoming instead tools of religious indoctrination. And any backsliding into the realm of objective scholarship is punished.

"I was once teaching an undergraduate course on the subject of Islam and women," said Professor Billings. "I wanted to go back to the Prophet, but this was thought irreligious and blasphemous because it dealt with concubines and sex with children. On another occasion, I remarked that suicide bombers posed a real problem because normal constraints don't apply if you think your death will lead to God. For this, I was reported to the vice-chancellor, who told me to back off."[59]

As Lamin Sanneh has written, British Muslims have resolved to make Islam count in the public realm, in schools and universities, the upbringing of children, marriage, divorce, property, inheritance, taxation, banking and trade, and to give the state a role in enforcing religious laws including rules against blasphemy. The secular state thus qualifies, he says, as a kind of surrogate Sharia institution. And so the public space abandoned by Christianity is filled.[60] By no means all Muslims want this to happen. A growing number of them are actually rather keen on benefiting from the personal freedoms and tolerance that are the British way. The problem is that the British no longer appear to agree.

CHAPTER SIX

SCAPEGOATING THE JEWS

In the attempt to establish whether "moderate" Muslim attitudes are truly moderate, there is one infallible litmus test that can be used. It is the attitude to Israel and the Jews. This issue is absolutely fundamental to understanding the terrorist threat against the Western world. Tragically, however, Britain has completely misunderstood it and consequently negated the message that it carries.

Many, if not most, people in Britain—certainly, the majority of the educated classes—believe that Israel is at the root of the terrorist threat. So it is—but not in the way they think it is. They have got it totally backwards. And this crucial error is preventing them from properly understanding the Islamist threat to themselves.

Many people in Britain think like this: They are aware that the conflict between Israel and the Palestinians is a principal and incendiary grievance among Muslims. They have a great deal of sympathy with this grievance. They think the root of it is that the Palestinians have been prevented from having a state of their own by Israel, which oppresses them. They believe it is this apparent injustice that is fueling the Muslim animus against the West. The United States has made itself into the principal target for Islamist aggression, they go on, only because of its slavish support for Israel in pursuing this agenda of stifling the Palestinians. That was why, after 9/11, there was a groundswell of feeling in Britain that the Americans "had it coming to them."

This analysis, which is based on widespread and profound ignorance of the history of the Middle East, is warped out of all recognition. In the vacuum created by the combination of this knowledge
deficit and the contemporary inability to distinguish between truth
and lies, the British have largely swallowed Muslim and Arab propaganda, which has denied historical evidence, replaced it by mythol-
ogy, lies and libels, and reversed victim and oppressor in the Middle
East conflict. As a result, the British have come to believe that Israel is
the oppressor and the Arabs are its victims. This is a total reversal of
the historical reality that Israel has been the target of annihilatory
aggression by the Arab world without remission since the institution
of the Jewish state in 1948, as the Jews of Palestine were the same target in the decades before its creation.

The British also think that Jews and Muslims coexisted perfectly
well until Israel was created. In fact, nothing could be further from
the truth. The only circumstances in which Muslims have been content to live alongside Jews are where Jews have been a powerless
minority within an Islamic society. Muslim hostility to Israel is
rooted in Muslim hostility to Jews. Drawing on a theological animosity, it is based on the belief that the Jews are a Satanic force and a conspiracy to destroy Islam and rule the world; and that, since the Jews
control Western society, it follows that Israel is the forward flank of
the West's attempt to subjugate Muslims everywhere.

At the core of the Arab and Muslim fight against Israel, therefore,
lies a visceral hatred and prejudice towards the Jewish people. Given
the belief that the Jews rule the West and want to take over the world,
the hatred of the Jews and of Israel lies at the heart of the hatred of
the West. It is not that Israel's behavior has inflamed the jihad against
the West (although it is certainly used to whip up hysteria and thus
recruitment). It is rather that the jihad, which views the West as a
threat to Islam, sees Israel's existence as living, breathing proof of the
Western and Jewish intention to rule the planet. The battle with
Israel is thus conceived as a metaphysical struggle between good—
the Islamic world—and evil—the Jewish-backed Western world.
Israel's struggle to defend itself against this monstrosity is therefore
the West's struggle to defend itself against the same monstrosity.

Israel's struggle is simply being played out in a unique place where metaphysics and geopolitics have become fused.

But Britain doesn't see it this way at all. Instead, it insists that the Middle East conflict is a dispute about land. Partly, this is because the empirical, rational British are incapable of understanding the hysteria and paranoia unleashed by religious fanaticism. They think that the only thing that could drive someone to the inhuman act of suicide bombing is the despair and rage caused by oppression. Because they put Israel in a box marked "territorial dispute," they cannot see that Israel is actually the front line of defense in the war that has been declared upon the United States and the United Kingdom, and that buses are being blown up in Jerusalem for exactly the same reason that Tube trains were blown up in London, and the Twin Towers and the Pentagon were hit in New York and Washington. Instead, they *blame* Jerusalem and Washington for the atrocities in London. While they loathe and fear Islamist extremism, they accuse the Jews of provoking it. While they detest the terrorism that results, they are dismayingly receptive to the very prejudices that fuel it.

To understand this lethally misguided mindset, we have to know a little more about what people in Britain believe about the Middle East. The general view is that, to assuage European guilt over the Holocaust, European Jews were given land belonging to the Palestinians, who were driven out by this process to the West Bank and Gaza. After 1967, Israel was determined to colonize these areas too—despite the fact that they were also Palestinian lands—thus frustrating the Palestinians' desire for a homeland of their own.

There are many more fundamental errors in this false analysis than can be dealt with here. They include the fact that Israel and parts of the West Bank were the ancient Jewish national home *before* this land was conquered by the Arabs; that half of Israel's Jewish population consists of Jews driven out of Arab countries; that the Palestinian Arabs were offered a state of their own in 1948 but refused and tried to wipe out lawfully constituted Israel instead; that they were not driven out of Israel but in the main fled; that the resulting war of annihilation against Israel has never stopped; that Israel's occupation of the West Bank and Gaza was legal because it was an action taken in

self-defense against combatants who have never stopped waging war
against it; and that these territories, far from belonging to the Palestinians, had previously been illegally occupied by Jordan and Egypt
and should more properly have been described as no-man's-land
since the end of the British Mandate in 1948. It is necessary to identify some of these errors because they are preventing Britain from
grasping the essential dimension of the Israel conflict that has such a
direct bearing on the jihad against the West. It is that the fight against
Israel is not fundamentally about land. It is about hatred of the Jews.
It is certainly *not* about the absence of a separate state of Palestine,
which was on offer in 1936, 1948 and 2000, and could have been
established at any time between 1948 and 1967 by Jordan and Egypt.
The agenda here remains the extermination of the Jewish state itself.
The reason is that the Jews are hated, the hatred is rooted in religion,
and this hatred lies at the core of the war against the West.

It is true that before the twentieth century, Muslims had not been
as savage towards the Jews as had been the Christians. Although there
are many vicious references to Jews in the Koran, it was traditionally
understood that the perceived faults of the Jews at the time of the
Prophet Mohammed did not devolve upon all Jews throughout time,
unlike the curse laid upon them in the New Testament. Accordingly,
Jews were allowed to live for long periods in a state of religious and
cultural autonomy within the Muslim lands they once inhabited—
but only as *dhimmi* people, or second-class citizens, since Islam could
not recognize unbelievers as equals. Although there were periods of
cultural flowering, these Jews nevertheless lived under varying degrees
of duress. Deeply rooted anti-Jewish feeling among Muslims was further inflamed and exploited by Christian Jew-hatred. Pogroms arising
from the blood libels against the Jews, initiated by Greek Christians in
the Ottoman Empire, spread during the nineteenth century to Beirut,
Antioch, Hamma, Tripoli, Damascus, Aleppo and Damanhur.[1]

During the 1930s, Nazi antisemitism, the demonizing of the Jews
as a subhuman race apart, found an eager echo in the Muslim world.
The Muslims of Palestine were already alarmed by the steady arrival of
Jews who they decided were secular communists, with women dressed
in shorts and enjoying sexual freedom and equality with men.[2] Fore-

shadowing Muslim concerns of today, they viewed this arrival of such free spirits as profoundly destabilizing and a threat to their religion and social order. Employing the language and imagery of the tsarist classic anti-Jewish forgery, *The Protocols of the Elders of Zion*, they seized upon the tropes of Christian antisemitism in claiming that revolution was inherent in the Jewish "character," which was to sow dissension, subversion and ruin everywhere.

Arab mobs were duly inflamed by the Grand Mufti of Jerusalem, Haj Amin al-Husseini, to commit massacres of Palestinian Jews. When Hitler came to power in Germany, Haj Amin avidly courted the Nazis. Landing up eventually in Berlin after having secured a commitment by Mussolini and Hitler to work for the "elimination of the Jewish national home in Palestine," he became active in the Nazi war effort, rallying Muslims everywhere to rise up against the Allies, dispatching Bosnian Muslims to fight under German command and urging the foreign minister of Hungary to prevent Jews from coming to Palestine and to send them to Poland instead—as a result of which, hundreds of thousands of Jews were sent to the extermination camps.[3] The history of the Palestinian Arabs is therefore inextricably bound up with their complicity in the Nazi Holocaust; the hatred for the Jews that they displayed during that period has been reflected ever since within their ranks and throughout the wider Arab and Muslim world.

During this period, a seismic development within the Arab world was to cement and expand the Muslim hatred of the Jews being fanned by the Nazi flames. The rise of Islamism, under such thinkers as Hassan al-Banna, Sayed Abu'l Ala Maududi and Sayed Qutb, and the emergence of the Muslim Brotherhood would bring to the fore a virulent interpretation of Koranic attitudes towards the Jews. Fixating upon the early conflict between the Prophet Mohammed and the Jewish tribes of seventh-century Arabia, the Islamists became obsessed with the archetype of a universal Jew, treacherous by nature, whose perfidy threatened not only Islam but all humanity.

This suited their Manichean mindset of a cosmic struggle between good and evil, which was central to their goal of purging society of un-Islamic teachings and practices, returning to Islam's original pure sources and establishing an ideal Islamic state. Seeing themselves as engaged in the final battle at the end of time, they needed to blame external forces for the intolerable situation in which they perceived Islam to be and thus devised conspiracy theories to fit. To excuse modern Muslim weakness and the sense of shame and humiliation it engendered, they targeted all Jews as scapegoats. It was the Jews who were behind the diabolical conspiracy of secularism, the Christian West and Freemasonry that made up the satanic, worldwide plot to exterminate Islam.[4]

In particular, it was Sayed Qutb's invective, through works such as his book *Our Struggle with the Jews* published in 1950, that turned antisemitism into the marker of Islamist movements and infected mainstream Muslim society with the virus. It was Qutb who made the Jews a metaphor for Western domination and immorality, representing a threat to the integrity of Islam. He accused the Jews of being the authors of Western decadence, having disseminated the doctrine of "atheistic materialism" through Karl Marx, "animalistic sexuality" through Sigmund Freud and sociology through Emile Durkheim.[5]

Jews, according to Qutb, were inherently evil because throughout the ages they had rebelled against God. "From such creatures who kill, massacre and defame prophets," he wrote, "one can only expect the spilling of human blood and dirty means which would further their machinations and evilness." They were characterized, he said, by ingratitude, selfishness, fanaticism, isolationism, and hatred for all others, always fomenting dissension in their host societies and exploiting all disasters to profit from the misery of others. Modern secular philosophy was a trap laid by worldwide Judaism in order to destroy the barriers of creed, weaken society and enable Jews to penetrate every country with their "satanic usurious activity," which would finally "deliver the proceeds of all human toil into the hands of the great usurious Jewish financial institutions." Zionism was but the latest in the long line of Jewish plots against Islam.[6]

The impact of such thinking by Sayed Qutb and other similar ideologues cannot be overstated. At around the same time that Nazi ideology was constructing its infernal vision of the Jews as a pestilential blight that had to be exterminated, Islamist ideology was constructing its own version of the same demonology. But whereas the

Holocaust forced the world to acknowledge the link between the Nazi demonization of the Jews and Hitler's program for global domination, the existence of Israel has made Britain deaf to the hatred of the Jews that underpins the Islamist threat. The anti-Jewish invective flowing from the mullahs of Iran or the leaders of al-Qaeda is thus all but ignored. Yet, in accordance with the thinkers who have inspired them, this egregious prejudice forms a key factor in their thinking. Thus Ayatollah Khomeini said in his "Programme for the Establishment of an Islamic Government" in 1970:

> We must protest and make the people aware that the Jews and their foreign backers are opposed to the very foundations of Islam and wish to establish Jewish domination throughout the world. Since they are a cunning and resourceful people, I fear that—God forbid!—they may one day achieve this goal and that the apathy shown by some of us may allow a Jew to rule over us one day. May God never let us see such a day.[7]

Osama bin Laden has claimed that the Jews want to divide the Muslim world, enslave it and loot its wealth, and that they use Western powers to achieve these aims. "The Jews in the past attacked the Prophets and accused Mary the mother of Jesus, who is revered in Muslim tradition, of a great sin," he said. "They believe all other humans were created to be exploited by them, and engage in killing, raping and stealing. They have managed to install governments in America that serve as their agents and do their bidding."[8]

Rashid al-Ghannushi, a Tunisian Islamist who lives in London, has spoken of "a Jewish-American plan encompassing the entire region, which would cleanse it of all resistance and open it to Jewish hegemony from Marrakesh to Kazakhstan." He did not speak of an Israeli-American plan. He believed in a wider Jewish conspiracy, of which Israel would be just one agency.[9]

There are many more such examples. But in addition to its deafness to the antisemitism of these radicals, Britain is even more oblivious to the hatred of the Jews that is central to Palestinian and other Arab terrorism. Britain is certain that the cause of the hatred is Israel in

particular rather than the Jews in general, the claim assiduously peddled by Muslim groups in Britain. It refuses to acknowledge that the
hatred of Israel arises *because* of the hatred of the Jews, a fact which is
overwhelmingly obvious from what such groups say.

The Iranian-backed Hezbollah, the "Party of God" which wants
to transform Islam into a universal power and establish Islamic rule,
negates Israel's existence based on Islamic precepts portraying Judaism
as the oldest and bitterest adversary of Islam. Hussain Fadlallah,
Hezbollah's most senior religious authority, has said: "We find in the
Koran that the Jews are the most aggressive towards the Muslims, not
because they are Jews or because they believe in the Torah but because
of their aggressive resistance to the unity of the faith."[10] The main
concern is with the perceived impediment to the imposition of Islam.

So Hezbollah presents the struggle between Islam and Judaism in
apocalyptic terms as the struggle between truth and falsehood, good
and evil. Thus: "The Jews are the enemy of the entire human race";
"Zionism dictates the world and dominates it"; "The Torah inspires
the Jews to kill"; and "The Jews constitute a financial power. . . . They
use funds to dominate the Egyptian media and infect its society with
AIDS." In another interview, Fadlallah is quoted as saying: "The
Jews want to be a world superpower. This racist circle of Jews wants
to take vengeance on the whole world for their history of persecution
and humiliation. In this light, the Jews will work on the basis that
Jewish interests are above all world interests. No one should imagine
that the Jews act on behalf of any super or minor power; it is their
personality to make for themselves a future world presence."[11] To that
end, it demonizes Israel as the source of all evil and violence in the
Middle East and, as a Western tool, an obstacle to Islamic unity. Thus
it freely interchanges the terms Zionism and Judaism and routinely
employs antisemitic motifs in its depiction of Israel. Typically, Israel's
alleged ruthlessness is illustrated by a soldier with a long, crooked
nose, long teeth and ears and a prickly chin, wearing an armband with
the Star of David and a steel helmet on his head, and holding a dagger
dripping with blood.[12]

In very similar terms Hamas, which defines itself as the military
wing of the Muslim Brotherhood, also presents the Arab-Israeli con-

flict as the epitome of an inherently irreconcilable struggle between Judaism and Islam. It is not a national or territorial conflict but a historical, religious, cultural and existential conflict between truth and falsehood, believers and infidels, prosecuted through jihad until victory or martyrdom. This ideology is represented in the movement's covenant, which in addition to declaring its aim of exterminating Israel displays the virulent and paranoid conspiracy theory that fuels it:

> The enemies [the Jews] have been scheming for a long time . . . and have accumulated huge and influential material wealth. With their money, they took control of the world media. . . . With their money they stirred revolutions in various parts of the globe. . . . They stood behind the French Revolution, the Communist Revolution and most of the revolutions we hear about. . . . With their money they formed secret organizations —such as the Freemasons, Rotary Clubs and the Lions—which are spreading around the world, in order to destroy societies and carry out Zionist interests. . . . They stood behind World War I . . . and formed the League of Nations through which they could rule the world. They were behind World War II, through which they made huge financial gains. . . . There is no war going on anywhere without them having their finger in it. . . . The Day of Judgment will not come about until Moslems fight Jews and kill them. Then, the Jews will hide behind rocks and trees, and the rocks and trees will cry out: "O Moslem, there is a Jew hiding behind me; come and kill him."[13]

Hamas leaflets further propagate this hatred of the Jews through a torrent of antisemitic motifs that are used to whip Muslims up to genocidal frenzy. Thus they call the Jews: "The brothers of the apes, the killers of the Prophets, blood suckers, warmongers"; "barbaric"; "cowards"; a "cancer expanding in the land of Isra' [Palestine] and Mi'raj [Mohammed's ascent to heaven] threatening the entire Islamic world"; "a conceited and arrogant people"; "the enemy of God and mankind"; "the descendants of treachery and deceit"; Nazis "spreading corruption in the land of Islam"; "the Zionist culprits who poisoned the water in the past, killed infants, women and elders"; and "thieves, monopolists, usurers."[14]

Such ravings demonstrate that the British view of Hamas and Hezbollah—that these are merely terrorist outfits formed to liberate the Palestinian people and secure their homeland—is totally misconceived. Indeed, the idea that Israel is the cause of the jihad against the West is demonstrably absurd. Ever since the 1930s, the Muslim Brotherhood had advocated jihad in defense of Egypt, Arabism and Islam against the British and the Jews—even calling Egypt's President Nasser the agent of a Jewish plot.[15] Hamas and Hezbollah are not fighting for national self-realization by the Palestinians. They are front-line soldiers in the jihad against the Western world. But because the British are certain that Israel is the cause and not the victim of Arab terrorism, they are ignorant of the Jew-hatred coursing through Islamist ideology and through its progeny among the Palestinian terrorists; they have been deaf to the anti-Jewish hatred that has been pouring out of the Arab and Muslim world for the past half-century, fusing Islamist conspiracy theory with the tropes of European Nazi Jew-hatred.

In his book *Holy War and Victory* published in 1974, Abd al-Halim Mahmoud, the rector of Cairo's Al-Azhar University—which has played a key doctrinal role in promulgating Islamist ideology—presented the Jews as a diabolical conspiracy:

> Among Satan's friends—indeed his best friends in our age—are the Jews. They have laid down a plan for undermining humanity, religiously and ethically. They have begun to work to implement this plan with their money and their propaganda. They have falsified knowledge, exploited the pens of writers and bought minds in their quest for the ruination of humanity. Thus they proceed from this to seizing power . . . domination, mastery and gaining full control.[16]

Throughout the Muslim world, the Nazi calumny and the tropes of medieval Jew-hatred have become assimilated into Islamic thinking. Thus in 1983 the Syrian defense minister, Mustafa Tlas, published *The Matzah of Zion*, which accepted as literally true the Damascus blood

libel of 1840 in which eight Jews were falsely accused of murdering a
Capuchin monk and his servant and using their blood to bake matzot,
the unleavened bread eaten at Passover. Such blood libels have been
regularly repeated. In March 2002, Dr. Umayma Ahmed al-Jalahma
stated in the Saudi government daily *Al-Riyadh*: "The Jews spilling
human blood to prepare pastry for their holidays is a well-established
fact, historically and legally, all throughout history. This was one of
the main reasons for the persecution and exile that were their lot in
Europe and Asia."[17] And the Iranian president Mahmoud Ahmadinejad, as a coda to his declared intention to "wipe Israel off the map,"
announced in December 2005 that "we do not accept" the claim that
"Hitler killed millions of innocent Jews in furnaces."[18]

The Protocols of the Elders of Zion is treated as a basic text and sold
throughout the Muslim world along with Hitler's *Mein Kampf*.[19] In
2003, Egypt TV aired a 41-part series, syndicated to more than twenty
other Arab TV stations, updating the *Protocols*. Muslim children
throughout the Arab world are taught to hate the Jews and regard
them as sinister and diabolical. Syrian school textbooks portray the
Jews as the enemies of Islam, of mankind and of God himself.[20] In
Egypt, a booklet for children tells them that the Jews "persistently
attempted to spread hate among the Muslims" and that "the only way
to eliminate the Jews is through holy war (jihad) for the sake of Allah
because they are the most villainous among Allah's creatures."[21]
Another book says: "No other nation in ancient and modern times
has carried the banner of fraud, evil and treachery as has the Jewish
nation." It accuses them of behaving throughout history in a "cruel
and corrupt manner," and of using "conspiracy and deceit" to carry
out their plans for "establishing their rule over the world."[22]

As for the Palestinian Authority—believed by the British public to
be a legitimate, non-extremist organization trying to secure statehood
and rights for the Palestinians—it is an unstoppable geyser of rabid
anti-Jewish prejudice. Through PA-controlled media including television sermons, radio and newspapers, it labels the Jews as the enemies of God and humanity whose annihilation is thus presented as a
legitimate self-defense and service to the world. In a sermon on PA TV,
Dr. Muhammad Mustafa Najem, a lecturer in Koranic interpretation

at Gaza's Al-Azhar University, preached that Allah described the Jews as "characterized by conceit, pride, arrogance, savagery, disloyalty and treachery . . . [and] deceit and cunning." Dr. Khader Abas, a lecturer in psychology at Gaza's Al-Aksa University, taught the origins of Jewish evil: "From the moment the [Jewish] child is born, he nurses hatred against others, nurses seclusion, nurses superiority."[23]

In 1999, a cartoon in the official PA daily *Al-Hayat al-Jadida* depicted a Jew as a subhuman dwarf with the caption: "The disease of the century." An opinion piece in the same paper said of the Jewish festival of Passover (an obsessive focus also for medieval Christian antisemitism): "This holiday has various meanings. . . . Murdering foreigners is a godly virtue that should be emulated. . . . There is nothing in history more horrible than the theft, the greatest crime in history, that the Jews carried out the night of their Exodus [from Egypt]. . . . In other words, robbing others is not only permitted, it is considered holy. Especially since this thievery was done under the direct command of God, [that is,] the God of the Jews."[24]

The PA's most popular imam, Ibrahim Mudayris, who has described the Jews as "a cancer," stated in May 2005 on PA TV:

> Read the history. . . . You'll find that Jews are behind every conflict on earth. The suffering of nations? The Jews are behind it! Ask Britain! What did it do to the Jews at the beginning of the sixth century? Chased them down, made them suffer, and prevented them from entering for more than three hundred years. . . . Ask France what it did to the Jews! They made them suffer, chased them down, and burned their Talmud, for the conflicts that they [Jews] tried to ignite in France. . . . Ask Portugal what it did to the Jews! Ask Czarist Russia—which hosted the Jews, and they plotted to murder the Czar! And they were massacred again and again. Don't ask Germany what it did to the Jews, since the Jews are the ones who provoked the Nazis so the world would go to war against it.[25]

This unending avalanche of hatred against the Jews is why, of all the iconic grievances for the Islamic world, Israel is the most important. Israel represents not a regional dispute but a metaphysical struggle between good and evil. That is why the cause of Palestine is key to the Islamists' demands. As Sheikh Yusuf al-Qaradawi has written: ". . . the Movement has never forgotten and will never forget the Palestinian cause, because Palestine is the first and foremost Islamic cause, and its liberation is the first and foremost duty . . . to adopt the Palestinian cause as part of a worldwide Islamic plan, with the policy plan and by means of jihad, since it acts as the keystone of the renaissance of the Arab world today."[26]

And this is why the attitude towards suicide bombings in Israel is the litmus test of a moral response to terrorism. Many people in Britain believe that there is no contradiction between having some sympathy with or even supporting suicide-bomb terrorism in Israel and opposing it in Britain. That is because they think that what caused the Middle East conflict is completely different from what lies behind Islamist terrorism. Not only is this attitude morally wrong, since opposition to terrorism must be indivisible or it is not opposition at all. It also means that the British cannot understand the enemy that threatens them; they are oblivious to the danger that Islamism poses to the entire Jewish people, and unaware that this danger to the Jews stands proxy for the threat to the West and to all free peoples.

That is why, despite claims by some in the British establishment that Qaradawi is a "moderate" because he opposes al-Qaeda terrorism in Britain, it is monstrous to regard him as such since he encourages human-bomb attacks in Israel and Iraq. His sermons often call for Jews to be killed on the basis that there is hardly any difference between Judaism and Zionism. He supports such assertions with libelous accusations and imputations of collective wrongdoing against the Jewish faith and its people. Thus he asserts that the Torah permits Jews to spill the blood of others and to seize their money and land, and that, "with the exception of a few honourable ones, the majority of Jews support Israel's policies."[27]

Qaradawi's virulent hatred of the Jews is unfortunately not uncommon among British Muslims. Indeed, the Muslim Council of Britain has said that he speaks for the majority of Muslims. But the MCB itself, despite being considered a mainstream representative organization, not only refuses unequivocally to condemn suicide bombings in Israel but has also associated itself with Holocaust denial and accused Jews of being Nazis.[28]

As a result of the relentless propaganda, lies, libels, paranoid delusions and diabolical images about both Jews and Israel that have suffused the Muslim world for decades, British Muslims subscribe in large measure to these attitudes. Walk down the Edgware Road, in the heart of London's Arab district, and you will find on open display in bookshop after bookshop copies of *The Protocols of the Elders of Zion* and *Mein Kampf*, books devoted to Holocaust denial and vilification of Israel, cartoons depicting George W. Bush wearing a skullcap with the Star of David on it, and countless other texts and images defaming both Israel and the Jewish people. Many British Muslims assume that the Jews are a malignant force in the world, driving America and global politics in their own self-interest and trampling down everything in their path. Wherever they may be, the Jews are assumed to comprise a sinister conspiracy not merely to maintain the State of Israel, but to eradicate Islam and take over the world. As a result, many Muslims ascribe virtually every misfortune in the world to the secret machinations of the Jews. They are pictured as the secret force behind the Asian tsunami on Boxing Day 2004, behind the 9/11 attacks—any and all calamities.

What makes such developments in Britain so chilling is the wider silence in which they occur. It is repeatedly said that the vast majority of British Muslims are moderate. But only a tiny handful denounce this hate-fest against Israel and the Jews—a statistically negligible number, well below the public radar. British Muslims often say their representative institutions do not reflect the views of the community. But nowhere is that community protesting in public that the Islamic world is consumed by hatred towards the Jews and towards Israel, and that this has got to stop. On the contrary, on February 2006, a poll of Muslims commissioned by a coalition of Jewish groups revealed that nearly two-fifths believed that the Jewish community in Britain was a legitimate target "as part of the ongoing struggle for justice in the Middle East," more than half believed that British Jews had "too much influence over the direction of UK foreign policy," and no fewer than 46 percent thought the Jewish community was "in league with Freemasons to control the media and politics."[29] And the wider, non-Muslim community is equally silent. The murderous rage against Israel, expressed by one Muslim organization after another, is greeted with indifference. Despite the plethora of antisemitic materials on sale in the bookshops, there are virtually no prosecutions because the prosecuting authorities believe these would not be "in the public interest"—in other words, they are afraid of a Muslim backlash.

One consequence has been a rise in physical attacks on British Jews. In 2004 the Community Security Trust, a Jewish defense organization, recorded 532 antisemitic incidents in Britain, up by 42 percent from the previous year and the highest number ever. These included assaults and threats, attacks on synagogues and desecration of cemeteries, abuse and hate mail.[30] In 2005 the number of antisemitic incidents was lower, but at 455 it was still the second highest on record and followed a warning by the chief rabbi, Sir Jonathan Sacks, that a "tsunami of antisemitism" was sweeping Europe.[31]

Towards all this, the British are generally indifferent. Indeed, such is the popular hostility towards Israel that when the British are presented with evidence of attacks on Jews in their own country, they often react with suspicion on the basis that such figures are exaggerated and a form of special pleading to camouflage Israel's misdeeds. The same people, however, are quick to claim "Islamophobia" when anything disobliging is said about Muslims, including any discussion about Islamist terrorism. Such is the moral and intellectual fallout of Londonistan, where, to a dismaying extent, the indigenous British have signed up to the false narrative of those who are laying siege to their society.

And at the very heart of that narrative of falsehood is the issue of Israel, the litmus test of morality, moderation—and the capacity of the West to secure its own survival.

· CHAPTER SEVEN ·

THE RED–BLACK ALLIANCE

When the Iranian president Mahmoud Ahmadinejad announced in October 2005 that he intended to "wipe Israel off the map," Britain, along with the rest of the civilized world, expressed shock and revulsion. Yet, two days later, thousands of demonstrators took to the streets of London to demand that Israel meet precisely such a fate.

While shocked demonstrators in Italy, Hungary, Austria and France waved around placards asking "Israel today, Europe tomorrow?", London resounded instead to shouts for Israel's destruction. Thousands of demonstrators marched through the city to mark "Al-Quds day"—when Muslims express solidarity with the Palestinian Arabs—on what was effectively a British march for genocide. The crowd chanted: "From the river to the sea, Palestine will be free," "Zionism, terrorism" and "We are all Hezbollah"; and no one turned a hair. All those who had expressed revulsion, shock and outrage two days previously at the outburst from Iran suddenly fell silent when confronted not merely by calls for Israel's annihilation but the spectacle of supporters of Iran's terrorist army on the streets of London calling for the destruction of a lawfully constituted, democratic country. "[The response] was great," said the event organizer Massoud Shadjareh, director of the Islamic Human Rights Commission. "It helped us gauge the reaction from the public, which was quite positive."[1]

One might have imagined that, in the wake of not just 9/11 but the

London bombings of 2005, Britain would have recoiled in horror at any such threat by Islamists and wished to express solidarity with the fellow democracy that was being thus threatened. One might have thought that, with Nazi-style demonization of the Jews pouring out of the Muslim world, the political left in particular would be springing to defend this beleaguered and tiny minority against the threat from clerical fascism. Doesn't the left, after all, make the most vigorous cause possible against racism and prejudice in all its forms?

On the contrary. Far from being seen as the mortal enemy of the causes that progressive opinion holds so dear, such as sexual freedom or equal rights for women and homosexuals, the Islamic jihad has turned into the armed wing of the British left. As soon as the issue of Israel enters the picture, the British reaction to terror becomes "quite positive." Far from springing to Israel's defense as a fellow target, the British become passive, mute and even sympathetic to the murderous sentiments being screamed by the marching jihadists.

For Israel is not viewed in Britain as it is in America, as the only democracy in the Middle East and one which has been under annihilatory attack by brutal tyrannies since its inception. It has instead become a pariah, viewed by "progressives" in the same way that they formerly viewed South Africa under apartheid. Many in Britain think it was a mistake that the Jewish state was ever created and would rather like it to vanish—not that they would condone any large-scale loss of life, you understand, but if it could be done without any nasty violence they would welcome its disappearance.

The argument that it has done nothing to deserve such a fate except fight for its existence is scorned. The argument that the Jews are as entitled to a state of their own as any other people, and that there are no similar calls to destroy any other nation-state, is received with hostile incomprehension. The argument that, uniquely among the peoples of the world, the Jews need a place of refuge is dismissed with contempt. After all, comes the riposte, have not the Jews now turned into the new Nazis in their treatment of the Palestinians? Thus the campaign to dehumanize, demonize and delegitimize Israel has done its dirty work. The big lie that has been rammed home about Israel has lodged deep in the British psyche. A key salient of the West's defense

—British public opinion—has thus been captured by the jihad.

How can this have happened? There are three issues that bind this unholy alliance together: America, Israel and the war in Iraq. At the very core of this troika is Israel—or to be more precise the Palestinians, who for the trendsetters among the British left have replaced the IRA as the terrorist fashion accessory *du jour* and have become the cause of choice for every heart that bleeds. For the left, Israel has filled the void created by the disappearance of the Latin American juntas, opposition to which once defined political virtue. When it is not marching against Israel or writing newspaper articles or making TV programs against it, the left is busy organizing academic and economic boycotts to bring it to its knees.

Much of the reason for this lies in the end of the Cold War. With the collapse of communism and the end of the dream of workers' control, the left alighted upon the Palestinians as the new proletariat whose cause could be championed as a weapon against Western society. Since the left demonizes America and Western capitalism, and lionizes the third world and all liberation movements, the Palestinian Arabs were a natural cause to be championed—victims of American imperialist power through the actions of its proxy, Israel.

There was a further and crucial cultural factor. With the fall of communism, the left shifted its focus from economics to issues of race, ethnic identity and the nation-state. If the notion of a dominant culture was now racist, the idea of a Jewish state was anathema; and the stand that America was taking in defense not only of Israel but of the Western nation-state and its values made it even more of an enemy.

Moreover, Jews were at the very heart of those Western values. Antonio Gramsci, the philosopher who became the iconic thinker of the 1960s, laid down the blueprint for precisely what has happened in Britain: the capture of all society's institutions, such as schools, universities, churches, the media, the legal profession, the police and voluntary groups. This intellectual elite was persuaded to sing from the same subversive hymn-sheet so that the moral beliefs of the majority would be replaced by the values of those on the margins of society, the perfect ambience in which the Muslim grievance culture could be fanned into the flames of extremism.

At the core of those Western majority values lay the Mosaic code, which first gave the world the concept of morality, self-discipline and laws regulating behavior. Who, then, could be surprised that the Jews found themselves in the left's crosshairs? As it took aim at morality and self-restraint, it seized a golden opportunity to pulverize the very people who invented the rules in the first place.

Of course, the communist left had always embodied a profound hatred of the Jews, and of America as the fount of capitalism, which it saw as a Jewish conspiracy against the masses. And as Richard Wolin has persuasively argued, "progressive" intellectuals have a long if unacknowledged history of a "fascination with fascism."[2] The Holocaust pushed this prejudice underground, but now it has resurfaced and regrouped around the issue of "Zionism." Far from being repelled by the Muslim view of America and Israel as the Great and the Little Satan, the left has enthusiastically embraced it.

This is all the more remarkable considering that the Islamists stand for precisely the kind of obscurantist and socially repressive values that the secular left—with its obsessive promotion of sexual freedom and the rights of women and gays—most detests. Yet it says it can put aside its differences with the Islamists simply because they too are against the state. In a long essay on the subject, Chris Harman of the revolutionary Trotskyite group the Socialist Workers Party argued that while the left could not support the Islamists, neither could it pass up the opportunity to exploit them. Their revolutionary capacity "could be tapped for progressive purposes," provided that socialists kept their distance. Where the Islamists were in opposition to the state, he wrote, the rule should be: "With the Islamists sometimes, with the state never."[3]

Despite their obvious differences, therefore, the far left and the Islamists have become a marriage made in hell. They have swallowed their profound differences to use each other to fight the West. Indeed, Marxism has had a considerable influence on Islamic radicals like Sayed Qutb, Sayed Maududi and Ali Shariati, the architect of the Iranian revolution who thought that Islam presented a better ideology and system than Marxism-Leninism for Muslims to topple the "imperialists."[4] And with the Iraq war, a cause arrived in Britain to give the Islamists and the far left a priceless opportunity to do just that.

The Muslim Association of Britain, the British arm of the Muslim Brotherhood, had already positioned itself as the spearhead of radical Palestinianism in the country. In April 2002 it organized a large pro-Palestinian rally in central London, where some demonstrators signified their approval for terrorism by dressing as suicide bombers and others carried placards downloaded from the MAB website equating Israel with Nazi Germany.[5]

With the Iraq war, the MAB realized the opportunity that was presented to vastly increase its own profile within the Muslim community. Its involvement in the Stop the War Coalition, led by the Socialist Workers Party (SWP) and the Communist Party of Britain, gave it real power. This antiwar coalition organized a series of rallies during 2003 that proved to be Britain's biggest-ever political demonstrations. The MAB influence resulted in the slogan "Don't attack Iraq/Free Palestine." Two important but separate issues, both key parts of the Muslim Brotherhood's agenda, were thus neatly conflated in the public mind.[6]

At a massive Stop the War rally held in Trafalgar Square in May 2003, Tony Benn, a former Labour MP and iconic politician of the left, called George Bush and Ariel Sharon the "two most dangerous men in the world," while Andrew Burgin of the Stop the War Coalition demanded the dismantling of the Jewish state. "The South African apartheid state never inflicted the sort of repression that Israel is inflicting on the Palestinians," he said to cries of "*Allahu akhbar!*" from the audience. "When there is real democracy, there will be no more Israel."[7]

In the wider community, the underlying agenda of hatred of the Jews was largely dismissed—not least by British Jews on the left. Not only did they too subscribe to the prevailing antiwar mood but, like many Britons, some of them actually endorsed the view that Israel was beyond the pale and dismissed any claims of resurgent antisemitism as special pleading. Nevertheless, three Jewish leftists wrote to the *Guardian* to express their shock and horror at being surrounded on such a march by "hate-filled chanting and images" in which anti-

Israel and anti-Jewish sentiments were blurred. "How else could we feel," they wrote, "when we saw placards featuring swastikas and the Star of David—an ancient symbol for all Jews everywhere, not just for the state of Israel—as synonymous symbols of oppression?"[8]

Such a protest fell on deaf ears. On the back of the Stop the War Coalition, a major plank of the Islamists' attack on the West was being promoted in London by two prominent British political figures.

London's Labour mayor, Ken Livingstone, has always espoused far-left views and has long enjoyed a reputation for being on the extreme edge of the Labour party. Indeed, in 2000 he was excluded from it altogether, having been thrown out when, while sitting in Parliament as a Labour MP, he stood as an independent candidate for the post of London's mayor.[9] In a remarkable volte-face he was brought back into the party by Tony Blair in 2004, when the prime minister realized in a panic that Livingstone was about to win that mayoral election.[10] The result is that London is governed by a mayor with far-left views who appears to be impregnable, because the public overlook these opinions as a result of Livingstone's populist charm and shrewd pavement politics.

Whereas once he was notorious for supporting the IRA, Livingstone's signature radicalism is now the Palestinian and Islamist cause. After the London bombings, the mayor's hostility to Israel and to the West burst into the open. Having first wept over the slaughter and declared that he did not support suicide bombers, he then effectively justified such terrorism on the grounds that the terrorists were "oppressed" by the people they murdered, blaming the West for "double standards" around the world that drove young Muslim men to turn themselves into human bombs because "they only have their bodies to use as weapons" while the Israelis had "done horrendous things which border on crimes against humanity in the way they have indiscriminately slaughtered men, women and children in the West Bank and Gaza for decades."[11] Subsequently, he claimed that Palestinian Arabs turned themselves into human bombs against Israelis because they did not have the vote, and compared the Likud party to Hamas, saying: "I think the Israeli hardliners around Likud and Hamas are two sides of the same coin, they need each other to drum up support."[12]

Even more astoundingly, he tried to draw an analogy between British Muslim suicide bombers and British Jews. "If a young Jewish boy in this country goes and joins the Israeli army, and ends up killing many Palestinians in operations and can come back, that is wholly legitimate," he said. "But for a young Muslim boy in this country, who might think, I want to defend my Palestinian brothers and sisters, and gets involved, he is branded as a terrorist. And I think it is this that has infected the attitude about how we deal with these problems."[13] But the equation was wholly false. British Jews do not serve in the Israel Defense Forces. "Jewish boys" serve in it only if they are Israeli citizens. And the actions of the IDF in defending Israel against terror are in a different moral universe from the actions of terrorists.

Deciding to ride the tiger of British Islamism to court the ever more significant Muslim vote, Livingstone embraced the Muslim Brotherhood—literally so. At a conference in London in July 2004, Livingstone publicly embraced Sheikh Yusuf al-Qaradawi, the Brotherhood's spiritual leader who has not only endorsed the use of human bombs against Iraq and Israel but denounced the "incomparable and overt" iniquity of the Jews and called for Jews and other infidels to be killed.[14]

The occasion was the annual session of the European Council for Fatwa and Research, held at London's City Hall. Livingstone later claimed that Qaradawi had been invited to City Hall to oppose the French ban on the Islamic headscarf.[15] But at the inaugural press conference, the mayor was the only person to mention the ban. Neither the MAB spokesman nor Qaradawi mentioned it, but concentrated instead on promoting the Fatwa Council's leadership role in the community. The main purpose of the conference was clearly to promote Qaradawi and the Fatwa Council, and the headscarf debate and the use of the mayor were just means to that end.[16]

What was so remarkable about Livingstone's embrace of Qaradawi was that the sheikh's virulent prejudices against homosexuals, women and "infidels" dramatically conflicted with Livingstone's carefully cultivated "rainbow coalition" of precisely such victim groups from which his original political power base had been formed. Nevertheless, the mayor insisted that his controversial guest was a beacon of modernity:

"Of all the Muslim leaders in the world today," he told the Commons Home Affairs Select Committee, "Sheikh Qaradawi is the most powerfully progressive force for change and for engaging Islam with western values. I think his is very similar to the position of Pope John XXIII."[17]

The mayor's erstwhile "rainbow" constituency took a very different view. An unprecedented coalition encompassing Sikhs, Hindus, Orthodox Jews, gays, lesbians and students produced a dossier detailing Qaradawi's many rabid utterances and accusing Livingstone of abusing his office. Livingstone reacted by accusing the opposition of being a Mossad plot to peddle a conspiracy theory to defame Islam.[18]

The fact is that Livingstone was extremely close to the Muslim Brotherhood, with whom his office enjoyed close links. But the Islamists opened up a second and even more powerful front with the election of George Galloway, another former Labour MP, who had been thrown out of the party for inciting British troops in Iraq to mutiny. Galloway, a defender of Saddam Hussein, Fidel Castro and Yasser Arafat, enjoyed five minutes of fame when he put on a characteristically swaggering performance in front of the Senate Foreign Affairs Committee and disclaimed any wrongdoing in the "oil for food" scandal in Saddam's Iraq. Now he had put himself at the head of the far-left/Islamist alliance in Britain with the creation of a new political party, Respect, of which he became the first MP.

Staffed mainly by the Socialist Workers Party and other hard-left groups, Respect targeted its message at Muslims in accordance with the same political strategy that had created the Stop the War Coalition. Riding the ever-rising wave of opposition to the Iraq war, Galloway used his formidable demagogic skills to whip up feeling among the disaffected Muslims of London's East End and defeat the sitting Labour MP, Oona King, at the 2005 general election, establishing Respect as a genuine force in a number of other constituencies too.

Such is the state of British politics that Oona King was herself a politician who had said of America: "It's a f***ing f***ed-up power man, it's a fundamentalist Christian power if we're not careful. It's terrifying."[19] In a newspaper article, she compared the Palestinians in Gaza to the Jews in the Warsaw ghetto.[20]

Nevertheless, what Galloway brought into being was a far more alarming development—sectarian politics, a specific appeal to Islamic religiosity through a political program skewed to foreign conflicts and tied up in the leftist projection of victimhood.

Narrow-minded, intrinsically intolerant, chauvinist, exclusivist and demagogic, and with a capacity to whip up anti-Western hysteria, it was thus profoundly dangerous to Britain, providing an unprecedented platform for the propagation of Islamist views in Britain. It was in exactly the same East End district that another demagogue, Oswald Mosley, had launched his Union of British Fascists in the 1930s. The appeasement-minded, reality-denying mood of the country then was similar in many striking respects to the mood of Britain today.

Galloway's startling trajectory was, however, to be brought to an abrupt and unforeseen halt in January 2006 after his Muslim constituents were appalled by his participation in a vulgar and sexually voyeuristic TV show. The wider community took a similarly dim view of his behavior. This was all the more startling since his pro-Islamist demagoguery—including a visit to Damascus, where he exhorted the Arab masses to rise up against the West—had been largely treated with indifference.

Neither Livingstone nor Galloway was taken seriously as a threat by the British public, who appeared almost wholly indifferent to the dangers they posed of whipping up Islamist extremism. One important reason was that the issue of Israel was central to their platform; and the British do not acknowledge the prejudice behind this onslaught against Israel because they tend to share it.

The reason is that Israel has now been delegitimized so it has become seen as on a par with apartheid-era South Africa. This is because extreme ignorance about the Middle East has led the British to swallow a campaign of demonization against Israel conducted by the media, who overwhelmingly subscribe to the worldview of the left. The unholy alliance between the left and radical Islamists is not confined to the revolutionaries of the Socialist Workers Party. Because of the iron grip exercised by the left on the British intelligentsia, its worldview has become the norm for most of the media class.

The result has been a media assault upon Israel of a kind that no other country in the world has endured. Of course, where Israel behaves controversially it should be criticized like anywhere else. But it has been demonized in a way that goes way beyond legitimate criticism, because the attacks are based on distortions, libels and outrageous double standards. The one democracy in the Middle East is being delegitimized as a pariah state while the media is relatively silent on the atrocities committed by the various despotisms that are trying to destroy it. Echoing the scapegoating of the Jews for people's troubles that has defined anti-Jewish hatred throughout the centuries, Israel has become a scapegoat for the violence of the Muslims and Arabs who attack both it and the free world.

Israel's history is routinely denied or ignored, so that the defense against attack that it has been forced to mount since its inception is falsely represented as aggression. It is the target of systematic and egregious lies and smears. Its every action is reported malevolently, ascribing to it the basest motives and denying its victimization. Instead of being the world's principal state-victim of terrorism, it is accused of being a terrorist state. So John Pilger, a persistent and egregious attacker, could write: "Thus, the state of Israel has been able to convince many outsiders that it is merely a victim of terrorism when, in fact, its own unrelenting, planned terrorism is the cause of the infamous retaliation by Palestinian suicide bombers."[21]

Israel is presented in the worst possible light by people who display an eagerness to believe that all its actions are malign, even where the facts clearly refute such assumptions. When Israel went into Jenin in 2002 to root out terrorists, the British media virtually without exception described the operation as a massacre, with hugely inflated figures of hundreds of dead Palestinians. Yet the facts were that only fifty-two Palestinians died, of whom the vast majority were armed men, and no fewer than twenty-three Israeli soldiers. But the false impression of a massacre, which ran in the press for days, has settled in the British psyche as a fact.

There is a refusal to report the nature and intensity of the attacks being perpetrated against Israel. Only a few of the most spectacular atrocities are reported in Britain; and since some 90 percent of attacks are thwarted by the Israelis, the full scale of the bombardment is vastly greater. Israel's attempt to defend itself is represented as a desire for vengeance or punishment—tapping into the ancient prejudice that the Jews are motivated by the doctrine of "an eye for an eye"—or sheer malice against the Palestinians.

But then, in much of the media, Israel's self-defense is regarded as intrinsically illegitimate. Thus Sir Max Hastings wrote in the *Guardian*: "Israel does itself relentless harm by venting its spleen for suicide bombings upon the Palestinian people." Attempts by Israel (or Russia) to defend themselves against terror by killing terrorists were described as the equivalent of Nazi tactics or war crimes. Hastings managed to present the Israeli victims of terror as Nazi-style butchers while the murderous aggression of the Palestinians, whose own demonology of the Jews is sometimes redolent of Nazi images of a subhuman race, was ignored altogether.[22]

But probably the greatest single reason for the obsessive and unbalanced focus on Israel is the prejudice and hostility of the BBC's reporting. Unlike newspapers, the BBC is trusted as a paradigm of fairness and objectivity. In fact, it views the world from a default position on the left. And since it regards this as the political center of gravity, it cannot acknowledge its own bias. The BBC is thus a perfectly closed thought system.

When it comes to Israel, the BBC persistently presents it in the worst possible light. The language and tone are loaded; Arab and Israeli interviewees are handled with a double standard; panel discussions are generally skewed, with two or three speakers hostile to Israel against one defender or, more often, none at all. Events in the Middle East are frequently decontextualized, so that reports of Israeli strikes against Palestinian terrorist targets downplay or even omit altogether any news of the attacks that prompted them. Thus Israel is transformed from victim to aggressor and presented as responsible for the violence in the Middle East when it is, in fact, the victim.

The BBC rarely talks of Arab or Muslim violence; when it does, reporters are keen to sanitize it and present Israelis as aggressors. Thus one correspondent described how a Palestinian suspected of collaborating with the Israelis had been beaten by other Palestinians and shot at close range in the side of the head, after which the mother of one of the men he betrayed was called forward to stab his lifeless corpse and pluck out his eyes—and the correspondent referred to this as "Old Testament-style brutality."[23]

The BBC never lost an opportunity to claim that the settlers in Gaza were "Jewish" and the land they were settling was "Palestinian." It wears its heart on its sleeve for the Palestinians, who are presented not as aggressors motivated to murder by brainwashing in hatred of Israel and the Jews, but as innocent victims. Reporter Barbara Plett actually burst into tears of sympathy when Yasser Arafat left the Muqata on his way to die in Paris.[24]

While one program even staged a mock "war crimes" trial for Ariel Sharon, with the verdict—that Sharon had a case to answer—never in doubt, Arafat received very different treatment. One thirty-minute BBC profile described him as a "hero" and "an icon" and spoke of him as having "performer's flair," "charisma and style," "personal courage," and being "the stuff of legends." Adjectives applied to him included "clever," "respectable" and "triumphant."

In addition, some BBC staff are open about their sympathies for Hamas. The senior BBC Arabic Service correspondent in the Gaza Strip, Fayad Abu Shamala, told a Hamas rally on May 6, 2001, that journalists and media organizations in Gaza, including the BBC, were "waging the campaign [of resistance/terror against Israel] shoulder-to-shoulder together with the Palestinian people." The BBC's response to requests from Israel that they distance themselves from these remarks was to issue a statement saying, "Fayad's remarks were made in a private capacity. His reports have always matched the best standards of balance required by the BBC."[25]

Despite the claim that this is simply "criticism of Israel" and in no way antisemitic, the language used by the media constantly elides Israel and the Jews, and—consciously or unconsciously—draws on ancient antisemitic tropes to do so, even in the most respectable outlets. For example, the *New Statesman* printed an investigation into the power of the "Zionist" lobby in Britain, which it dubbed the "kosher conspiracy" and illustrated by a cover depicting the Star of David piercing the Union Flag. After protests, the editor apologized for the cover but saw nothing wrong in running an article based on the premise that there was something untoward about Jewish influence.

But then, the *New Statesman* has run piece after piece defaming Israel. A typical column by John Pilger stated:

> The Zionist state remains the cause of more regional grievance and sheer terror than all the Muslim states combined . . . the equivalent of Madrid's horror week after week, month after month, in occupied Palestine. No front pages in the west acknowledge this enduring bloodbath, let alone mourn its victims. Moreover, the Israeli army, a terrorist organisation by any reasonable measure, is protected and rewarded in the west. . . . The "neoconservatives" who run the Bush regime all have close ties with the Likud government in Tel Aviv and the Zionist lobby groups in Washington.[26]

Not only was Israel "the guiding hand" behind American foreign policy that was responsible for outrages like Madrid, but "middle-class Jewish homes in Britain" were also guilty of "virulent" and "destructive" Zionist complicity. Thus British Jews were lumped into the world Jewish conspiracy. Similarly, the *Independent* newspaper illustrated an article on the Israel lobby in America with a picture of an American flag on which the stars were replaced by gold Stars of David.

The ancient antisemitic claim of a global Jewish conspiracy has now become a commonplace in British public discourse. When the Labour backbencher Tam Dalyell claimed in 2003 that both Tony Blair and George Bush were influenced by a "cabal" of powerful Jews—including people who were not Jews at all, but merely had some Jewish ancestry—his remarks were brushed aside indulgently as an embarrassing outburst by a venerable eccentric. The following day, BBC TV's *Newsnight*—far from asking how such an ancient prejudice could have been revived—devoted a substantial item to asking whether Dalyell's claims were true in the United States, and left the impression that there was indeed a tightly knit group of Jews in America who wielded far too much power.

The much-abused term "neoconservatives" has become code in Britain for Jews who have suborned America. In *The Times*, Sir Simon

Jenkins wrote approvingly of the thesis of two American authors that "a small group of neo-conservatives contrived to take the greatest nation on Earth to war and kill thousands of people," that they were "traitors to the American conservative tradition" who achieved a "seizure of Washington (and London) after 9/11," and that their "first commitment was to the defence of Israel." "With the coming to power of President Bush," he wrote, "the neocons deftly substituted the threat of Islam for the threat of communism" and on that basis "sought a 'comprehensive revamping of American foreign policy.'"[27]

So, according to Jenkins—who in 2006 was to write that "there never was a 'terrorist threat' to western civilisation or democracy, only to western lives and property'" and that "only those with money in security have an interest in presenting Bin Laden as a cosmic threat"[28] —the neocons possessed extraordinary and sinister power, which they exercised in a covert way to advance the interests of Israel and harm the rest of mankind. Thus they had "seized" Washington, were "traitors" to the conservative tradition and by implication to America itself, disdained law and diplomacy because they were driven by the desire to kill people, and so "deftly" provided a new threat to terrify the world after communism. It was hard to believe that such opinions could be published in *The Times*, the purported notice-board of the British establishment.

Far from denouncing the Islamists' view of the global Jewish conspiracy, therefore, respectable commentators merely endorsed it. Such a view has brought liberals and left-wingers into an even more extraordinary alliance with the far right. Sentiments, images and tropes appearing in the literature of the left and of the Islamists are similar to—and sometimes even drawn from—the outpourings of neo-Nazis and white supremacists.

In addition to its open support for the Holocaust denier David Irving, the Muslim Public Affairs Committee has leveled accusations of "Zionist" media and political control, listed Jewish donors to New Labour, and asked whether the Talmud is "the most powerful and racist book in the world."[29] The Muslim Association of Britain and the General Union of Palestinian Students have both published *The Franklin "Prophecy,"* an antisemitic hoax originally published by the

American Nazi William Dudley Pelley in 1934.[30] The pro-Hamas *Palestine Times* has promoted work by Michael Hoffman II, a revisionist historian whose website has links to Holocaust denial material.[31]

The far-right British National Party advised its members to read the *Guardian* for information about "the Zionist cabal around President Bush."[32] The day after the BNP claimed that U.S. policy was being driven by "the Zionist and Christian fundamentalist zealots around Bush,"[33] the Muslim Council of Britain described the war as "part of a plan to redraw the map of the Middle East in accordance with the agenda of Zionists and American neo-Conservatives."[34]

The British people once fought against Nazism and fascism, which were intent on annihilating the Jews as part of a bid for global domination. Now, the British appear not to care that the toxic prejudices of the far right have been infiltrated, through the alliance of Islamists and the left, into mainstream political discourse under the grotesque umbrella of a "human rights" opposition to Israel.

Meanwhile, the Islamist agenda for global domination is sanitized out of existence. Islamists who variously subscribe to these anti-Jewish, anti-Israel and anti-Western views are regularly trotted out by the media as "moderate" spokesmen. After the London bombings, the BBC TV show *Newsnight* used the Muslim Brotherhood activist and Hamas supporter Dr. Azzam Tammimi as a quasi reporter. He was given several minutes of broadcasting time to narrate a film on this topic, which placed him in a much more authoritative position than a mere interviewee. He used the opportunity to argue that a major factor behind the bombings was British foreign policy—complete with an implicit threat in his payoff line that unless this policy was changed there would be more such attacks.[35]

The *Guardian* managed to turn itself into a virtual mouthpiece for the Muslim Brotherhood. Thus Anas al-Tikriti, president of the Muslim Association of Britain, wrote in its pages that Israel's killing of the Hamas head Sheikh Ahmad Yassin was "an example of state terrorism";[36] Azzam Tammimi of the MAB decried the elections taking place in Iraq and the Palestinian Authority;[37] Osama Saeed of the MAB claimed that it was wrong to expect British Muslims to take any responsibility for defeating Islamist terror and said that attacking the idea of the caliphate was "the equivalent of criticising the Pope";[38] Sohaib Saeed of the MAB claimed that Sheikh Qaradawi was "scholarly" and "moderate" and had been traduced by media labels of extremism.[39]

The relative tolerance of the British public, in the face of such outrageous encroachment by people who, in any sane world, should be regarded as the enemies of the West and a danger to the state, is due not only to the issue of Israel but also to the impact of the war in Iraq. It is impossible to overstate the extent to which the Iraq war has poisoned British political life and shifted the political center into a dangerously irrational frame of mind. For although the running against the Iraq war has been made by the left, aided by the Islamists, profound opposition to the war is deeply entrenched across the political spectrum.

The issue is not just opposition to the war itself but, much more remarkably, a view of the world that would once have been confined to the wilder fringes of the far left but now is commonplace among conservatively minded middle Britain, the equivalent of the "red states" in America. If one travels around Britain as a member of radio panel discussions, for example, one finds just such conservative audiences literally cheering the view that America is the fount of world terror, that George W Bush is a war criminal, and that the nuclear-armed state that poses the biggest threat to the world is Israel.

These are the people who believe that the root of Muslim rage is Israel's "oppression" of the Palestinians, that America is a target only because of its support for Israel, and that Britain is a target only because of its support for America. Because they are conservative in their approach, they make a fetish of "stability" and so would prefer to have Middle Eastern tyrants in place rather than upset the regional status quo. As a result, and because of the failure to find any weapons of mass destruction in Iraq and the messy aftermath of the war in which so many mistakes have been made, what started out as a perfectly reasonable difference of views about the best way to contain the threat of Saddam Hussein has mutated into a settled conviction that Saddam never posed a threat at all and the British were taken to war on a series of lies.

This belief has become the prism through which every development in the Iraq crisis has been viewed. As a result, history has simply been rewritten and the British have been consumed by a dangerous climate of irrationality, whipped up by a media coverage that has been as unbalanced as it has been relentless.

For the BBC and other media, there was always one story about Iraq from the very start. This was that the war was a criminal folly. Their original predictions that Saddam would not be toppled, of mass uprisings all over the Arab world and of hundreds of thousands of Iraqis turned into refugees proved wrong. So they kept shifting the goalposts and rewrote history to prove that Bush and Blair were malign or stupid or both. When no weapons of mass destruction were found, they seized on this to claim that the war was fought only because we were told there were WMD stockpiles. Thus Sir Max Hastings wrote in the *Guardian*: "Yet it bears stating again and again that we went to war, launching thousands of British soldiers into Iraq, on a pretext now conclusively exposed as false."[40]

It was not the pretext for war that was false but arguments of people like Hastings and countless other prominent journalists and armchair generals who have rewritten history. It is not true that we went to war on account of the stockpiles. From the actual speeches and written statements by Tony Blair or the foreign secretary, Jack Straw, it is clear that the overwhelming emphasis was on Saddam's refusal to obey the binding UN resolutions, his resulting failure to prove that he had destroyed his WMD programs and renounced his intention to continue developing WMD, and the dangers posed by the axis of rogue states, WMD and terrorism.

A genuine difference of opinion over policy is one thing. A credulity towards distortion is quite another. It is disturbing to find that when presented with the recorded facts about the case set before the public for going to war, people tend to brush them aside because they are sure that the whole saga was based on a succession of government lies. This has happened in part because of widespread distrust of the prime minister, and a resulting cynicism so corrosive that anything he says is now dismissed as a fabrication. The distortions provided by the media, which now form an impenetrable crust over the whole issue, reinforce people's unshakeable conviction in the truth of their analysis. Refusing to accept the metaphysical wellsprings of Islamist terrorism, they believe that any terrorist threat to Britain is caused instead by the stupidity of government policy in turning Britain into a target.

Beneath all this runs the poisonously false belief that it wasn't Saddam who threatened the security of the world as much as Israel. Scratch an implacable opponent of the Iraq war, the kind who doesn't just think the decision to go to war was wrong but that the whole terrorist threat to Britain has been exaggerated by Tony Blair, and you will usually find a hostility to Israel as deep as it is ignorant. Many articles denouncing the Iraq war have contained the giveaway view that it diverted attention from the real cause of global instability, the Israel/Palestine conflict. And some go further. One prominent and distinguished military historian told me that the real issue behind the Islamic jihad was Israel. "Really," he said, "it would have been better if Israel had never been created."[41]

The effect of all this has been to create a climate in Britain that has alarming echoes of Weimar in the 1930s. There is the same combination of amorality and appeasement, of decadence and denial. The narrative of Islamists who threaten the West has been widely adopted as the default political position. Members of the intelligentsia, the class that sets the tone for a culture, support the murder of innocents whom they choose to represent instead as oppressors. Ted Honderich, for example, a former professor of logic at University College, London, has written:

> I myself have no serious doubt, to take the outstanding case, that the Palestinians have exercised a moral right in their terrorism against the Israelis. They have had a moral right to terrorism as certain as was the moral right, say, of the African people of South Africa against their white captors and the apartheid state. Those Palestinians who have resorted to necessary killing have been right to try to free their people, and those who have killed themselves in the cause of their people have indeed sanctified themselves. This seems to me a terrible truth, a truth

that overcomes what we must remember about all terrorism and also overcomes the thought of hideousness and monstrosity.[42]

A number of public figures have posed as virtual cheerleaders for suicide bombers under the guise of "compassion." The former Liberal Democrat MP Jenny Tonge was sacked by her party after she had expressed sympathy for suicide bombers. "I am a fairly emotional person and I am a mother and a grandmother," she said. "I think if I had to live in that situation [under Israeli rule], and I say this advisedly, I might just consider becoming one [a suicide bomber] myself."[43] Within a short time, however, her party elevated her to the House of Lords. The prime minister's wife, Cherie Blair, was forced to apologize for saying, hours after twenty Israelis died in a suicide bombing in Jerusalem, that young Palestinians "feel they have got no hope but to blow themselves up."[44] But others sprang to endorse her remarks. A former Foreign Office adviser and critic of government policy, David Clark, sneered that her remark pointed up the distance the government had traveled between "emoting about the suffering of the Palestinians to falling in behind Washington's one-sided support for their tormentors in Israel's Likud government,"[45] and thirty-seven Labour MPs signed a Commons motion supporting her.[46]

Meanwhile Canon Paul Oestreicher, former chairman of Amnesty International, appeared to be endorsing the "resistance" to both U.S. troops in Iraq and Israeli troops in the disputed territories. He equated this with the French resistance against the Germans, thus also implying that the Americans and the Israelis were akin to the Nazis:

Yesterday's front page describing the crimes of the US military in Iraq and the Israeli military in Palestine denote for me, late in the day, a crossing of the Rubicon. I have until now, perhaps foolishly, been prepared to admit that in both situations one could agree to differ with the apologists. But no longer. These are not "military actions" but crimes against humanity. The occupations in both cases have no basis in law. They amount to the brutal repression of civilian populations. As a British citizen

I am ashamed to be party to all that. Those old enough to remember will recollect that the French Resistance were held to be heroes when they killed the German occupiers. I did not rejoice at German deaths then, any more than I rejoice at Israeli, American and, yes, British deaths now. But there is no difference.[47]

Such inflammatory and grotesquely unjust comments, the relentless demonizing of America and Israel and the never-ending uproar over "atrocities" being committed against Iraqis and Palestinians with no attempt at either balance or truthfulness, has created a dangerous eruption of hatred in Britain and an escalating subcurrent of violence and intimidation. The effect of such incendiary rhetoric upon young Muslims who were already inflamed against the West has been incalculable. Being fed a daily dose of invective about Jews, Israelis and evil Americans has almost certainly reinforced their sense of victimization and turned up the temperature of an already overheated grievance to boiling point.

For British Jews in particular, an idyll has been brought abruptly to an end. For decades, this small community told itself that, while it knew that antisemitism never died but only slept, there was no reason to think that Jews were other than wholly accepted into British life as equal citizens and any threat to them that might arise would be seen off by their decent, tolerant, fair-minded British compatriots. They have now experienced the rudest of awakenings. Jewish nationhood is being delegitimized; antisemitic libels out of the European nightmare have become commonplace in polite society; and attacks on Jews are increasing. But the British are responding with indifference or worse.

On campus, Jewish students run a gauntlet of insults and intimidation. They are spat at; they have to be smuggled out the back doors of meetings because of fears for their safety; they are baselessly accused of conspiracies.[48] In British cities on a Saturday, you will find stalls advocating a boycott of Marks & Spencer because it stocks Israeli produce. Such stalls proclaim "End Israeli Apartheid" and "The Wall Must Fall." One such stall in Newcastle-upon-Tyne displayed a banner depicting a sinister, hook-nosed Jew as a truck driver with skull-shaped smoke emerging from the exhaust, and distributed leaflets stating that Israel deliberately steals Palestinian land and water, and murders "peace activists."[49]

At a social level, dinner party conversation is now likely to throw up not just the same kind of demonization of Israel but prejudiced remarks about Jews being too powerful, all sticking together and so on. Any attempt by a British Jew to challenge the current prejudice and lies about Israel is likely to provoke the accusation of double loyalty. At a debate organized by the *Economist* magazine on a motion suggesting that those who claimed there was a resurgence of antisemitism in Britain were "the new McCarthyites," a former Conservative MP, Robert Jackson, accused British Jews of dual loyalty and said their Britishness was conditional on their explicit repudiation of the policies of Ariel Sharon.[50] For the Jews alone, it seems, British identity now appears to depend on the opinions they hold about the policies of another country.

Far from the British springing to the defense of the Jews against the lies and libels of Muslim antisemitism, it appears that the issue of Israel has enabled hatred of the Jews once again to become respectable. One prominent liberal editor said candidly that it was a "great relief" that Britain no longer had to worry about what it said about the Jews because of the way Israel was behaving. "Ever since the war we were told that because of their suffering the Jews were above criticism. But now that's no longer the case."[51]

So now it's open season. In the House of Lords, a meeting was told that the Jews control the British media. One peer told another: "Well, we've finished off Saddam. Now your lot are next."[52] A fashionable poet, Tom Paulin, called for the Israeli settlers to be shot. For this incitement to mass murder, he continued to be lionized by the BBC. The *Independent* published a cartoon depicting a monstrous Ariel Sharon biting the head off a Palestinian baby. For this, the cartoonist received first prize in a prestigious national cartoonists' competition. At one point, the *Sun* newspaper became so alarmed at the firestorm of anti-Israel and anti-Jewish hatred blazing through British society that it felt the need to publish a full-page leading article telling its readers: "The Jewish faith is not an evil religion."[53]

While those who seek to defend Israel are pilloried, those who seek to prevent Israel from defending itself against mass murder are turned into heroes. Thus fashionable London purred over the production in 2005 of the *Cantata for Rachel Corrie*, an opera celebrating the International Solidarity Movement activist who was killed by an Israeli military bulldozer as she tried to prevent the Israel Defense Forces from demolishing houses in Rafah where Palestinians were suspected of smuggling weapons into Gaza.

In Britain, the notion of Jewish victimhood has now been all but expunged. In its place has come "Islamophobia." While the Jews are defamed as Nazis, the Palestinians are considered to be the "new Jews." Thus have the Islamists captured the citadels of thought at the heart of the Western alliance.

CHAPTER EIGHT

ON THEIR KNEES
BEFORE TERROR

O n the Sunday after the London bombings, the parish priest of
the church that stands a few yards away from where the number
30 bus was blown up in Russell Square delivered a sermon in which,
having urged his congregation to rejoice in the capital's rich diversity
of cultures, traditions, ethnic groups and faiths, he added: "There is
one small practical thing that we can all do. We can name the people
who did these things as criminals or terrorists. We must not name
them as Muslims."[1]

When a memorial service for the victims of the London bombings
was being planned for St. Paul's Cathedral, church leaders wanted to
invite the families of the bombers. Two senior bishops believed that this
would "acknowledge their own loss and send a powerful message of
reconciliation to the Muslim community." Jack Nicholls, bishop of
Sheffield, said: "We have to look forward, not back, forward to a society
in which Muslims and Christians live together amicably in an integrated community."[2]

After relatives of the murdered victims expressed their outrage at
this suggestion, the government declined to accept it. The reaction of
these churchmen was typical. The first instinct of many British clerics
was to empathize and agonize not with the victims of the atrocity but

with the community of the faith in whose name it had been committed—and to deny that religion had had anything to do with it at all.

Those who might have thought the Church of England would hold
the line as the last redoubt against both the attack upon the West from
Islamism and the attack upon its values from within—which has so
weakened its defenses against the onslaught from without—are in for
a shock. Far from defending the nation at the heart of whose identity
and values its own doctrines lie, the Church of England—Britain's
established church—has internalized the hatred of the West that
defines the shared universe of radical Islamism and the revolutionary
left. At a clergy gathering on 9/11, as clerics watched the horror
unfold on a large TV screen, one turned to another and said: "I hope
Bush doesn't retaliate. The West has brought this judgment on
itself."[3] The Church of England is on its knees before terror.

In America, the churches have been in the forefront of the defense
of Western values. Some of the strongest support for Israel comes from
evangelical Christians. In Britain, by contrast, the Church of England
has been in the forefront of the retreat from the Judeo-Christian heritage. At every stage it has sought to appease the forces of secularism,
accommodating itself to family breakdown, seeking to be nonjudgmental and embracing multiculturalism.

Presented with a society that has lost its moral compass and
descended into the nihilism of moral relativism, the Church has feebly
followed suit. The prevailing view, as one bishop observed, is that
"there is no one truth, and we all have to respect each other's truths."[4]
A church that can no longer distinguish the truth from a lie no longer
believes that its own message is true.

Peter Mullen, rector of St. Michael's Cornhill in London, has
written in despair of his church's "mania for self-destruction." The
majestic Book of Common Prayer and the Authorised Version of the
Bible, he wrote, had been replaced by evasive, sentimentalized and
vacuous texts that sounded as if they had been "written by a committee made up of Tony Blair, Karl Marx and Noddy."[5]

How has this happened at the heart of the Anglican Communion?
As the former archbishop of Canterbury, Lord Carey, puts it: "Britain's
unthinking secularism is the context for the Church's attitudes,

shapeless form and its lack of any underpinning values."[6] During the 1960s, the view expressed by radical theologians that traditional belief was no longer possible in a secular age was absorbed by the Church of England as a fact that could not be challenged. This was because, unlike the American churches where evangelical Christians are in the majority, the Church of England is dominated by liberals who control its bureaucracy and its thinking process. In addition, because it is the established church of the nation it is governed by the belief that it has to be—literally—a broad church embracing everyone. Such a drive to be consensual means that it tends to go with the flow, even when that flow is in the direction of religious, moral and social collapse.

The outcome for the Church has been that faith in God and belief in the fundamental doctrines of Christianity have been replaced by worship of social liberalism. The Church stopped trying to save people's souls and started trying instead to change society. It signed up to the prevailing doctrine of the progressive class that the world's troubles were caused by poverty, oppression and discrimination. Miracles were replaced by Marx. Accordingly, it soaked up the radical message coming out of the World Council of Churches, under the influence of liberation theology, that the problems of the poor peoples of the south were social and economic, and emanated from the capitalist West and America in particular. At home, absorbing the prevailing utilitarianism which preached the creed of lifestyle choice, the Church came to believe that it too was in the business of delivering the greatest happiness to the greatest number. So it went with the flow of permissiveness, supporting the liberalization of abortion, homosexuality and divorce. And as post-moral Britain demanded that ever more constraints be knocked away, the Church was forced further and further into hollowing out its own identity.

As it renounced its own culture, it embraced others, while never ceasing to grovel for its onetime sin of believing in itself. As secular society denounced the crimes of British cultural and political imperialism, so the Church of England abased itself for its own crime of religious imperialism. The archbishop of Canterbury, Dr. Rowan Williams, apologized for bringing Christianity to the world. Addressing the Anglican conference in Cairo in 2005, he said that the Church had taken "cultural captives" by exporting hymns and liturgies to remote parts of the world.[7] The fact that Christianity had brought civilization to these remote parts of the world, for the very good reason that it was superior to traditional practices in those parts, was not acknowledged. For the implicit assumption was that Christian values are trumped by the belief that everyone's culture is of equal value and so no one has the right to overlay any other. That of course leads directly to the view (not stated by the Church) that polygamy, female circumcision or the stoning of adulterers must be regarded as of equal merit to the concept of human dignity at the heart of Christianity. It took a black Ugandan cleric, Dr. John Sentamu, when he was enthroned as archbishop of York in 2005, to scorn publicly this white postcolonial and post-missionary guilt by denouncing multiculturalism, defending the British Empire and praising the English culture it spread around the world.[8]

One of the most striking features of the Church's instinct for self-immolation is that it abases itself particularly towards those ideologies that are out to destroy it, notably secularism and radical Islamism. As it progressively lost its way, it developed an obsessive enthusiasm for interfaith dialogue. While few would decry the importance of forging links between faiths to create better understanding, the interfaith industry acts as a positive bar to understanding by dangerously sanitizing differences that can explode into aggression and violence. This is because interfaith work has become an end in itself, skating over the really difficult areas of hostility or hatred between faiths just to keep everyone on board and ensure that the dialogue continues.[9] As a result, the message coming out of these interfaith groups is that the Church has no real problem with either Islam or Judaism, and that there is no real difference between the Church's relationship with Judaism and its relationship with Islam. After all, the argument goes, all three faiths are the children of Abraham.

This has managed to obscure two absolutely fundamental problems for the Church. The first is that the dominant contemporary political force within Islam is an ideology that seeks to destroy Christianity and its values. The second is that, because the Church has failed to resolve its deeply ambiguous and conflict-laden attitude towards the Jews, it cannot recognize the threat posed by Islamism to the Jews and beyond them to the free world. Instead, it has allowed itself to absorb much of the Islamist and Arab narrative of hostility to Israel and the Jews, thus positioning itself as an unwitting ally of those who would destroy Christianity itself.

The result is an astounding silence by the Church about the persecution by Muslims of millions of Christians around the world. Churches are being burned down and Christians terrorized and killed by Muslims in Sudan, Congo, Egypt, Indonesia, Pakistan, Nigeria, Lebanon, Somalia, the Philippines and elsewhere. Yet in the face of this global persecution of its followers, the church that represents them is almost totally silent. It has abandoned its own flock and sucked up to their persecutors instead. When it does tiptoe into the subject—as Dr. Williams did in an article in December 2005 about the burning of churches and Bibles in the Punjab[10]—it is done in such a limp and oblique way as to make a bad situation even worse.

One churchman who *has* spoken out about the way Islam treats Christians is the former archbishop of Canterbury, Lord Carey. He says the Church is overly apologetic to Islam for a number of reasons, including fear that any protest might make the situation of Christians in such countries even worse. In 2004, Lord Carey made a speech in Rome that caused a stir. He said that although the vast majority of Muslims were "honourable and good people who hate violence," Islam stood in opposition to "practically every other world religion— to Judaism in the Middle East; to Christianity in the West, in Nigeria, and in the Middle East; to Hinduism in India; to Buddhism, especially since the destruction of the Temples in Afghanistan."[11]

What was particularly striking was this passage: "Sadly, apart from a few courageous examples, very few Muslim leaders condemn, clearly and unconditionally, the evil of suicide bombers who kill innocent people. We need to hear outright condemnation of theologies that state that suicide bombers are 'martyrs' and enter a martyrs' reward. We need to hear Muslims expressing their outrage and condemning such evil."[12]

This was notable because no other church leader in Britain had dared criticize this most glaring omission. As a result, Lord Carey found himself criticized—from within his own church. "The following week I went to Leicester and the canon of Leicester Cathedral told me that I had done a great deal of damage because I had rattled the cage," he said.[13]

The essential problem that Lord Carey had laid his finger on was that Muslims had failed to acknowledge that the problem lay in their religion. Unlike other church leaders, he saw very clearly that it was not enough for them to say how much they deplored violence if at the same time they were denying its nature as an expression of religious fanaticism rooted in Islamic theology. "What appalled me about the reaction was the way they distanced themselves from the essential problem," he said. "They said the problem was that this was coming from 'extremists.' They didn't seem to see there was a link between themselves and these people: they were 'not real Muslims' at all. So they pushed the problem away to safeguard the heart of Islam, without realizing that the theological issue is what drives fanatics. In the long history of Christian or Jewish martyrdom, there wasn't one person who killed *another* to be a martyr. But here was a theology of Muslim martyrdom where you kill innocent people and go to heaven and God will bless a terrible act like that. I have said to Muslims, 'You've got to condemn it' and they say 'I have condemned it.' But they don't condemn the theology behind it."[14]

It is perhaps no surprise that Lord Carey, an evangelical with a very strong belief in the truth of Scripture, takes such a clear moral view. In stark contrast, the current archbishop of Canterbury, Dr. Williams, has responded to Islamist terrorism with repeated examples of moral equivalence and appeasement. In *Writing in the Dust*, a meditation he wrote after 9/11 when he was still archbishop of Wales, he wrote of the West: ". . . we have something of the freedom to consider whether or not we turn to violence and so, in virtue of that very fact, are rather different from those who experience their world as leaving them no other option."[15]

So according to this, Islamists were driven to mass murder because they had "no other option." He also observed of the Palestinian/Israeli deadlock that "both sides know what it is to be faced with regular terror" and that "the Muslim world is now experiencing—as it has for some time, but now with so much more intensity—that 'conscription' into someone else's story that once characterized the Church's attitude to Jews."[16]

Dr. Williams's prose style is famously opaque. But the man who was shortly to become the leader of the Anglican Communion appeared to be saying that Israeli self-defense against terror was morally equivalent to that terror, that attitudes to Muslims in the wake of 9/11 were morally equivalent to the Church's persecution of the Jews, and that 9/11 had happened because its perpetrators couldn't help themselves.

His remarks after he became the archbishop of Canterbury continued in the same vein. At the memorial service for fallen British soldiers after the defeat of Saddam Hussein, he used his sermon to attack the prime minister for the war, with the implication that all killing was wrong regardless of factors such as aggression, motivation or responsibility.[17] In a subsequent lecture to the Royal Institute for International Affairs, he effectively said that a state had no right to seek to defend itself by military means if other countries were opposed to such a course of action.[18] And he chose one of the major seats of Islamic learning, Al-Azhar University in Cairo, to mark the anniversary of 9/11 in 2004 by saying that people should not take the action that might be necessary to prevent themselves and others from being murdered:

> We may rightly want to defend ourselves and one another—our people, our families, the weak and vulnerable among us. But we are not forced to act in revengeful ways, holding up a mirror to the terrible acts done to us. If we do act in the same way as our enemies, we imprison ourselves in their anger, their evil. And we fail to show our belief in the living God who always requires of us justice and goodness. So whenever a Muslim, a Christian or a Jew refuses to act in violent revenge, creating terror and threatening or killing the innocent, that person bears witness to the true God. They have stepped outside the way the faithless world thinks. A person without faith, hope and love may say, If I do not use indiscriminate violence and terror, there is no safety for me. The believer says, My safety is with God, whose justice can

never be defeated. If I defend myself, I seek to do so only in a way that honours God and God's image in others, and that does not offend against God's justice. To seek to find reconciliation, to refuse revenge and the killing of the innocent, this is a form of adoration towards the One Living and Almighty God.[19]

This was a quite remarkable doctrine. Ostensibly evenhanded, it actually represented a startling moral inversion and a rubric against all military self-defense. Christians and Jews do not use "indiscriminate violence and terror" against Muslims; it is Muslims who are indiscriminately murdering Christians and Jews. Attacks on Muslims by Jews, Christians or others who have themselves been attacked are conducted solely in self-defense and in an attempt to prevent further acts of mass murder. To equate such acts of self-defense with truly indiscriminate acts of barbarism is moral illiteracy. Condemning self-defense or the defense of others against murder as "revenge" or "indiscriminate violence and terror" condemns the innocent to death in the guise of godliness. If followed, such guidance would turn Christianity into the handmaiden of evil. It implies that if the Nazi Holocaust were to happen again, the Church would once again stand aside. In the current war being waged against the West, the head of the Anglican Church is telling it to turn the other cheek.

Such a near-pacifist attitude—despite many pious allusions to "just war" theory—is reflected in the Church's visceral hostility to the war in Iraq. This opposition also draws upon a deep well of anti-Americanism among the clerics—not least because of their distaste, droll as this may seem, for the "Christian fundamentalists" supporting President Bush and their loathing of the "Christian right." For the English clerics believe that the Christian left is a benchmark of virtue that brooks no alternative, and that belief in Biblical truth is a psychological flaw.

In the Church's General Synod, only two people spoke in favor of the war in Iraq.[20] This reflected not merely an opposition to the war itself, but a view that the best way of dealing with Islamism was to appease it. A report by the Church's House of Bishops argued that it was important to win Muslim hearts and minds, and that to do so required "an understanding of what is being thought and felt in the Islamic world, together with active steps to address legitimate concerns, such as the ongoing Middle East conflict." Although it hastily denied that such an approach amounted to appeasement, it went on: "A political settlement that meets some of the terrorist concerns, while rejecting others, can help in undercutting the terrorists by reducing the pool of political support."[21]

The way the Church could aid this process, the report suggested, was to apologize both for the Iraq war—which "appeared to be as much for reasons of American national interest as it was for the well-being of the Iraqi people"—and for everything the West had ever done in relation to Iraq, including its previous support for Saddam Hussein and the sanctions used against him. The bishops said that since the government was unlikely to show remorse, the churches should do so instead by organizing a major gathering with senior figures from the Muslim community to make a "public act of repentance."[22]

The first and obvious question this raised was to whom the bishops wanted to apologize. To the Ba'athists, perhaps, for removing Saddam, along with an apology to the Iraqis he terrorized? This moral muddle was amplified by the precedents they cited for such an act of reconciliation: the official statements by the Vatican expressing sorrow for the Christian persecution of the Jewish people throughout the ages, the repentance by the Anglican Church in Japan for its complicity in Japanese aggression during the Second World War, and the regret expressed by leaders of the Dutch Reformed Church in South Africa for their theological and political backing of apartheid.

In other words they were comparing the *removal* of Saddam Hussein to the persecution of the Jews, the axis against democracy in World War II, and South African apartheid. But it was Saddam Hussein, the butcher of his own people and sponsor of terrorist murder against Israel and America, who was the brother in blood to the tyrants of history. To the bishops, however, it was "not terrorism but American foreign policy and expansionism that constituted 'the major threat to peace.'" So the global jihad, the intention to restore the medieval caliphate, 9/11 and the many attacks on America and other Western interests that preceded it apparently did not constitute "the major threat to peace." Only America, a principal victim of this threat, filled that role in this hall of moral mirrors.

But then, how could the bishops be expected to formulate a principled response to the threat of Islamist terrorism when in the next breath they revealed that they did not understand the difference between legitimate and illegitimate regimes? The bishops wrote:

> The Third Reich began as a democratic response to an "emergency" facing the German nation. Thereafter, whenever Adolf Hitler required more power he created emergencies, real or imagined, so as to justify the democratic suspension of democratic safeguards. Military coups in Africa and Latin America were all mounted on the basis of a "national emergency," and to the extent that they received popular support, they were based on disillusionment with a democratic politics that had descended into chaos and the fear that things could only get worse. While it is evident that Western democracies are built on substantial foundations, it is equally clear that 9/11 represents a real and major escalation in the threats to such societies.[23]

But although the Germans did originally elect Hitler, Nazism was never a democratic ideology; nor are military coups anything other than usurpations of the democratic political process. Yet on the basis of these entirely spurious analogies, the bishops argued against measures to protect Britain from further attack. The bishops thus displayed their profound lack of understanding not merely of religious fanaticism but of the moral difference between fascism and self-defense. Far from "undercutting" terrorism, their naïve and muddled proposals would hand it a clear victory.

It is, perhaps, no surprise therefore that the Church should have taken the side of the Palestinian Arabs in the Israel/Arab impasse. A letter to the prime minister about the Iraq war, from the archbishops of Canterbury and York backed by every diocesan, suffragan and assistant bishop in the Church of England, showed how deeply the Church's views about Iraq were dominated by the issue of Israel, which they approached solely from the perspective of Arab and Muslim opinion. There was no mention in this letter of the rights of Israel or the Jews as the principal victims of annihilatory aggression and prejudice. Instead, they wrote:

> Within the wider Christian community we also have theological work to do to counter those interpretations of the Scriptures from outside the mainstream of the tradition which appear to have become increasingly influential in fostering an uncritical and one-sided approach to the future of the Holy Land.[24]

Their target was the Christian Zionists, regarded by the Church with as much horror as the "Christian fundamentalists" and "Christian right," who it believes have hijacked American foreign policy; indeed, they are synonymous. Christians who support Israel take a variety of views about its policies, but the Anglicans see Christian Zionists as supporting an expansionist policy of "Greater Israel" that would colonize the disputed territories—which the Anglicans see as "Palestinian"—on the basis of the Biblical promise of the land made by God to the Jews. Indeed, for many Anglicans this aggressive form of Zionism *is* Zionism. They don't believe there is any other form. And they don't believe that Israel, however controversial some of its behavior might be, is fundamentally trying to defend itself against a war of extermination.

Part of this flows from the simple fact that the Church has lost its moral compass along with its faith, a loss that now appears to prevent it from distinguishing between victim and victimizer whether it is looking at a Palestinian suicide bomber, the fall of Saddam Hussein, or a teenage serial mugger in the largely black south London district of Brixton. Partly, it is the defensive response of a religion that feels the ground disappearing beneath its feet. According to Canon Andrew White, the Church's foremost Middle East specialist, demographic change has played upon a profound ignorance of the Middle East, both past and present. "Church knowledge of the Middle East is very superficial," he said. "During the 1980s, the Church watched Islam becoming an increasingly significant force in Britain and the second largest religion. And the core cause for British Muslims was Palestine."[25] As a result of this deep ignorance and instinct for appeasement, along with the prevailing view among the Christian and non-Christian left that the peoples of the third world were universal victims of Western society, the Anglicans and their counterparts in Scotland and Wales subscribed unquestioningly to the narrative of the Arab and Muslim world that painted Israel as a genocidal oppressor of the Palestinians, who only wanted a homeland of their own.

This viciously unbalanced view is heavily promulgated by Christian NGOs. Christian Aid, for example, has presented for years a wholly one-sided and malevolently distorted account of Israel's history and present actions, demonizing it as a ruthless aggressor and oppressor of innocent Palestinians, whose own violence towards Israelis is barely touched upon and, where it is, effectively justified. Many of Christian Aid's assertions about Israel's history have been the myths peddled by Palestinian propaganda, with manipulated images and half-truths designed to present Israel in the worst possible light.

Israel's antiterror policies have been depicted as an attempt to ruin the Palestinian economy and destroy its infrastructure. In Christian Aid's materials, the oppression of the Palestinians has never been a "claim" but an objective reality. Israeli security measures have been repeatedly condemned without any acknowledgment that they are a response to terrorist violence. Christian Aid has failed to examine Palestinian incitement to hate and murder Israelis, or to acknowledge the humanitarian aid that Israel brings the Palestinians. And having thus demonized Israel, it has dwelt obsessively upon it, devoting infinitely less attention to the persecution of Christians by Muslims worldwide—which one might have thought would be the major preoccupation for a Christian charitable organization.[26]

There are indications that Christian Aid may now be moderating its attitude in response to growing complaints; but its materials have had a huge effect on British attitudes. At a time when politicians have lost public trust, such NGOs are relied upon as dispassionate arbiters of truth. The result is that the distortions and libels that Christian Aid dispenses about Israel have been believed, not just among Christians but in the wider community. Not surprisingly, when the organization takes people on visits to the Holy Land they return filled with virulent prejudice against Israel, with the settled conviction that it is doing an evil that has provoked an understandable reaction by the Arab Muslim world. And it is not just Christian Aid that has had this effect. Thousands of British Christians go every year on pilgrimages to the Holy Land run by organizations with similar attitudes. Such pilgrims spend virtually all their time visiting holy sites in Palestinian-run territory, staying in Palestinian hotels and listening to Palestinian tour guides. As a result, people who start out on such pilgrimages in a state of almost total ignorance of Israel and the Jews return filled with hatred towards them.[27]

The result is a virulent animosity towards Israel in the established churches in Britain, which promulgate inflammatory libels against it. The archbishop of Wales, Dr. Barry Morgan, said in a lecture in 2003 on the relationship between religion and violence: "Messianic Zionism came to the fore after the Six Day War in 1967 when 'Biblical territories were reconquered', and so began a policy of cleansing the Promised Land of all Arabs and non-Jews rather than co-existing with them."[28] But there has been no such "cleansing" at all in the disputed territories. The only attempt at "cleansing" has been the Palestinian attempt to kill as many Israelis as possible. The same archbishop eulogized upon the death of Yasser Arafat:

> Yasser Arafat has given his life to the cause of the Palestinian people and will be remembered for his perseverance and resolve in the face of so many challenges and set-backs. When I heard the news of his death this morning, my initial reaction was to pray that in death Yasser Arafat will find that peace which only God can give and which was denied him in life.[29]

So the Church all but canonized a terrorist mass murderer. In September 2004, it proceeded further to punish his victims. Despite an attempt by the archbishop of Canterbury to draw the sting from the decision, the Anglican Consultative Council commended the American Episcopal Church for divesting from companies whose corporate investments "support the occupation of Palestinian lands or violence against innocent Israelis" (the last phrase being plainly a meaningless gesture towards evenhandedness).

Worse still, the ACC also endorsed an accompanying report by the Anglican Peace and Justice Network, a piece of venomous and mendacious Palestinian propaganda that provided a travesty of both history and present reality. Ignoring the offer by Israel in 2000 of a state of Palestine based on more than 90 percent of the disputed territories, it asserted that "there have been no significant positive steps towards the creation of the state of Palestine. On the contrary, the state of Israel has systematically and deliberately oppressed and dehumanized the people of Palestine." It presented Israel's military actions as a deliberate policy of oppression which had made Palestinian lives a misery, whereas the only reason that normal Palestinian life was impossible was the Palestinian war of terror against Israel. It described Israel's security barrier as an "apartheid/segregation" wall and compared the territories to the "bantustans of South Africa," despite the fact that the Arabs in Israel have full civil rights and the Arabs outside Israel are by definition not its citizens. Most egregiously of all, it compared "the concrete walls of Palestine" to "the barbed-wire fence of the Buchenwald camp." Thus the Anglicans compared the Jews of Israel to the Nazis on account of a measure that aimed to prevent them from being murdered.[30]

In February 2006, there was a repeat performance. This time, the Synod backed a call from the Episcopal Church in Jerusalem and the Middle East for the Church Commissioners to divest from "companies profiting from the illegal occupation," such as Caterpillar Inc. An American company, Caterpillar manufactures bulldozers used by Israel in clearance projects in the disputed territories, and is also used by Palestinians in their own rebuilding work.[31] This decision, which was backed by the archbishop of Canterbury (but which was revoked a month later purely on practical grounds), caused grave disquiet among a number of Christians in Britain and provoked a crisis in relations between the Church and Britain's Jewish community. The chief rabbi, Sir Jonathan Sacks, launched a blistering attack, arguing that Israel needed "support, not vilification" when it was facing enemies such as Iran and Hamas that were sworn to eliminate it, and that the decision would have "the most adverse repercussions" on relations between Christians and Jews in Britain.[32]

The extreme viciousness behind such a wholesale inversion of truth and morality by the Church, and the extent to which this monstrous mindset has captured its establishment, cannot be explained simply by the Church having lost its way, succumbed to left-wing orthodoxies or panicked in the face of British demographic change. The real motor behind the Church's engine of Israeli delegitimization is theology—or, to be more precise, the resurgence of a particular theology that had long been officially consigned to ignominy. This is "replacement theology," sometimes known also as "supercessionism," a doctrine going back to the early Church Fathers and stating that all God's promises to the Jews—including the land of Israel—were forfeit because the Jews had denied the divinity of Christ.

This doctrine lay behind centuries of Christian anti-Jewish hatred until the Holocaust drove it underground. The Vatican officially buried it, affirming the integrity of the Jewish people and recognizing the State of Israel. This was because the Catholic Church faced up to the excruciating role it had played over centuries in dehumanizing and demonizing the Jewish people, a process which had paved the way for the Holocaust. But the Anglican Church failed to conduct a similar process, leaving unaddressed and unresolved the key issue of how in doctrinal terms it should regard the Jews. The ancient calumny that the Jews were the murderers of God and had denied His love thus still had resonance for Anglicans. So when Arab Christians reinterpreted Scripture in order to delegitimize the Jews' claim to the land of Israel, this kick-started replacement theology, which roared back into the imaginations, sermons and thinking of the Anglican Church.

This revisionism held that Palestinian Arabs were the original possessors of the land of Israel. The Anglican bishop of Jerusalem, Riah Abu el-Assal, claimed of Palestinian Christians: "We are the true Israel. . . . no-one can deny me the right to inherit the promises, and after all the promises were first given to Abraham and Abraham is never spoken of in the Bible as a Jew. . . . He is the father of the faithful."[33]

Another Palestinian Christian cleric, Father Naim Ateek, is a favorite thinker among many Anglican bishops, with whom he enjoys personal friendships going back many years. His influence in the Church is immense, not least through his Sabeel Centre in Jerusalem, a source of systematic demonization of the Jewish state. Ateek, who claims to accept Israel's existence, profoundly undermines it on a theological level by attempting to sever the special link between God and the Jews. His book *Justice and Only Justice* inverts history, defames the Jews and sanitizes Arab violence. Modern antisemitism gets precisely one paragraph; Zionism is portrayed not as the despairing response that it was to the ineradicable antisemitism of the world, but as an aggressive colonial adventure. Courageous Jews are those who confess to "moral suicide" and who say that Judaism should survive without a state; real antisemitism, says Ateek, is found within the Jewish community in its treatment of the Palestinians.

The real sting of this analysis lies in the liberation theology on which it is based. Ateek makes clear that the existence of the Jewish state has thrown the interpretation of Scripture into turmoil for Palestinian Christians, for whom this calamity calls into question the integrity of God. There is no indissoluble link, he says, between Israel and God, who is a deity for the whole world. Zionism was a retrogression into the Jews' primitive past. God's choice of Israel for the Jews was merely a paradigm for His concern for every land and people. While such a universal blessing does not exclude Jews or Israel, he writes, "neither does it justify their invoking an ancient promise—one that betrays a very exclusive and limited knowledge of God in one stage of human development—in order to justify their uprooting an entire people and expropriating their land in the twentieth century. To cling only to the understanding of God in those limited and exclusive passages is to be untrue to the overall Biblical heritage."[34]

Ateek thus uses the Bible to delegitimize the Jewish state by misrepresenting the Jews' relationship with God. He goes further: having accused the Jews in Israel of systematically oppressing the Palestinians, he inverts God's promise to the Jews by saying that God takes the side of the oppressed and "can only will and affirm a state that is based on justice." Not only is this not true, but it is not relevant to Israel's existence, which was not based on divine revelation but on a resolution of the United Nations.

Elsewhere, Ateek has recycled the charge of deicide against the Jews and directed the hostility it arouses against Israel. In December 2000, he wrote that Palestinian Christmas celebrations were "marred by the destructive powers of the modern-day 'Herods' who are represented in the Israeli government." In his 2001 Easter message, he wrote: "The Israeli government crucifixion system is operating daily. Palestine has become the place of the skull." And, in a sermon in February 2001, Ateek likened the Israeli occupation to the boulder sealing Christ's tomb. With these three images, Ateek has figuratively blamed Israel for trying to kill the infant Jesus, crucifying him and blocking the resurrection of Christ.[35]

This fusion of ancient theological prejudice and modern politics has found echoes in Britain, as illustrated by the revised version of *Whose Promised Land?* by the highly influential Anglican thinker Colin Chapman. Though Chapman carefully condemns antisemitism and says the Christians have not superseded the Jews, his book is a poisonous travesty that uses theology to delegitimize Israel. Although the Jews are still in a special relationship with God, he says, their only salvation is through Christ when they will be "grafted back" onto their own olive tree. Christians have come to share the Jews' privileges; through Christ, the division between Jews and Christians has broken down and they have become as one new man. These "new men" don't believe it is important to have a Jewish state. In his conclusion, Chapman explicitly delegitimizes Israel on theological grounds:

> When seen in the context of the whole Bible, however, both Old and New Testaments, the promise of the land to Abraham and his descendants does not give anyone a divine right to possess or to live in the land for all time because the coming of the kingdom of God through Jesus the messiah has transformed and reinterpreted all the promises and prophecies in the Old Testament. . . . Jesus the messiah who lived, died and was raised from death in the land has opened the kingdom of God to people of all races, making all who follow him into one new humanity.[36]

This is replacement theology masquerading as a dispassionate analysis of the tragedy of Israel and the Palestinians. Indeed, the very premise of the book is suspect. It investigates the claim to the land based on Biblical exegesis. But the Jews' claim to Israel was not based on the Bible. Certainly, the dream of Zion is integral to Jewish attachment and religious focus, and a minority of Jews believe in the literal truth of prophecy. But that wasn't why Israel was founded. Zionism was never a religious movement. Israel was established because after the Holocaust, the world finally decided to enact the undertaking made thirty years previously to re-establish the Jews in their ancient homeland.

Chapman's version of replacement theology is based on the premise that the existence of Israel has to be justified. It does not. To single out Israel's existence in this way is without precedent in the world and is itself evidence of prejudice. Moreover, replacement theology is not just a form of anti-Zionism; it directly attacks Jewish religion, history and identity.

At the same time, Chapman's history grossly downplays the extent of Arab violence against Jews in the decades of Jewish immigration to Palestine before the State of Israel was created. His conclusion that Zionism was an innate deception and that violence was always implicit is a baseless slur, as is the confusion of Jewish self-determination with racism. Not surprisingly, this elides seamlessly into the anti-Jewish trope of Jewish power over America, repeating the absurd claim that no U.S. president could win without Jewish votes. Since American Jews are overwhelmingly Democrats, the victory of Republican presidents must remain, on this theory, a complete mystery.

According to Canon Andrew White, replacement theology is dominant in the Church of England and present in almost every church, fueling the venom against Israel. Lord Carey agrees that replacement theology is the most important driver behind the Church's hatred of Israel.[37]

David Ison, the canon of Exeter Cathedral, took a party of pilgrims to the Holy Land in 2000 at the start of the intifada. They had a Palestinian guide, visited only Christian sites in Arab East Jerusalem and the West Bank, and talked to virtually no Jews. "The Old Testament is a horrifying picture of genocide committed in God's name," he said. "And genocide is now being waged in a long, slow way by Zionists against the Palestinians." Asked what he made of Yasser Arafat's rejection of the offers presented by Israel at Camp David and Tabah, Ison said he knew nothing about it. Indeed, he said, he knew nothing about Israel beyond what he had read in a book by an advocate of replacement theology, with which he agreed, and what he had been told by the Palestinians on the pilgrimage.[38]

The bishop of Guildford, Dr. John Gladwyn, who said he particularly admired Bishop Riah and Naim Ateek, shared the view that the Jews have no particular claim to the promised land. Christianity and Islam, he said, could lay equal claim. And although he said Israel's existence was a reality that must be accepted, his ideal was very different. A separate Palestinian state would be merely a "first step." "Ultimately, one shared land is the vision one would want to pursue, although it's unlikely this will come about."[39]

Stephen Sizer, the vicar of Christ Church, Virginia Water, is a leading crusader against Christian Zionism. He believes that God's promises to the Jews have been inherited by Christianity, including the land of Israel. He has acknowledged that Israel has the right to exist, since it was established by a United Nations resolution. But he has also said it is "fundamentally an apartheid state because it is based on race" and "even worse than South Africa" (this despite the fact that Israeli Arabs have the vote, they are members of the Knesset and one is even a Supreme Court judge).

Asked whether Israel's existence could be justified, Sizer replied that South African apartheid had been "brought to an end internally by the rising up of the people." So, despite saying he supported Israel's existence, he appeared to be suggesting that the Jewish state should be singled out for a fate imposed on no other democracy properly constituted under international law. But perhaps this was not surprising, given his attitude towards Jews. "The covenant between Jews and God," he stated, "was conditional on their respect for human rights. The reason they were expelled from the land was that they were more interested in money and power and treated the poor and aliens with contempt." Today's Jews, it appeared, were no better. "In the United States, politicians dare not criticize Israel because half the funding for both the Democrats and the Republicans comes from Jewish sources."[40]

In a lecture in 2001, Canon Andrew White observed that Palestinian politics and Christian theology had become inextricably intertwined. The Palestinians were viewed as oppressed and the Church had to fight their oppressor. "Who is their oppressor? The State of Israel. Who is Israel? The Jews. It is they therefore who must be put under pressure so that the oppressed may one day be set free to enter their 'Promised Land' which is being denied to them."[41]

The essential problem, he observed, was the lack of will in the Church to face the difference between Judaism and Islam. "They don't want to recognize that their faith comes from Judaism," he said. "They talk instead of the 'children of Abraham' as if we are all in it together. The reality is, however, that although Islam and Judaism have a lot in common in terms of customs, they are as far apart as Christianity is from heathenism."[42]

The revival of replacement theology, the ancient theological prejudice against the Jews, has achieved two results. The first is that the Church has lent its weight to the delegitimization of Israel. The second is that this conflation of revisionist Christian theology with an Arab agenda has delivered a victory to the Islamists. A view which holds that the enemies of civilization are not the Islamists but the Jews transfers righteous opposition from those who threaten the free world to their victims. This feeds into and is in turn fed by the Church's perverse desire at home to surrender to those who wish to obliterate Christianity from the British public sphere. As Lord Carey observed:

> The net victors in all this are the Muslims. Through all that has happened they have positioned themselves very well through violence to gain a greater niche in British society. Their voice has been heard. People are reading the Koran and taking an interest, so they stand to gain a great deal. Muslim leaders have done a very successful job in separating the tenets of Islam from the extremists. So there's been a reversal: instead of people saying, "I abhor an ideology which does such terrible things," they say, "of course these people were not doing it in the name of Islam, which is a tolerant and benign faith."[43]

The net losers in this process are the Church, steadfastly immolating itself at the shrine of interfaith vacuities, and the nation it has defined but whose spiritual light is now all but extinguished.

CHAPTER NINE

THE APPEASEMENT OF
CLERICAL FASCISM

After the London bombings in July 2005, Tony Blair appeared to
have understood just what Britain was facing. He spoke of the
need to confront a strain of Islam that was an "evil ideology." "It cannot be beaten except by confronting it, symptoms and causes, head-on,
without compromise and without delusion," he declared.[1] Crucially, he
recognized that the ideological component of the struggle with radical
Islamism was as important as the military and operational aspects—if
not even more so. He said he would close mosques that fomented
hatred, vet foreign imams and outlaw extremist groups such as Hizb
ut-Tahrir and al-Muhajiroun that are known to be ideological organizations rather than ones with a direct connection to terrorism.

By setting the ideology of radical Islamism firmly in his sights, the
prime minister appeared to have got the point. But it was not always
so. In the immediate aftermath of 9/11, he had declared after meeting
a group of Muslim community leaders: "What happened in America
was not the work of Islamic terrorists, it was not the work of Muslim
terrorists. It was the work of terrorists, pure and simple."[2]

Following the American atrocities, the British government had
bent over backwards to avoid saying that they had anything to do with
Islam at all. It was all to do instead with grievances, discrimination and

"Islamophobia." A former Foreign Office minister, Denis MacShane, has said that he tried to push for a more hard-line approach but was rebuffed because of concerns that Muslims would be offended. "My generation of Labour MPs don't want to indulge in anything that smacks of Muslim typecasting or hostility," he said; ". . . it's fair to say we failed to work out an adequate political response to Islamist politics in the UK."[3]

Despite the apparent change in Tony Blair's attitude, however, neither the rest of his government nor the wider British establishment seems yet to have worked out an adequate political response to Islamism even after the London bombings; all are still paralyzed by the terror of Muslim hostility. According to a *Guardian* poll carried out a month after the London attacks, almost three-quarters of the public believed that it was right to give up civil liberties to improve security.[4] Nevertheless, opinion in political, judicial and intellectual circles was very different. Indeed, Mr. Blair found that in his attempt to beef up the country's security he was all but outnumbered.

After the bombings, he issued a blunt warning to the country's judges. "The independence of the judiciary is a principle of our democracy and we have to uphold it but . . . it is important that we do protect ourselves," he said. "Let no one be in any doubt, the rules of the game are changing."[5] With that one statement, he set the British government on a collision course with the country's judiciary. He was reflecting a widespread feeling that one of the main reasons why Britain had laid itself wide open to terrorism was that the courts had made it impossible for it to defend itself.

A harsh spotlight was suddenly being shone on the culture of human rights and the role played by the judiciary in enforcing it, apparently privileging the rights of extremists over the right to life and limb of everyone else. For the first time, the prime minister floated the possibility of amending Britain's Human Rights Act—the measure that his own government had introduced with enormous fanfare. It was Mr. Blair who, by this measure, had given the judges a far more powerful role in British public life. Now he was trying to rein them in, threatening "a lot of battles" with the courts if they used human rights grounds to block his new resolve to deport extremists.

But the judges made it clear that they were not going to cooperate. Lord Ackner, a retired law lord, said: "The judiciary will oppose attempts to undermine its independence. These suggestions that we [politicians and judges] are all a team and should pull together is such rubbish that the judiciary will ignore it."[6]

The judges were part of a widespread establishment mood that did not think the case had been made for encroaching upon Britain's jealously protected liberties. There was deep hostility to the American "war on terror," particularly over detention without trial in Guantanamo Bay, and fury that the prime minister had yoked Britain to President Bush's coattails; skepticism that the terrorist threat to Britain was as great as Blair said it was, simply because it was Blair who was saying it; disbelief that the threat from al-Qaeda was any different from previous terrorist threats from the IRA; suspicion of police incompetence, especially after the debacle at Stockwell Tube station in south London shortly after the bombings, when an innocent Brazilian electrician was shot dead by the police who thought he was a suicide bomber; and a deep fear of upsetting British Muslims and provoking a backlash against them.

The result was that Blair's antiterrorism measures became mired in a welter of confusion and recrimination. One proposal, to make it an offense to "glorify terrorism," provoked a struggle between both houses of Parliament as the government tried to fight off attempts to remove it by an alliance of liberals and the Conservative party.[7] Another proposal, to shut down extremist mosques, was withdrawn after objections by the police that this would damage relations with the Muslim community. Yet another, to require imams to be tested on their knowledge of Britishness, was shelved (to the irritation, in fact, of the Muslim Council of Britain).[8]

The most controversy, however, was aroused over a proposal to detain terrorist suspects for ninety days without charge to allow the police time to build up a case against them. In an unusually powerful document, the Anti-Terrorist Branch of the Metropolitan Police spelled out why this was necessary. The new terrorist threat to inflict mass civilian casualties, it said, posed an unprecedented dilemma. The police could no longer afford to build up the evidence necessary to support legal charges because the risk to the public was simply too great. They therefore had to arrest suspects before they had enough evidence that would stand up in court. Since al-Qaeda was a global network requiring police inquiries in many jurisdictions and with possibly dozens of computers and hundreds of hard drives to analyze, the two-week detention deadline under existing antiterror laws was clearly hopelessly inadequate. They needed ninety days instead.[9]

But Parliament wasn't having any of it. Instead, it was prepared to increase the detention period by only two weeks. In November 2005, the government was defeated and the ninety days maximum was reduced to four weeks.

The fight over these proposals, however—in which the government was pitched against Parliament, the Conservative opposition, the media, the human rights industry and the rest of the intelligentsia— served to obscure a more fundamental and dangerous problem. The government had understood from the police and security service that existing laws were inadequate to deal with the terrorism the country was now facing. But the fact that they grasped that there was an entirely new kind of terrorist threat did not mean they understood what lay behind it.

They knew well enough that it involved suicide bombing and the deliberate mass targeting of civilians and that it was intended to involve weapons of mass destruction. But with the exception of the prime minister and a handful of others, they continued to go to great lengths to deny its most obvious characteristic: that it was rooted in a religious ideology. They believed instead that it was merely the violent expression of various grievances by a small handful of unrepresentative extremists. They thought therefore that they could buy it off. They imagined that by doing so they would damp down Muslim rage. And, within the Labour party, they thought it would buy them Muslim votes.

Labour was traditionally the party that appealed most to new immigrants, and Britain's Muslims were no exception. Many Labour MPs, including the foreign secretary, Jack Straw, found themselves representing constituencies with significant Muslim populations. This had a number of consequences, one of which was that some Labour politicians allowed Pakistani politics to influence British politics. On the

day of the 2005 British general election, Faisal Bodi wrote in the
Guardian:

> Labour politicians have cultivated the "community leader",
> the modern-day equivalent of the village chief, whose unique
> selling point is that he can bring in the vote of the particular
> ethnic sub-category he belongs to, be it by fair means or rigged
> postal votes. Jack Straw's Blackburn constituency typifies this
> type of Indian subcontinent politics. Here Adam Patel was
> raised to the peerage in 2000, with an unwritten brief to deliver
> the Indian Muslim vote. He has used his influence to insulate
> mosques against anti-Labour sentiments and protect his mas-
> ter's 9,000 majority.[10]

According to the bishop of Rochester, Dr. Michael Nazir-Ali, himself
of Pakistani origin, a number of Labour MPs with large numbers of
Muslim voters need the support of various Islamic leaders in Pakistan
who tell their followers in Britain how to vote. He claimed that one
such leader who was close to al-Qaeda, Maulana Fazlur Rahman, had
been welcomed to Britain by the Foreign Office because of his great
influence over certain sections of British Muslims. "I asked the government why they had allowed him in," said Dr. Nazir-Ali, who was
outraged that someone with such an extremist record should have
been given red carpet treatment. "They said he had a very strong following in Britain."[11]

It might be no coincidence, therefore, that the foreign secretary
was given to denouncing the West and extolling the Muslim world. In
2002, Straw blamed many of the world's problems on the legacy of
British imperialism.[12] In September 2005, he told the United Nations
General Assembly that Muslims had given the world mathematics
and the digital age, and that only "terrorists and the preachers of hate"
wanted people to believe "that Islam and the West are fundamentally
different."[13]

Such Labour efforts to suck up to the Muslim community, however, were badly undermined after 9/11 when Britain supported first
the war in Afghanistan and then the war in Iraq. This enraged Britain's

Muslims, who appeared inclined to support the antiwar Liberal Democrats instead. An opinion poll in 2004 showed that Labour support in the Muslim community had halved from 75 percent at the 2001 general election to 38 percent.[14] In the event, the Muslim Labour vote held up pretty well at the 2005 general election, with only a few Labour scalps going to the Liberal Democrats. But what was more notable was the arrival of sectarian politics in Britain, with the emergence of Muslims voting en bloc for candidates on the basis of whether or not they were delivering a Muslim agenda.

A group called VoteSmart set up a website linked to the Muslim Council of Britain that asked, "Will your MP support Muslim issues in the next Parliament," and rated them on a variety of issues from plus five to minus five.[15]

Some Labour MPs were the targets of gross intimidation by Muslims who decided they were not acting in Muslim interests and accordingly organized campaigns to unseat them. Lorna Fitzsimons, for example, the Labour MP for the northern town of Rochdale, lost her seat to the Liberal Democrats after the Muslim Public Affairs Committee (MPACUK) sponsored hundreds of leaflets that wrongly claimed she was Jewish and called on residents to vote against her. One leaflet said: "Lorna Fitzsimons is an ardent Zionist and a member of the most powerful anti-Muslim lobby in the world, the Israel lobby." Told that she was not Jewish, MPACUK issued a statement apologizing for any "offence" caused.[16]

Mike Gapes, MP for the east London suburb of Ilford South, told the House of Commons how Muslim groups were trying to unseat him because he was an officer of the Parliamentary Labour Friends of Israel and supported both a two-state solution in the Middle East and the government's antiterrorist legislation. After being harangued and harassed in the street with taunts of "Racist," "Murderer" and "How many children have you killed today?" he was sent a distorted digest of his views by Inayat Bunglawala, the public affairs officer of the Muslim Council of Britain and his constituent, with the implied threat that this would be used to persuade Ilford's Muslims not to vote for him.

Following this, leaflets were distributed with the heading "Mike Gapes: No Friend of the Muslims" and stating among other things:

"Note there are 300,000 Jews in Britain but over 2 million Muslims in Britain. The Jewish community has over 20 declared MPs while the Muslims have only one MP." A further batch of leaflets included a photograph of an Israeli tank and a Palestinian boy throwing a stone at it, along with other, similarly inflammatory pictures. The wording said: "Getting rid of Mike Gapes will send a massive shock wave throughout the pro-Israel lobby and make it clear that Muslims are not to be trifled with."[17]

Gapes was interviewed by Faisal Bodi for the BBC Radio program *The World Tonight*. Unknown to Gapes, as he subsequently told the Commons, Bodi was a Hamas supporter who had previously written an article published in the *Guardian* stating that Israel had no right to exist. The Bodi item transmitted by the BBC show allowed Gapes's opponents to state without challenge that he was an "Islamophobe" and "a proven enemy of Muslims." Following complaints, the BBC decided not to use Bodi again; after which he wrote a two-page attack published in the *Guardian*, singling out Gapes for having gotten Bodi "banned" by the BBC.[18]

In 2003, the government's pusillanimity in the face of such intimidation claimed a ministerial scalp. Denis MacShane, then a junior Foreign Office minister, accused British Muslims of failing to do enough to counter extremism and suggested that some were aggravating terrorism by showing understanding for the politics of terror. "It is time for the elected and community leaders of British Muslims to make a choice," he said. "It is the British way, based on political dialogue and non-violent protests, or it is the way of the terrorists against [whom] the whole democratic world is now uniting."[19]

MacShane's comments enraged Muslims in his northern constituency of Rotherham and were criticized as "an outrage and extremely disgraceful" by Anas al-Tikriti of the Muslim Association of Britain.[20] But what finished him was being hung out to dry by the Labour government of which he was a member. Having been made to grovel to both the MCB and the MAB, he was then stripped of his ministerial post. The reason for this shameful capitulation almost certainly did not lie in Rotherham but in Blackburn, where the foreign secretary was struggling with a Muslim bloc formed from his own

Muslim activists. MacShane was the bone that Straw threw them to save his own political skin.

The extent to which a panicky Labour government was going to appease the Muslim bloc was laid bare in an article published in *The Muslim Weekly* a few months before the 2005 general election. In this another minister, Mike O'Brien, pleaded for votes by boasting of the lengths to which the government had gone to accede to British Muslim demands. Two weeks after the Muslim Council of Britain had asked for a new law banning religious discrimination, he said, Tony Blair promised he would provide it. "It was," wrote O'Brien, "a major victory for the Muslim community in Britain."[21]

This was the proposed law against incitement to religious hatred, which provoked widespread opposition because of fears that it would criminalize legitimate comments about religion. In February 2006, it was defeated in Parliament by a combination of rebellion in Labour's ranks and tactical incompetence by the government. But a law that had the power to shut down necessary debate about Islam, and potentially put Christians, Jews, Hindus, Sikhs, secularists and others in the dock for speaking the truth, had been introduced to buy Muslim votes. The price to be paid for invading Iraq, in other words, was to have been Britain's freedom of speech.

Even worse, O'Brien appeared to be openly pandering to Muslim anti-Israel and anti-Jewish prejudice. He wrote: "The reality is that the only way a Palestinian state will be created is if Israel is prepared to concede land it currently occupies on the West Bank and Gaza. Whether we in Britain like it or not, the reality of the modern world is that only the Americans can influence Israel. And it seems only Tony Blair has any influence with the Americans."[22] With these words, O'Brien lent the British government's authority to the prejudice that the Middle East impasse was Israel's fault. He made no mention of the need to stop Arab and Muslim terror as a precondition to peace and a Palestinian state. Instead, he tried to turn Blair's support for Bush on its head by claiming that only Blair was worth the Muslims' vote because only Blair could put pressure on the Americans to bring Israel to heel.

As if all this weren't bad enough, O'Brien then implied heavily that Muslims should not vote for Michael Howard, the Conservative opposition leader at the time, because he was a Jew. He wrote:

> Ask yourself, what will Michael Howard do for British Muslims? Will his foreign policy aim to help Palestine? Will he promote legislation to protect you from religious hatred and discrimination? Will he give you the choice of sending your children to a faith school? Will he stand up for the right of Muslim women to wear the hijab? Will he really fight for Turkey, a Muslim country, to join the EU? These are not academic questions. Remember, the last thing we want is to vote in anger and repent at leisure as Michael Howard, with a big smile on his face, walks through the door of No 10.[23]

O'Brien denied pandering to anti-Jewish prejudice, claiming that he was not attacking Howard personally but as leader of the Conservative party. But in fact the Conservatives, who called this attack "despicable," said they actually supported most of the policies he listed. Small wonder that Mohammad Sawalah, the deputy head of the Muslim League in Britain, gloated: "Such Muslim campaigns have actually paid off and scared away the Zionist lobby and the extremist right-wing."[24]

The Labour party, in short, had been taken captive by the constituency for whose votes it was groveling.

There was, however, an even deeper problem than crude electoral politics that was preventing Britain from facing up to Islamist extremism even after the London bombings. This was a profound reluctance among the official class—the senior civil servants who run the country and the intelligence world that guards it—to acknowledge the true nature of the threat. Crucially, these officials appeared incapable of recognizing that behind the terror lay an ideology whose grip extended far beyond those who were actually engaged in terrorism. They did not grasp that this had created a hysterical communal fervor made up of grievance, victimization and paranoia in the holy cause of defending God against the infidels, which was swelling the sea in which terrorism swam.

Instead, they thought al-Qaeda was a protest movement. An unprecedentedly dangerous one, certainly, but a protest movement nevertheless, inspired by certain discrete grievances around the world. The idea that those grievances were all linked by an ideology that had made them into grievances in the first place was simply denied. "We don't know what these people actually want," they said. But wasn't it clear that al-Qaeda wanted to Islamize the world? Not so, they said, it was all very incoherent beyond wanting to restore the medieval Islamic caliphate. But there was no threat to Britain or America as such, no intention to Islamize those countries or destroy Western civilization; just a set of specific geopolitical grievances over which America and Britain were being attacked because they were on the wrong side. Whatever this was, it was not a religious war.[25]

Such arguments revealed a lethal ignorance at the very heart of the British political and security establishment. These were the people who ran Britain, who were responsible for its security and provided the analysis that underpinned its whole strategy for combating Islamist extremism. Yet in saying that this terrorism was all about specific grievances, they failed to look more deeply into the motivation to purify the world of non-Islamic tendencies. To deny that these were all fundamentally religious conflicts was to reveal an astounding misreading of those conflicts.

And to say that al-Qaeda had never expressed a desire to Islamize the non-Muslim world simply wasn't true. In his "Letter to the American People" in 2002, for example, after a long litany of global grievances Osama bin Laden announced what he wanted of the West: "The first thing that we are calling you to is Islam." This was at the very top of his list of demands. Straight after that came this:

> The second thing we call you to, is to stop your oppression, lies, immorality and debauchery that has spread among you. . . . We call you to be a people of manners, principles, honour, and purity; to reject the immoral acts of fornication, homosexuality, intoxicants, gambling, and trading with interest. We call you to all of this that you may be freed from that which you have become caught up in; that you may be freed from the deceptive

lies that you are a great nation, that your leaders spread amongst you to conceal from you the despicable state to which you have reached.[26]

There was much more in this vein. It was only a long way down this diatribe against the Western way of life and his demand that the West embrace instead the principles of Islam that he arrived at the demand to stop supporting Israel, Kashmir and so forth, and to get out of "Muslim lands."

By focusing on the geopolitical grievances, therefore, the British were mistaking the satellites for the sun. Despite their avowals that this was a completely new phenomenon, they seemed to be still trapped in the Northern Ireland mindset. This was not surprising, since so many of them had forged their careers in the crucible of Northern Ireland's bloody terrorist war against the British state. That really *was* a discrete geopolitical grievance. Although it was fought out between Catholic republicans and Protestant nationalists, this was not a religious but a political war. The aim of Irish republicanism was not to Catholicize Britain—or even the six counties of Northern Ireland— but to unify Ireland by ending British "colonial" rule over the north.

This was completely different from Islamism, which aimed to spread Islam to a world that had either departed from or never embraced its precepts. What Britain was now facing, therefore, was a war prosecuted in the name of religion. But the British simply refused point-blank to accept this. They were terrified that if they did so, they would be effectively demonizing an entire community. Yet this did not follow at all. Islamism is a particular interpretation of authentic Islamic principles. This does not mean that all Muslims subscribe to this interpretation; indeed, many do not, which is why the greatest number of victims of Islamist oppression have been Muslims. Many British Muslims repudiate Islamism and themselves need to be defended against this life-denying ideology. But this in turn does not mean that the ideology is not rooted in the religion. If the Islamist nature of the terrorism is denied, it is not understood; and a country cannot defend itself or its citizens, Muslim as well as non-Muslim, against a phenomenon that it refuses to understand or even name.

The British establishment is unfortunately locked into just such a lethal state of denial. With very few exceptions, politicians, Whitehall officials, senior police and intelligence officers and academic experts have all failed to grasp a key fact. It is not only the terrorists who have a totally nonnegotiable agenda; they are fueled by an ideology that itself is nonnegotiable and forms a continuum that links peaceful, law-abiding but nevertheless intensely ideological Muslims at one end and murderous jihadists at the other. Transfixed by the artificial division it has erected between those who actively espouse violence and those who do not, the British establishment rejects the idea that the hatred of the Jews, Israel, America and the West that suffuses the utterances of the Muslim Brotherhood forms an ideological conveyor belt to the terrorism to which it gives rise.

The result of this institutionalized denial has been that the British government has settled upon a disastrously misguided strategy. Believing that Islamist terrorism is merely about grievances, it thinks it can appease Muslim rage in Britain by pandering to extremism. The head of the civil service, Cabinet Secretary Gus O'Donnell, caused widespread astonishment when the Civil Service Islamic Society, of which he is patron, invited an extremist cleric, Sheikh Abu Yusuf, to address senior officials at a Whitehall function to mark Eid. Sheikh Yusuf had praised Muslims who shed blood in the cause of jihad and had made jokes about "Jew York, sorry, New York."[27] The invitation was abruptly canceled after it was exposed in the press.

But the government's strategy of appeasement goes much deeper than such gestures. Dismissing the idea that this is a religious war and that ideology is its principal weapon, the government thinks it can prevent young Muslims from falling into the clutches of al-Qaeda by promoting nonviolent religious extremists. And so, far from regarding the Muslim Brothers as a seditious force imperiling the country, it is recruiting them into the heart of the establishment.

In 2004, leaked briefing papers from the apex of government laid this appeasement strategy bare. A paper sent by Sir Andrew Turnbull, who as cabinet secretary was head of the civil service, to John Gieve, who was the permanent secretary or top civil servant in the Home Office, revealed the government's counterterrorism strategy, Operation

Contest. The aim, it said, was "to prevent terrorism by tackling its underlying causes, to work together to resolve regional conflicts to support moderate Islam and reform, and to diminish support for terrorists by influencing relevant social and economic issues."[28]

The problem was its definition of "underlying causes." These did not include religious ideology. Instead, the paper identified British foreign policy and discrimination and poverty among British Muslims. So instead of challenging the grievance culture that lay at the root of Islamist extremism, the government chose to endorse it. Far from challenging the Muslim community to sort itself out, its questions were all as self-flagellatory as they were agonized. Was the government listening enough to Muslims? Was it communicating the right messages, both to and about Muslims? And even more ominously: "Foreign policy— should our stance (e.g. on MEPP [Middle East peace process] or Kashmir) be influenced more by these concerns?"[29]

In reply, John Gieve voiced the governing concern of British officials that extremism could not be confronted without the cooperation of British Muslims, and that this provided "added reason for tackling their 'social exclusion.'"[30] But what if they would not cooperate because the extremism was more widely and deeply seated than the government acknowledged? And what if their "social exclusion" had come about, not through any sin of omission or commission by the British state, but through their own wish to exclude themselves from it because they were hostile to its whole way of life?

None of this occurred to John Gieve. The Home Office program was based, he said, on dialogue with the police, engagement with young Muslims, combating "Islamophobia," enlisting "MPs with large Muslim constituencies as partners in Government's dialogue"—the very MPs, no doubt, who had been targeted for intimidation by Islamist radicals—and circulating to government departments "guidance on Muslim sensitivities and appropriate non-inflammatory terminology."

Worse was to come in the accompanying paper Gieve sent to Turnbull written jointly by the Home Office and the Foreign Office, "Young Muslims and Extremism."[31] Not once did any of these officials suggest challenging the concept of a "truly globalised community," the *ummah*, which sets up a conflict with the West. Nor did they confront the myths and prejudices at the core of Islamist extremism, the bigotry against the Jews, the demonization of Israel, the mischaracterization of the West as a conspiracy against Islam. They averred that "public challenges to Muslims to decide where their loyalties lie are counterproductive."[32]

Instead, the government would take on "Islamophobia" by combating "distorted public and media perceptions of Islam and Muslims" and collaborating with "moderate Muslim bodies," amongst which it counted the Muslim Council of Britain. Even more dangerously, it suggested that the government should "encourage, assist and promote mainstream Muslim communication channels, i.e. radio stations, newspapers aimed at British Muslims, and television channels."[33] But Muslim newspapers and TV channels such as Al-Jazeera and Al-Arabbiya actively spread distortions about the West and provide a powerful emotional stimulus to the call to jihad.

The paper recommended avoiding the term "Islamic fundamentalism" because "some perfectly moderate Muslims are likely to perceive it as a negative comment on their own approach to their faith."[34] But such reasoning exposed a logical flaw: If Muslims were so likely to be pushed towards extremism, then they could hardly be called moderate—at least, not according to any definition that would command widespread understanding in Britain.

A graphic illustration of the extent of official confusion over what constituted a Muslim moderate was provided by the government's attitude to Sheikh Qaradawi, the Muslim Brotherhood zealot. The issue was whether or not Qaradawi, who by now had attained some notoriety in Britain as a result of the Livingstone episode, should be allowed back into the country. The *Observer* newspaper obtained a leaked memo by a Foreign Office adviser, Mockbul Ali, in which he recommended that Qaradawi not be excluded from Britain, presenting him as someone who—while saying some things with which the government would not agree—was nevertheless "the leading mainstream and influential Islamic authority in the Middle East and increasingly in Europe, with an extremely large popular following and regular shows on al Jazeera."[35]

Some might have thought this was all the more reason for the government to exclude him from the country. Ali's argument, however, was that excluding him would drive more Muslims into the arms of extremists, and would pass up a golden opportunity for such Muslims to hear the words of wisdom of an Islamic authority who disapproved of al-Qaeda. The fact that he also supported human-bomb terrorism in Israel and said it was a duty to fight the coalition in Iraq apparently made the opportunity no less golden. The Foreign Office duly agreed to support Qaradawi's visa application (although the cleric later canceled his visit).

If there was any residual doubt about Mockbul Ali's less than moderate personal agenda, it was surely dispelled by his next comments:

> A significant number of the accusations against al Qaradawi seemed to have been the result of a dossier compiled by the Board of Deputies, based on information from Middle East Media Research Institute (MEMRI). The founding president of MEMRI is retired Colonel Yigal Carmon, who served for 22 years in Israel's military intelligence service. MEMRI is regularly criticised for selective translation of Arabic reports.[36]

In fact, MEMRI's translations have never been found to be anything other than scrupulously accurate and fair. And to imply that information is suspect simply because it emanates from the Jewish community in Britain or an Israeli who was once in the service of the military intelligence of Israel—a British ally, moreover—betrays a telling prejudice against the Jews, which is startling in a Whitehall official.

After the London bombings, it appeared for a brief while that this policy of appeasement had been overturned by events. Tony Blair met Muslim representatives and announced that a "task force or network" would be created to tackle extremism "head on." It would go into communities to actively confront what he called an "evil ideology" based on a perversion of Islam, and "defeat it by the force of reason."[37] And he urged people to speak out in Muslim communities against what he called the "Crusader Zionist Alliance rubbish" on Islamist websites and the claims—also "rubbish"—that the United States sought to suppress Islam.[38]

Such a committee network was duly set up. But it turned out to include a number of radical Islamists and anti-Jewish bigots whom the government had seen fit to appoint to this task. One of these was Ahmad Thomson, a barrister and member of the Association of Muslim Lawyers. After his appointment, Thomson claimed that a secret alliance of Jews and Freemasons had shaped world events for hundreds of years and now controlled governments in both Europe and America. He said the prime minister was the latest in a long line of British politicians to come under the control of this "sinister" group, and that the invasion of Iraq and the removal of Saddam Hussein were part of a master plan by Jews and Freemasons to control the Middle East. "Pressure was put on Tony Blair before the invasion," he said. "The way it works is that pressure is put on people to arrive at certain decisions. It is part of the Zionist plan and it is shaping events."[39]

Next, government officials had invited onto the task force Inayat Bunglawala, media secretary of the Muslim Council of Britain and the persecutor of Mike Gapes MP. In 2001, before the 9/11 atrocities, Bunglawala distributed an e-mail to hundreds of British Muslims praising Osama bin Laden as a "freedom fighter." He subsequently said his words were "ill-chosen."[40] In January 1993, Bunglawala had called the blind Sheikh Omar Abdel Rahman "courageous" one month before he bombed the World Trade Center in New York.[41] In a youth magazine he once edited, Bunglawala wrote that Hamas is "an authentically Islamic movement" and "a source of comfort for Muslims all over the world." In the same article, according to a report by the Institute for the Study of Islam and Christianity, he supported radical Wahhabi clerics in Saudi Arabia who were later linked to Osama bin Laden, and the Islamic Salvation Front in Algeria; in other issues, he supported other Islamist terror groups.[42]

Bunglawala's past comments also included the allegation that the British media were "Zionist-controlled." In 1992, for example, he wrote: "The chairman of Carlton Communications is Michael Green of the Tribe of Judah. He has joined an elite club whose members include fellow Jews Michael Grade [then the chief executive of Channel 4 and now BBC chairman] and Alan Yentob [BBC2 controller and friend of Salman Rushdie]. The three are reported to be 'close friends' . . . so that's what they mean by a 'free media.'"[43] And on another occasion: "The Jews consider themselves to be God's chosen people—although the blessed prophet Jesus called them the children of the Devil (John 8:44)—and so can do just whatever the hell they like."[44] Citing claims that the Zionist movement was "at the core of international banking and commerce," he asked: "Nonsense? You be the judge."[45]

Despite this startling record of gross anti-Jewish prejudice and support for terrorism, Bunglawala was a convener of Tony Blair's task force against extremism.

The most eye-catching recruit to this task force, however, was Professor Tariq Ramadan. His previous claim to fame was being banned from entering the United States and France because of his alleged links with terrorism—allegations he strenuously denies. A Swiss philosophy teacher, he happens to be the grandson of Hassan al-Banna, the founder of the Muslim Brotherhood. While his ancestry should not be held against him, he is widely thought to be close to the Brothers—some even think they appointed him to be their principal representative in Europe—and he has a record of extremist statements and telling evasions.

Asked by one Italian magazine if the killing of civilians was morally right, he replied: "In Palestine, Iraq, Chechnya, there is a situation of oppression, repression and dictatorship. It is legitimate for Muslims to resist fascism that kills the innocent." Asked if car-bombings were justified against U.S. forces in Iraq, he answered: "Iraq was colonised by the Americans. Resistance against the army is just," and has described the terrorist attacks on New York, Bali and Madrid as merely "interventions."[46]

Ramadan has blamed Jewish intellectuals for their support of the war in Iraq, and has accused them of placing their allegiance to Israel above their conscience. In his book, *The Islam in Question*, he wrote that he strongly favored the death of the "Zionist entity"—the term used by Islamists who refuse even to pronounce Israel's name.[47] His message that Islam is the solution to the problems of the West—coincidentally the slogan of the Muslim Brotherhood—has proved as slippery as it is intoxicating to young Muslims. Some commentators think that the immensely charismatic Ramadan was highly influential in radicalizing French Muslim youths who rampaged through the *banlieues* of France during the autumn of 2005.

The researcher Caroline Fourest, who has made an exhaustive study of Tariq Ramadan's works, says that he speaks with two voices. To the non-Muslim world, she says, he presents himself as a man of dialogue with no links to the Muslim Brotherhood. But in his cassettes and books, distributed in radical Islamist libraries and shops, he explains and praises the teachings and methods of Hassan al-Banna without any critical analysis. He has extolled Sheikh Qaradawi, openly supported Hamas as a "resistance" movement, and when asked whether he approved of the killing of an eight-year-old Israeli child who would grow up to be a soldier, he replied: "That act in itself is morally condemnable but contextually explicable," since "the international community has put the Palestinians in the arms of the oppressors."[48] In response to Fourest's observations, Ramadan claimed on oumma.com, the website of the UOIF (the main French Muslim organization linked to the Muslim Brotherhood), that she was "a long-time militant for whom every criticism of Israel is antisemitism" and was an agent of Israel.[49] The laughable Israel smear is, of course, an Islamist giveaway.

Given the composition of the task force committees, it was perhaps not surprising that their first public utterance was to call for Britain's Holocaust Memorial Day to be scrapped because it offended Muslims. Instead they wanted a "Genocide Day" that would recognize, as they put it, the mass murder of Muslims in Palestine, Chechnya and Bosnia as well as people of other faiths.[50] The Home Office was quick to knock down the suggestion—the same Home Office that had appointed these extremists to this task force in the first place.

This was merely a foretaste, however, of what was to come. The task force's final report reflected the view that the fault for Islamist terrorism lay as much with the government as with the bombers, and that the causes were deprivation, discrimination and Islamophobia. Confronting extremism and radicalization in all its forms was the "responsibility of society as a whole" and the solutions were to be found in "tackling inequality, discrimination, deprivation and inconsistent Government policy, and in particular foreign policy."[51]

The task force wanted more services and opportunities for Muslim youths. It effectively proposed more, not less, Islamic separatism with more Islam in the school curriculum and Islamic education and Arabic lessons for women (which were supposed to empower them). It opposed just about every government antiterrorist proposal. It wanted changes in British foreign policy, which it said was a "key contributory factor" for "criminal radical extremists," with the implied threat that if foreign policy didn't change there would be more attacks. It wanted government-funded Muslim propaganda, with an Islamic media unit to "encourage a more balanced representation of Islam and Muslims in the British media, (popular) culture and sports industries," a steering group to "draw up a strategy on combating Islamophobia through education," and a touring exhibition promoting the "Islamic way of life." And it wanted a rapid rebuttal unit for "Islamophobic" sentiments and a prohibition of the term "Islamic extremism" because "the language suggests that the terrorism we are facing today is 'a Muslim problem'—created by Muslims and to be resolved by Muslims."[52]

What had started as an exercise to get the Muslim community to grapple with the sources of extremism in its midst had been transformed into a demand for Britain to treat that community as a principal *victim* of British society and to make amends by dancing to its tunes—including dictating how people talked and thought about Islam, and censoring and suppressing anyone who dissented.

No other minority in Britain had ever presented the state with a shopping list of demands for special treatment, let alone in the context of a continuing terrorist threat to the country emanating from within that same community. Dismayingly, however, the government did not seem to see it that way. The home secretary, Charles Clarke, said he had "no problem" with most of the task force's recommendations, with the exception of the requirements that British foreign policy be changed and that a public inquiry be held into the July 2005 bombings. He maintained, however, that the committees were being wound up, their recommendations would largely be shelved and their members— of whom he granted that "one or two" had been appointed without enough being known about them—would have no further standing in Whitehall.[53] Yet the government had prepared a grid detailing a schedule for implementing the task force's recommendations. The conveners were meeting the foreign secretary, Jack Straw—despite the assurance that foreign policy would not be changed. And there was no indication that the Islamic road shows or educational materials would not be dominated by the Muslim Brotherhood. No assurance was given that Sheikh Qaradawi, for example, would not be used on any such speakers' panels; indeed, all the indications were that he would.

The government had quite simply handed over policy on extremism to the extremists. This was no accident but a deliberate policy of riding the Islamist tiger. Asked why the government was using radicals in this way, Clarke replied that it was to demonstrate to the Muslim community that democracy entailed engaging with a range of views rather than blowing up one's opponents.[54] Clarke appeared to think that he could use dialogue with the Islamists as a kind of role-play, which would have no effect on government policy but would show that talking was "the British way."

This was hopelessly naïve. It took no account of the fact that it raised the profile of such radicals and gave them credibility and thus even more clout within their community. Above all it showed that, like so many others, Clarke did not grasp that religious ideology rather than bombs was the principal weapon in this war. While he accepted that religion could not be divorced from this particular terrorism, he thought that what was driving it was more like "nihilism." "I don't believe this is a jihad," he said, "because that implies an organizing force that is greater than exists."[55]

In fact, the strategy of riding the Islamist tiger appeared to have been even more recklessly developed within the British intelligence world. In another leaked internal government paper, William Ehrman, the top intelligence official at the Foreign Office, revealed that this ministry planned to spread "black" anti-Western propaganda as a way of first gaining the trust of Islamist extremists and then using that trust to argue that violence was not the way forward. Ehrman proposed that spies should infiltrate extremist websites and develop "messages aimed at more radicalized constituencies who are potential recruits to terrorism." These extremists would not listen to the traditional calls for the Middle East to become a zone of peace and prosperity, said

Ehrman. "They might, however, listen to religious arguments about the nature of jihad, that, while anti-Western, eschew terrorism."[56]

A more dangerous and deluded approach could scarcely be imagined than using a lesser form of Islamist extremism to counter the greater. The thinking behind this strategy was alluded to in an unremarked lecture delivered in 2004 by a former head of MI6, Sir Colin McColl. He delicately referred to the British habit of adding a "political ingredient" to the recipe for combating terror, as had been done in Cyprus and Northern Ireland—which appeared to mean giving the terrorists what they wanted. He went on to say that hearts and minds needed to be won back within the Muslim world to staunch the flow of new recruits to terror. To do this, he suggested repeating what he claimed had been done in the fight against communism. This had consisted of providing more attractive ideas than communism for young people, through moves that would "outflank communism on the left" and thus demonstrate "the total phoniness of, for example, the Soviet version of democracy."[57]

The same approach, he said, could be used against al-Qaeda to show young Muslims that continued violence was counterproductive. What was needed, he mused, was the emergence of "a new Islamist leader, both charismatic and positive, an Islamic Pied Piper who will take the young Muslims down a creative and non-violent path to a better world and make Osama bin Laden look like yesterday's man."[58] He could have been writing the job description for Tariq Ramadan.

And here was the sting: "Central to such an effort, of course, is a willingness to see published attacks on some of the sacred cows of western policy—the universality of western values, Israeli-tilted policies on nuclear proliferation and Palestine, western farming subsidies and the joys of globalization." This, he suggested, would show that the fight was against the killers and not Islam, and would demonstrate the futility and destructiveness of violence.[59] On the contrary: it would show that violence pays. The "political ingredient" would be the very change in British foreign policy demanded as the price for an end to terror.

Despite the government's strenuous protestations that foreign policy would not be thus offered up as a propitiatory sacrifice, others were tripping unconcernedly down precisely this primrose path to appeasement. The Labour MP John Denham, chairman of the Commons Home Affairs Select Committee—a parliamentary committee concerned with terrorism—said in an interview that the alienation of young British Muslims was the government's fault for failing to give the "issues and concerns raised within the Muslim community any priority till after the London bombings."[60]

These issues and concerns were Israel/Palestine, Kashmir and Chechnya. Startlingly, Denham suggested that foreign policy should now take into account the possible risk to British security:

> We need to recognise that some foreign policy has now a very direct impact on domestic policy. And we may well need to give [these things] higher priority and more energy, and indeed be prepared to change the emphasis of our foreign policy in order to safeguard our own security. . . . It is no exaggeration to say that Israeli policy in the occupied territories is not simply a matter of foreign policy—it is a matter for British domestic security policy too.[61]

So what Israel did, or was perceived to do, to the Palestinian Arabs was the cause of Islamist terrorism against the British. The reasoning behind this remarkable sentiment was that the subjective perception of British Muslims was all that mattered. If they said that Israel was committing ethnic cleansing against the Palestinians or murdering their children, then this was the grievance that had to be addressed in order to avert terrorism against Britain. The fact that such perceptions might be untrue, misguided or malevolent did not seem to enter Denham's head. "Terrorism," he said, "is rarely defeated until serious efforts are made to engage with the political and social problems that give rise to it in the first place" and "if a substantial section of the population believes that it is in any case subject to arbitrary injustice —at home or abroad—then it is much more difficult to win consent."[62]

But what if this "substantial section of the population" believes—as it does—that the very existence of Israel is an injustice? Or—as it does —that Israel's attempts to protect its citizens from mass murder are an injustice? Or—as it does—that the Jews control America and thus the West? Or—as it does—that the West wants to take over and destroy the Islamic world? The real problem that surely has to be engaged with if terrorism is to be defeated is that all these perceptions are simply wrong. The alternative, as defined by Denham, is not just surrender to violence but the endorsement of injustice, oppression and lies.

The British government is now in danger of falling into the same trap as the French. After the Muslim riots in France in autumn 2005, the French government, unable to regain control, went in desperation to those who had radicalized the community's youths in the first place and begged them to restore order. The result was a huge increase in political power for the Muslim Brotherhood. Now the British are doing the same thing. Instead of exiling the radicals, they are recruiting them.

A decision was taken to strengthen the "Engaging with the Islamic World" unit in the Foreign Office. It was given its own support staff and a wider brief to work across all areas of government. And the person put in control of it was none other than Mockbul Ali, the young adviser who had recommended Sheikh Qaradawi as a role model for Britain's Muslim youth.[63]

The *Observer* revealed that Ali shocked senior officials by arguing that the Muslim Brotherhood was a "reformist" and moderate group. He pushed yet again for Qaradawi to enter the UK, and hinted how he and the Muslim Brotherhood could become increasingly important to the Foreign Office. "Qaradawi would be the first port of call when encouraging statements against terrorism and the killing of Muslim civilians in Iraq."[64]

Four months after he wrote this, Ali's prediction came true. When the British antiwar campaigner Bruce Kember was taken hostage in Iraq in late 2005, the British authorities turned to the Muslim Brotherhood to try to secure his release. After consultations with the Foreign Office, the Muslim Association of Britain dispatched to Iraq its president, Anas al-Tikriti, to negotiate with the kidnappers. The MAB also persuaded Qaradawi, as well as the leaders of Hamas, Hezbollah and twenty-three other Muslim organizations, to sign a press release calling for Kember and three other hostages to be freed. Abu Qatada also appealed for their release from his prison cell, as did Moazzam Begg, the British man who had previously been detained at Guantanamo Bay, while Muslims at the Finsbury Park mosque—now run once more by the Brotherhood—said prayers for Kember's safe return, which were played on televisions across the world.[65] Similar initiatives occurred when the Britsh aid worker Kate Burton and her parents were kidnapped by Palestinians in Gaza in December 2005. Before they were released, Ziad Aloul of the MAB was preparing to travel to Gaza as an "envoy" on behalf of British Muslim and Palestinian groups to plead for the family's release,[66] a plea entered also by Sir Iqbal Sacranie, who urged the kidnappers to release them as soon as possible.[67]

No one saw fit to observe that a group of people who were said to have "nothing to do with terrorists" because they were merely austere religious puritans were suddenly the only people with the credibility to negotiate with those terrorists. And virtually no one wondered what would be demanded in return by Islamists who were thus being courted and built up by the British state they vowed to usurp.

The British government thinks it is using Islamist radicals in a sophisticated strategy. The reality is that it is being used by an enemy it does not understand.

CONCLUSION

———————◇———————

B ritain is in denial. Having allowed the country to turn into a global hub of the Islamic jihad without apparently giving it a second thought, the British establishment is still failing even now—despite the wake-up calls of both 9/11 and the London bomb attacks of 2005—to acknowledge what it is actually facing and take the appropriate action. Instead, it is deep into a policy of appeasement of the phenomenon that threatens it, throwing sops to both radical Islamism and the Muslim community in a panic-stricken attempt to curry favor and buy off the chances of any further attacks. This disastrous policy ignores the first law of terrorism, which is that it preys on weakness. The only way to defeat it is through strength—the strength of a response based on absolute consistency and moral integrity, which arises in turn from the strength of belief in the values that are being defended. By choosing instead the path of least resistance, Britain is advertising its fundamental weakness and is thus not only greatly enhancing the danger to itself but also enfeebling the alliance in the defense of the West.

Britain has a long and inglorious history of appeasing terrorism, thus bringing true the aphorism, in which its ruling class so cynically believes, that "terrorism works." Now, however, this dubious national trait has been cemented even more firmly into the national psyche by the governing doctrine of multiculturalism, which has made it all but impossible even to acknowledge that this is a problem rooted within the religion of a particular minority community. The fervent embrace of "victim culture" means instead that this minority has to be treated on its own assessment as a victim of the majority and its grievances attended to on the grounds that it is these grievances that are the cause of terrorism. At the same time, however, this minority disavows any connection with terrorism and vilifies anyone who dares suggest the contrary. Thus Britain is being forced to act on the basis that if it does not do so it will be attacked—by people who claim that terrorism runs totally counter to the values of their religion, but then demand that the grievances of members of that religion are addressed as the price of averting further attacks. This deeply manipulative and mind-twisting behavior is the equivalent of holding a gun to Britain's head while denying that this is being done, and threatening to run out of town anyone who points it out.

The intersection of an aggressive religious fanaticism with the multicultural ideology of victimhood has created a state of paralysis across British institutions. The refusal to admit the religious character of the threat means that Britain not only is failing to take the action it should be taking but, worse still, is providing Islamist ideologues with an even more powerful platform from which to disseminate the anti-Western views that have so inflamed a section of Britain's Muslims. The refusal to acknowledge that this is principally a war of religious ideology, and that dangerous ideas that can kill are spread across a continuum of religious thought which acts as a recruiting sergeant for violence, is the most egregious failure by the British political and security establishment. The deeply rooted British belief that violence always arises from rational grievances, and the resulting inability to comprehend the cultural dynamics of religious fanaticism, have furthermore created a widespread climate of irrationality and prejudice in which the principal victims of the war against the West, America and Israel, are demonized instead as its cause.

This mindset and the corresponding terror of being thought "Islamophobic" have prevented the British from acknowledging the eruption of Islamist violence not just in Britain but around the Western world. The British media either ignore it—as with disturbances in Sweden or Belgium—or, when they do report it, insist that Islam has nothing to do with it. When Muslim riots engulfed France in November

2005, the reaction of most of the British (and European) media was that they were caused by the poverty, unemployment and discrimination endured by the alienated youths who torched the country from Normandy to Toulouse. One writer suggested that those who saw Islamism on the march in France were merely exponents of a particularly virulent form of conservative thinking, expressed variously around the world through Russian racism, demagogic Hindu nationalism, Gallic exceptionalism, U.S. Christian fundamentalism and Muslim fundamentalism, which were all marching shoulder to shoulder in an attempt to stop the clock of history.[1]

Yet the vast majority of the French rioters were Muslims; the rioters screamed "*Allahu akhbar*,"[2] talked about jihad[3] and expressed admiration for Osama bin Laden;[4] and, more pertinently still, the French government asked Muslim imams to calm the unrest, which they did "in the name of Allah" and issued a fatwa telling the rioters that such behavior went against the religion.[5] Yet despite all this evidence, British commentators insisted that Islam was irrelevant.

There was a similar reaction to the riots in Australia involving Lebanese Muslims in December 2005. Trouble flared on Cronulla Beach in New South Wales when thousands of drunken white youths went on the rampage, attacking police and people of Middle Eastern appearance. It spread later with retaliatory attacks by groups of Arab youths who stabbed one man and smashed dozens of cars. Almost universally, the media described what happened as white racists attacking Arabs and referred to the disturbances, which went on for several days, as "race riots."

But race was not the issue here. It was culture. There had never been any trouble with Lebanese Christians in Australia, who had integrated well and were prospering. Although white racists were certainly involved, the unrest was actually sparked by Lebanese Muslim attacks on two white Australian lifeguards, the tip of an iceberg of aggression by this minority, which had gone all but unreported. It was the Muslim community that for years had been giving rise to a major problem of aggression, which Australia's rigid multiculturalist mindset had transformed into Muslim grievances and never properly addressed.[6]

One of the reasons why people shy away from acknowledging the religious aspect of this problem is, first, the very proper respect that should be afforded to people's beliefs and, second, the equally proper fear of demonizing an entire community. There is indeed a risk of such a discussion exposing innocent Muslims to attack. But there is a greater risk to the whole community if the roots of the problem are censored and never dealt with.

The key issue is the inability to grasp that just because a problem has a religious character, this does not mean that all members of that religion suffer from that problem. There is a distinction to be drawn between Muslims and Islamists. Islamism is the politicized interpretation of the religion that aims to Islamize societies. Many Muslims in Britain and elsewhere would not subscribe to this ideology. But it is the dominant strain throughout the Muslim world, and so far there has been no serious challenge to it—not least because those who do speak out against it run the risk of being killed.

Because it is so dominant, backed by powerful Muslim states and even more crucially by Islamic religious authorities, it constantly spreads its extremist messages of religious fanaticism and political sedition. That is why the development of the Muslim Brotherhood infrastructure in Britain was so calamitous. It is also why the most bitter criticism of the government's subsequent appeasement of the Brotherhood has come from liberal British Muslims, who understandably feel betrayed as the ground is cut from under their feet.

The charge that pointing out the religious nature of this extremism is an act of bigotry against Muslims is deployed to shut down a vital debate that urgently needs to be held, not least within the Muslim community itself. The claim is a form of crude intimidation, and the fact that Britain is so cowed by it in itself shows how far it has already traveled down this dangerous path.

It also ignores the fact that some Muslims themselves are speaking out in a similar vein. Sheikh Abd al-Hamid al-Ansari, the former dean of the Faculty of Sharia at the University of Qatar, wrote in the London-based Arabic-language daily *Al-Hayat*:

Why won't we take the opportunity of the appearance of the 9/11 Commission's report to ponder why destructive violence and a culture of destruction have taken root in our society? Why won't we take this opportunity to reconsider our educational system, our curricula, including the religious, media, and cultural discourse that cause our youth to live in a constant tension with the world?[7]

Aisha Siddiqa Qureshi wrote in *Muslim World Today* that "radical Islam threatens to subjugate the world and murder, enslave or convert all non-Muslims," that radical Muslims "share Hitler's goal," and that liberals were not willing to defend their own institutions against this threat.[8]

And Mansoor Ijaz wrote in the *Financial Times* shortly after the first set of London attacks:

> It is hypocritical for Muslims living in western societies to demand civil rights enshrined by the state and then excuse their inaction against terrorists hiding among them on grounds of belonging to a borderless Islamic community. It is time to stand up and be counted as model citizens before the terror consumes us all.[9]

Such courageous Muslims are being betrayed by Britain's pusillanimity. The Muslim community has got to come up with a response other than blaming Britain and the West. While no one has the right to tell it how to organize its own religion, it does have a responsibility to address those aspects of its culture that threaten the state. Britain does this community no favors by pandering to its own tendency to self-delusion.

For Britain to start to address this properly, it would have to take a number of steps that showed unequivocally that it was refusing to compromise not just with terror but with the ideology that fuels it. This would mean showing that, while it had no problem with the practice of Islam as a minority faith that observed the same rules as all other minority faiths, it would not countenance the practice of Islamism, or clerical fascism, and would take measures to stop it.

Britain would first have to take robust steps to counter the specific threat posed by Islamist terrorism. To do this properly, it needs to recognize that this particular threat really is something new and does not properly correspond either to our definition of terrorism or to our definition of war but sits somewhere between the two. Consequently, it needs to develop new structures and new principles to deal with this new phenomenon. A start would be to construct special courts to deal with particularly sensitive cases in which intelligence could safely be brought forward as evidence, which is not the case at present.

To enable it to expel foreign radicals, Britain would repeal its Human Rights Act and either derogate or withdraw from both the European Convention on Human Rights and the UN Convention on Refugees, drafting its own legislation to define refugee status. The claim that abolishing human rights legislation would be a regressive move that would leave Britain a less free society is very wide of the mark. Britain was arguably a freer society before European human rights law eroded the foundation of British liberty, the common law.

A properly motivated Britain would put a stop to the funding and recruitment for terrorism taking place under the umbrella of charitable work through intensive investigation of such organizations. It would shut down newspapers and television stations spreading incitement to terrorism and war against the West. It would ban extremist organizations like Hizb ut-Tahrir and the Muslim Association of Britain, recognizing that while they may not advocate terrorism, their advocacy of Islamization creates a conveyor belt to violence. It would certainly not grant Sheikh Qaradawi an entry visa. And it would introduce surveillance of subversives on campus through targeted covert work, as suggested by Professor Anthony Glees and Chris Pope.[10]

Recognizing that Islamist ideology is a conveyor belt to terror, it would end its strategy of using Islamist radicals. Instead, any materials advocating an Islamic takeover of the West would be treated as subversion, sedition or even treason, and be prosecuted. The curricula used in Muslim schools would be inspected by Arabic speakers, and if they contained similar incitement, they would be similarly dealt with. Imams would be regulated and monitored. Extremist imams would be expelled and extremist mosques closed down.

The message conveyed by all such moves would be that Britain has no problem with Islam as long as it poses no danger to the state. Since the Muslim community insists that it is moderate and has no truck with extremism, it should have no objection to such measures, which would ensure that this would be the case.

Next, a properly motivated nation would set about the remoralization and reculturation of Britain by restating the primacy of British culture and citizenship. To do this, it would recognize that British nationhood has been eviscerated by the combination of three things: mass immigration, multiculturalism and the onslaught mounted by secular nihilists against the country's Judeo-Christian values. It would institute tough controls on immigration while Britain assimilates the people it has already got. The principal reason behind the cultural segregation of Britain's Muslims is their practice of marrying their young people to cousins from the Indian subcontinent. That has got to stop because it is a threat to social cohesion. The usual charges of racism would be faced down by reaffirming two things simultaneously: that Britain values its immigrants who make a great contribution to the country; and that in order to integrate them properly into the society, Britain must control their numbers.

It would abolish the doctrine of multiculturalism by reaffirming the primacy of British values. It would ensure that British political history is once again taught in schools, and that Christianity is restored to school assemblies. It would stop the drift towards the creation of a parallel Islamic jurisdiction under Sharia and would no longer turn a blind eye to the practice of polygamy, following the recommendation of Dr. Ghayasuddin Siddiqui that imams should be allowed to officiate at marriages only upon the production of a civil marriage certificate.[11]

It would halt the drift towards social suicide by ending the culture of equal entitlement ushered in by the application of secular human rights doctrine. An agenda that seeks to destroy Western values by abolishing moral norms altogether and replacing them with transgressive behavior has been serviced by human rights law. An end to this victim culture is essential both to restore social order to Britain and to give it back its sense of its own identity. While it is being undermined from within, it is not able adequately to defend itself against the threat from without.

Finally, it would undertake a major educational exercise for both Muslims and non-Muslims. It would teach Muslims what being a minority means, and that certain ideas to which they may subscribe are simply unacceptable or demonstrably untrue. It would say loud and clear that the double standards from which Muslims think they suffer are actually a form of doublethink. Any administration that was really concerned to fight racism would educate the nation in the historical truths about Israel and the Arabs, and would tell Muslims that they have systematically been fed a diet of lies about Israel and the Jews.

If Britain really understood the threat to the West, this is the kind of program it would now be introducing. Unfortunately, there is very little chance of any of this happening. Britain is currently locked into such a spiral of decadence, self-loathing and sentimentality that it is incapable of seeing that it is setting itself up for cultural immolation. In the short term, this is likely to lead to the increasing marginalization of British Jews, Hindus, Sikhs and other minorities caught in a pincer movement between radical Islamists on the one hand and, on the other, a craven establishment that is pandering to Islamist extremism. So much for the multicultural nirvana.

America's principal ally is currently at a crossroads. With Islamist terrorism having erupted in London and still worse atrocities feared to be in the offing, the British government has even now only tightened up a few procedures. If there were to be more attacks, it is possible that it would finally be forced to take a more tough-minded approach. But to date, Londonistan still flourishes. Yes, a few more extremists have been locked up. Yes, a few thinkers have now questioned the wisdom of multiculturalism. But the push for Islamization continues, British Muslims are still being recruited for the jihad, and the country's elites are still in the grip of the nation-busting, universalist mindset that has hollowed out Britain's values and paralyzed it in the face of the assault by Islamism. A liberal society is in danger of being destroyed by its own ideals.

The emergence of Londonistan should be of the greatest concern to America, for which it poses acute dangers. Clearly, the fact that Britain has become Europe's Islamist terror factory presents immediate and obvious risks to America's physical security. On another level, there is the danger that Britain might cease to play such a staunch role in the continuing defense of the West. Tony Blair has said he will not stand again as Labour's leader. Given the hostility of his party towards America, Israel and Iraq, his successor is unlikely to share his passion for the cause. As for the Conservative party, which might come to power instead, it has lost its ideological way, with many in its ranks having come to share the shrill prejudices of the left and with a new leader, David Cameron, who has announced that he "loves Britain as it is, not as it once was."

At a deeper, cultural level there is now a risk of the special relationship between Britain and America fracturing as Britain slides further into appeasement. But there is a more subtle peril still for America. After all, if Britain slept on its watch, so too did America and for similar reasons. Like British politicians and British intelligence, successive American administrations along with the CIA and the FBI similarly failed to pay attention to or understand the rise of fanatical Islamism and what this meant for the world. Like their British counterparts, American officials dismissed the warnings they were given by occasional farsighted officials and other players who did understand that a religious war was brewing. Indeed, America has an even greater horror than Britain of encroaching on religion's private space. It too has gone to great lengths to avoid referring to the religious nature of the war declared on the West, calling the struggle instead—absurdly—a "war on terrorism." As a Pentagon briefing paper observed, "America's political leaders still think Muslim terrorists, even suicide bombers, are mindless 'criminals' motivated by 'hatred of our freedoms' rather than religious zealots motivated by their faith. And as a result, we have no real strategic plan for winning a war against jihadists."[12]

The cultural deformities of moral relativism and victim culture that have done such damage in Britain are present in American society too. At present, they are locked in conflict with traditional values in America's culture wars. But it doesn't take too much imagination to envisage that, if a different administration were installed in the White House, Britain's already calamitous slide into cultural defeatism might boost similar forces at play in the United States.

Britain is the global leader of English-speaking culture. It was

Britain that first developed the Western ideas of the rule of law, democracy and liberal ideals, and exported them to other countries. Now Britain is leading the rout of those values, allowing its culture to become vulnerable to the predations of militant Islam. If British society goes down under this twin assault, the impact will be incalculable— not just for the military defense of the West against radical Islamism, but for the very continuation of Western civilization itself.

The West is under threat from an enemy that has shrewdly observed the decadence and disarray in Europe, where Western civilization first began. And the greatest disarray of all is in Britain, the very cradle of Western liberty and democracy, but whose cultural confusion is now plain for all to see in Londonistan. The Islamists chose well. Britain is not what it once was. Whether it will finally pull itself together and stop sleepwalking into cultural oblivion is a question on which the future of the West may now depend.

NOTES

INTRODUCTION

1 *Draft Report on Young Muslims and Extremism*, Foreign and Commonwealth Office/Home Office, 2004; Robert Winnett and David Leppard, *Sunday Times*, 10 July 2005.

2 Bruce Bawer, *While Europe Slept: How Radical Islam Is Destroying the West from Within* (Doubleday, 2006); Claire Berlinski, *Menace in Europe: Why the Continent's Crisis Is America's, Too* (Crown Forum, 2006).

3 Tony Blair speech, 16 July 2005; Tony Blair, Downing Street press conference, 21 July 2005.

4 Dundan Gardham and George Jones, *Daily Telegraph*, 8 February 2006.

5 Sean O'Neill, Daniel McGrory and Philip Webster, *The Times*, 9 February 2006.

6 John Steele and George Jones, *Daily Telegraph*, 9 February 2006.

7 David Blunkett, *Sun*, 9 February 2006.

8 Paul Reynolds, *BBC News Online*, 6 February 2006, http://news.bbc.co.uk/1/hi/world/south_asia/4686536.stm; Hjörtur Gudmundsson (with Filip van Laenen), *Brussels Journal*, 14 January 2006, http://www.brusselsjournal.com/node/668

9 Amir Taheri, *New York Post*, 9 February 2006.

10 David Rennie, Julian Isherwood and Jack Barton, *Daily Telegraph*, 4 February 2006.

11 *BBC News Online*, 9 February 2006.

12 U.S. State Department press briefing, 3 February 2006.

13 Press Association newswire, 3 February 2006.

14 Steve Bird and Daniel McGrory, *The Times*, 4 February 2006.

15 Press Association newswire, 9 February 2006.

16 Ibid.

17 Prince of Wales, "Islam and the West," speech at Oxford Centre for Islamic Studies, 27 October 1993; text, *MSANEWS*, Ohio State University.

18 Tony Brooks, *Daily Express*, 24 October 2005.

19 Steve Doughty, *Daily Mail*, 18 October 2005.

CHAPTER 1: THE GROWTH OF LONDONISTAN

1 Trevor Phillips, speech to Manchester Council for Community Relations, 22 September 2005.

2 Stephen Ulph, "Londonistan," *Terrorism Monitor* (Jamestown Center), vol. 2, no. 4 (26 February 2004).

3 Rachel Ehrenfeld, *FrontPageMagazine.com*; July 20, 2005.

4 Reda Hussaine, interview with author, 2005.

5 Jonathan Spyer, *Ha'aretz*, 15 July 2005.

6 Reda Hussaine interview.

7 *United States of America v. Usama bin Laden, et al.*, U.S. District Court, Southern District of New York, 2001.

8 Maureen O'Hagan and Mike Carter, *Seattle Times*, 29 December 2004.

9 Interview with Navid Akhtar, *BBC Radio Five Live*, 7 March 2004.

10 Michael Whine, "The Penetration of Islamist Ideology in Britain," *Current Trends in Islamist Ideology* (Hudson Institute), vol. 1 (April 2005).

11 Alex Alexiev, "Violent Islamists in the UK and Europe," *Internationale Politik* (Berlin), September 2005.

12 BBC TV *Panorama*, 21 August 2005.

13 Alexiev, "Violent Islamists in the UK and Europe."

14 Sue Reid, *Daily Mail*, 3 September 2005.

15 Dr. Ghayasuddin Siddiqui, interview with author, 2005.

16 Bishop Michael Nazir-Ali, interview with author, 2005.

17 Dr. Ghayasuddin Siddiqui interview.

18 Steve Coll, *Ghost Wars* (Penguin, 2004).

19 *Globe and Mail* (Toronto), 9 December 1992.

20 Stewart Tendler, Andrew McEwen and Nicholas Beeston, *The Times*, 15 February 1989.

21 Amit Roy, *Sunday Times*, 22 October 1989.

22 Ibid.

23 Joanna Coles, *Guardian*, 14 February 1990.

24 Amit Roy and Greg Hadfield, *Sunday Times*, 12 March 1989.

25 *Independent*, 3 June 1989.

26 *Prospect*, October 2005.

27 *Independent*, 5 June 1989.

28 *BBC News Online*, 26 November 2001,
   http://news.bbc.co.uk/1/hi/uk/1564626.stm

29 Reda Hussaine interview.

30 Ian Bruce, *Herald* (Glasgow), 9 July 2002.

31 Ulph, "Londonistan."

32 *Mail on Sunday*, 12 November 1995.

33 "Insight," *Sunday Times*, 7 August 2005.

34 *Daily Mirror*, 7 September 1996.

35 Robert Leiken, *Bearers of Global Jihad: Immigration and National Security after 9/11* (Nixon Center, 2004).

36 Ulph, "Londonistan."

37 Leiken, *Bearers of Global Jihad*.

38 Sean O'Neill, *Daily Telegraph*, 21 January 2003.

39 *Daily Telegraph*, 18 October 2003.

40 Jessica Berry and Nick Fielding, *Sunday Times*, 13 February 2005.

41 Bishop Michael Nazir-Ali, interview.

CHAPTER 2: THE HUMAN RIGHTS JIHAD

 1 Robert Leiken, *Bearers of Global Jihad: Immigration and National Security after 9/11* (Nixon Center, 2004).
 2 Cited in Reuven Paz, "Middle East Islamism in the European Arena," *MERIA*, vol. 6, no. 3 (September 2002).
 3 James Slack, *Daily Mail*, 22 December 2005.
 4 Abul Taher, *Sunday Times*, 20 November 2005.
 5 John Fonte, "The Ideological War within the West," *Watch on the West* (Foreign Policy Research Institute), vol. 3, no. 6 (May 2002).
 6 Lord Bingham, speech to Commonwealth Law Conference, 14 September 2005.
 7 Ibid.
 8 David Selbourne, *The Principle of Duty* (Sinclair-Stevenson, 1994; revised, Abacus, 1997).
 9 Francesca Klug, *Values for a Godless Age* (Penguin, 2000).
10 Clare Dyer, *Guardian*, 9 March 2006.
11 Joshua Rozenberg, *Daily Telegraph*, 3 March 2005.
12 *A [et al.] v. Home Department*, Session 2004–05 [2004] UKHL 56 (16 December 2004).
13 Ibid.

CHAPTER 3: THE SECURITY DEBACLE

 1 Elaine Sciolino and Don Van Natta Jr., *New York Times*, 10 July 2005.
 2 James Sturcke, *Guardian*, 19 July 2005.
 3 Anthony Barnett and Martin Bright, *Observer*, 2 October 2005.
 4 Vikram Dodd, *Guardian*, 26 October 2005.
 5 *Responsibility for the Terrorist Atrocities in the United States, 11 September 2001—An Updated Account*, HMG, 2001.
 6 Kathryn Knight, *Mail on Sunday*, 23 September 2001.
 7 Rory Carroll, *Guardian*, 24 June 1999.
 8 Marie Colvin and Dipesh Gadher, *Sunday Times*, 17 January 1999.
 9 Ely Karmon, International Policy Institute for Counter-Terrorism at the Interdisciplinary Center Herzliya (Israel), interview with author, 2005.
10 Philip Johnston, *Daily Telegraph*, 28 September 2001.
11 Stephen Ulph, "Londonistan," *Terrorism Monitor* (Jamestown Center), vol. 2, no. 4 (26 February 2004).
12 *BBC News Online*, 26 September 2001, http://news.bbc.co.uk/1/hi/uk/1564626.stm
13 Elaine Sciolino and Don Van Natta Jr., *New York Times*, 10 July 2005.
14 Richard Beeston and Michael Binyon, *The Times*, 10 August 2005.
15 Jimmy Burns and Stephen Fidler, *Financial Times*, 12 July 2005.
16 James Woolsey, interview with author, 2005.
17 Kathryn Knight, *Mail on Sunday*, 23 September 2001.

18 Anthony Glees and Chris Pope, *When Students Turn to Terror: Terrorist and Extremist Activity on British Campuses* (Social Affairs Unit, 2005).
19 Oliver Revell, interview with author, 2005.
20 Lord Carey, interview with author, 2005.
21 Marquess of Salisbury, interview with author, 2005.
22 Interview with official, 2005.
23 David Blunkett, interview with author, 2005.
24 Reda Hussaine, interview with author, 2005.
25 Sue Reid, *Daily Mail*, 3 September 2005.
26 Reda Hussaine interview.
27 Jason Burke, *Observer*, 26 January 2003.
28 *Al-Sharq al-Awsat*, 22 August 1998.
29 Bishop of Rochester, interview with author, 2005.
30 David Blunkett interview.
31 Marquess of Salisbury interview.
32 Oliver Revell interview.
33 Interview with official, 2005.
34 David Blunkett interview.
35 Nicole Martin, *Daily Telegraph*, 26 June 2005.
36 Ian Herbert, *Independent*, 8 July 2005.
37 Jasper Gerard, *Sunday Times*, 6 February 2005.
38 *BBC News Online*, 12 August 2005.
39 *Daily Express*, 1 August 2005.
40 *Daily Mail*, 2 December 2005.
41 *Daily Express*, 1 September 2005.
42 Interviews with participants, 2005.
43 Memo by Mockbul Ali, Foreign Office, 14 July 2005.
44 John Mintz and Douglas Farah, *Washington Post*, 11 September 2004.

CHAPTER 4: THE MULTICULTURAL PARALYSIS

1 Lord Swann, *Education for All: The Report of the Committee of Inquiry into the Education of Children from Ethnic Minority Groups*, HMSO, 1985.
2 Fred Naylor, *Dewsbury and the School above the Pub* (Claridge Press, 1989).
3 Andrew Norfolk, Sean O'Neill and Stewart Tendler, *The Times*, 20 July 2005.
4 Office for National Statistics.
5 *The Future of Multi-Ethnic Britain: The Parekh Report* (Profile Books, 2000).
6 Richard Ford, *The Times*, 12 October 2000.
7 Leo McKinstry, *Spectator*, 24 September 2005.
8 *Sun*, 1 October 2005.
9 Steve Kennedy, *Sun*, 16 September 2005.
10 Martin Evans, *Daily Express*, 16 November 2005.

11 Sarah Harris and Laura Clark, *Daily Mail*, 9 April 2002.

12 Dalya Alberge, *The Times*, 24 November 2005.

13 Trevor Phillips, speech to Conservative Party conference, September 2005.

14 Dave Walker, *Humanities Resource*, Spring 1995/1996.

15 John Beck, "Nation, Curriculum and Identity in Conservative Cultural Analysis: A Critical Commentary," *Cambridge Journal* (University of Cambridge Institute of Education), no. 2 (1996).

16 Bruce Carrington and Geoffrey Short, "What Makes a Person British? Children's Conceptions of Their National Culture and Identity," *Educational Studies*, vol. 21, no. 2 (1995).

17 Bernard Barker, *Anxious Times: The Future of Education* (Stanground College, Peterborough, 1995).

18 Tom Leonard, *Daily Telegraph*, 14 July 2005.

19 FaithWorks case studies, 2005.

20 Steve Doughty, *Daily Mail*, 18 October 2005.

21 Stephen Bates, *Guardian*, 16 November 2005.

22 Roy Hattersley, *Guardian*, 21 November 2005.

23 Andrew Alderson, *Sunday Telegraph*, 30 October 2005.

24 Prince of Wales, "Islam and the West," speech at Oxford Centre for Islamic Studies, 27 October 1993; text, *MSANEWS*, Ohio State University.

25 Ibid.

26 Ruth Gledhill, *The Times*, 14 December 1996.

27 Daniel McGrory, *The Times*, 21 January 2003.

28 Kenan Malik, "Too Much Respect," *Prospect*, October 2005.

29 Home Office Race, Equality, Faith and Cohesion Unit website, http://communities.homeoffice.gov.uk/raceandfaith/com-cohesion/comm-coh/asp-of-citizenship/

30 Stephen Glover, *Daily Mail*, 23 August 2005.

31 BBC/ICM poll, November 2001; *Guardian*/ICM poll, June 2002; *Guardian*/ICM poll, March 2004.

32 *Guardian*/ICM poll, July 2005.

33 Jamie Doward and Gaby Hinsliff, *Observer*, 30 May 2004.

34 Clare Garner, *Independent*, 21 February 1997.

35 Kenan Malik, *Guardian*, 7 January 2005.

36 Private correspondence, July 2005.

CHAPTER 5: THE ALIENATION OF BRITISH MUSLIMS

1 Fiona Govan, Neil Tweedie and Paul Stokes, *Daily Telegraph*, 2 September 2005.

2 Nick Britten, *Daily Telegraph*, 28 July 2005.

3 BBC *News 24*, 17 July 2005.

4 *Evening Standard*, 24 July 2005.

5 Joint statement from Muslim groups, 16 August 2005.

6 Koran, sura 5:32.
7 "Fatwa: Religious Decree in Response to the London Bombings," *British Muslim Forum*, July 2005.
8 *Draft Report on Young Muslims and Extremism*, Foreign and Commonwealth Office/Home Office, 2004.
9 Robert Winnett and David Leppard, *Sunday Times*, 10 July 2005.
10 BBC/ICM poll, November 2001.
11 *Guardian*/ICM poll, March 2004.
12 *Guardian*/ICM poll, July 2005.
13 Eastern Eye/MORI poll, November 2001; BBC/ICM poll, December 2002; *Telegraph*/ YouGov poll, December 2002.
14 *Telegraph*/YouGov poll, 23 July 2005.
15 Letter from John Gieve to Sir Andrew Turnbull, 10 May 2004.
16 Nazih N. Ayubi, *Political Islam: Religion and Politics in the Arab World* (Routledge, 1991); in Daniel Benjamin and Steven Simon, *The Age of Sacred Terror* (Random House, 2002).
17 M. Ali Kettani, "Problems of Muslim Minorities and Their Solutions," in *Muslim Communities in Non-Muslim States* (London: Islamic Council of Europe, 1980), pp. 96–105; from *Islamization of Europe*, Barnabas Fund, 11 August 2005.
18 Srdja Trifkovic, "The Islamic Conquest of Britain," *Chronicles*, 20 December 2002, www.chroniclesmagazine.org/News/Trifkovic/NewsST122002.html
19 BBC TV *Panorama*, 21 August 2005.
20 Ibid.
21 John Calvert, "Sayyid Qutb in America," *Newsletter of the International Institute for the Study of Islam in the Modern World*, no. 7 (March 2001), p. 8, www.isim.nl/files/newsl_7.pdf; in Benjamin and Simon, *The Age of Sacred Terror*.
22 *Young Muslims and Extremism*.
23 Theodore Dalrymple, "The Suicide Bombers Among Us," *City Journal*, Autumn 2005.
24 Charles Clarke, speech to Heritage Foundation, 5 October 2005.
25 *Young Muslims and Extremism*.
26 BBC TV *Panorama*, 21 August 2005.
27 Leeds Grand Mosque statement, 7 July 2005.
28 This sermon, preached in March 2004, was originally published on the website of the Leeds Grand Mosque, http://www.leedsgrandmosque.org.uk/; it now appears to have been removed.
29 Chris McGreal, Conal Urquhart in Jerusalem and Richard Norton-Taylor, *Guardian*, 1 May 2003.
30 *Young Muslims and Extremism*.
31 Anthony Glees and Chris Pope, *When Students Turn to Terror: Terrorist and Extremist Activity on British Campuses* (Social Affairs Unit, 2005).

32 Ibid.

33 Phil Baty, *Times Higher Educational Supplement*, 14 October 2005.

34 Mashuq Ally, in *The Muslim*, vol. 25, no. 1 (January–March 1990).

35 Yusuf al-Qaradawi, in ibid.

36 Umm Mohammad Azzam, in *The Muslim*, vol. 25, no. 4 (October–December 1990).

37 David Leppard, *Sunday Times*, 23 January 2005.

38 *Jewish Chronicle*, 27 May 2005.

39 *BBC News Online*, 8 July 2004.

40 *Jewish Chronicle*, 27 May 2005.

41 BBC TV *Panorama*, 21 August 2005.

42 Answer to personal question by author, 13 January 2005.

43 Martin Bright, *Observer*, 14 August 2005.

44 Laura Clark, *Daily Mail*, 16 February 2006.

45 Professor Paul Winston, Leicester council, interview with author, 2005.

46 Tom Gross, "Living in a Bubble: The BBC's Very Own Mideast Foreign Policy," *National Review Online*, 18 June 2004.

47 Abul Taher, *Sunday Times*, 27 November 2005.

48 Alex Alexiev, "Tablighi Jamaat: Jihad's Stealthy Legions," *Middle East Quarterly*, vol. 12, no. 1 (January 2005).

49 M. Ali Kettani, "Problems of Muslim Minorities and Their Solutions"; see n. 17 above.

50 *Guardian*/ICM poll, November 2004.

51 BBC Radio 4 *Sunday*, 6 February 2005.

52 *Young Muslims and Extremism*.

53 Islamic Sharia Council website, http://www.islamic-sharia.co.uk/preface.html

54 "Mortgage and Islamic Ethics: Report from European Council for Fatwa and Research," *Bohra Chronicle*, March 2001; in *Islam in Britain*, Institute for the Study of Islam and Christianity, 2005.

55 Nicholas Hellen, *Sunday Times*, 26 December 2004.

56 Dr. Ghayasuddin Siddiqui, interview with author, 2005.

57 Alasdair Palmer, *Sunday Telegraph*, 19 February 2006

58 Dr. Ghayasuddin Siddiqui interview.

59 Professor Alan Billings, interview with author, 2005.

60 Lesslie Newbigin, Lamin Sanneh and Jenny Taylor, *Faith and Power: Christianity and Islam in "Secular" Britain* (SPCK, 1998).

CHAPTER 6: SCAPEGOATING THE JEWS

1 Robert Wistrich, *Antisemitism: The Longest Hatred* (Methuen, 1991).

2 Ibid.

3 Howard M. Sachar, *A History of Israel from the Rise of Zionism to Our Time* (Alfred Knopf, 2003); *The Arab Higher Committee: Its Origins, Personnel and Purposes*, documentary record submitted to the United Nations, May 1947.

4 David Zeidan, "The Islamic Fundamentalist View of Life As a Perennial Battle," *Middle East Review of International Affairs*, vol. 5, no. 4 (December 2001).

5 Wistrich, *Antisemitism*.

6 Zeidan, "The Islamic Fundamentalist View of Life."

7 *Islam and Revolution: Writings and Declarations of Imam Khomeini* (Berkeley, 1981), quoted in Wistrich, *Antisemitism*.

8 John Miller, ABC News interview with Osama bin Laden, 28 May 1998, http://abcnews.go.com/sections/world/dailynews/terror_980609.html; in Zeidan, "The Islamic Fundamentalist View of Life."

9 Martin Kramer, "The Salience of Islamic Antisemitism," *Institute of Jewish Affairs Report* no. 2 (October 1995).

10 Esther Webman, *Anti-Semitic Motifs in the Ideology of Hizballah and Hamas*, Project for the Study of Antisemitism, Tel Aviv University, 1998.

11 Ibid.

12 Ibid.

13 Hamas Covenant, article 22 and article 7.

14 Webman, *Anti-Semitic Motifs*.

15 Wistrich, *Antisemitism*.

16 *Al Jihad wa an-Nasr*, 1974; in Wistrich, *Antisemitism*.

17 Wistrich, *Antisemitism*.

18 Robert Tait, *Guardian*, 9 December 2005.

19 *"Hate Industry": Anti-Semitic, anti-Zionist and anti-Jewish Literature in the Arab and Muslim World* (Part 1), Intelligence and Terrorism Information Center at the Center for Special Studies, Information Bulletin No. 4 (September 2002).

20 *Incitement and Propaganda against Israel, the Jewish People and the Western World, Conducted in the Palestinian Authority, the Arab World and Iran*, Intelligence and Terrorism Information Center at the Center for Special Studies, Information Bulletin No. 1 (January 2002).

21 Mas'ud Sabri, "The Wars of the Prophet: The Wars against Bani Qainuqa," cited in *"Hate Industry,"* Intelligence and Terrorism Information Center, Bulletin No. 4.

22 Abdallah Nasih Alwan, cited in *"Hate Industry,"* Intelligence and Terrorism Information Center, Bulletin No. 4.

23 Itamar Marcus and Barbara Crook, "Kill a Jew—Go to Heaven: The Perception of the Jew in Palestinian Society," *Jewish Political Studies Review*, vol. 17, no. 3–4 (Fall 2005).

24 Ibid.

25 Ibid.

26 Yusuf al-Qaradawi, *Priorities of the Islamic Movement in the Coming Phase* (1990).

27 Evidence to Foreign Office by Community Security Trust, 2004.

28 *Jewish Chronicle*, 27 May 2005.

29 *The Times*, 7 February 2006.

30 Community Security Trust, *Antisemitic Incidents Report* 2004.

31 Community Security Trust, *Antisemitic Incidents Report* 2005; Jonathan Petre, *Daily Telegraph*, 3 February 2006.

CHAPTER 7: THE RED-BLACK ALLIANCE

1 *Islam Online*, 31 October 2005.

2 Richard Wolin, *The Seduction of Unreason: The Intellectual Romance with Fascism from Nietzsche to Postmodernism* (Princeton University Press, 2004).

3 Chris Harman, "The Prophet and the Proletariat," *Marxism Online*, 1994, http://www.marxisme.dk/arkiv/harman/1994/prophet/ch10.htm

4 Mustafa Akyol, "Free Muslims Against Terrorism," Free Muslim Coalition website, http://www.freemuslims.org/document.php?id=55

5 "FBI Sets Up Shop in Yemen," *Time*, 9 August 2003; "Failure to Communicate," *Newsweek*, 4 August 2003; in Michael Whine, "The Penetration of Islamist Ideology in Britain," *Current Trends in Islamist Ideology* (Hudson Institute), vol. 1 (April 2005).

6 Whine, "The Penetration of Islamist Ideology in Britain."

7 Robert Wistrich, *Jerusalem Post*, 15 July 2005.

8 Reva Klein, Edie Friedman and Francesca Klug, letter to *Guardian*, 1 October 2002.

9 Seumas Milne, *Guardian*, 4 April 2000.

10 Hugh Muir, *Guardian*, 7 January 2004.

11 Ken Livingstone, press conference, London, 19 July 2005.

12 BBC Radio 4 *Today*, 20 July 2005.

13 Livingstone press conference.

14 Sheikh Qaradawi's sermons, in *Mayor Livingstone and Sheikh Qaradawi: A Response by a Coalition of Many of London's Diverse Communities*, 2004.

15 Ken Livingstone, letter to Jack Gilbert, 27 October 2004.

16 News transcript of the press conference, Inaugural Session of the European Council for Fatwa and Research, www.mabonline.net; in *Mayor Livingstone and Sheikh Qaradawi*.

17 Philip Johnston, *Daily Telegraph*, 14 September 2005.

18 Mayor of London, *A Reply to the Dossier against the Mayor's Meeting with Dr. Yusuf al-Qaradawi*, Greater London Authority, January 2005.

19 Simon Hattenstone, *Guardian*, 12 May 2003.

20 Oona King, *Guardian*, 12 June 2003.

21 John Pilger, *New Statesman*, 20 September 2004.

22 Max Hastings, *Guardian*, 6 September 2004.

23 Tim Butcher, *BBC News Online*, 14 May 2005.

24 BBC Radio 4, *From Our Own Correspondent*, 30 October 2004.

25 Tom Gross, "Living in a Bubble: The BBC's Very Own Mideast Foreign Policy," *National Review Online*, 18 June 2004.

26 *New Statesman*, vol. 17, no. 799 (22 March 2004), reproduced in *Morn-*

ing Star, 20 March 2004; David Rich, *The Barriers Come Down: Anti-semitism and Coalitions of Extremes* (JPR/Institute for Jewish Policy Research, 2003).

27 Simon Jenkins, *Times*, 2 July 2004.

28 Simon Jenkins, *Sunday Times*, 19 February 2006.

29 Rich, *The Barriers Come Down*.

30 *The New Dawn* (monthly newsletter of the Muslim Association of Britain), no. 2 (October–November 2000); also General Union of Palestinian Students leaflet, "Prophecy of Benjamin Franklin in Regard of the Jewish Race," distributed at Manchester University, March 2002; in Rich, *The Barriers Come Down*.

31 *Palestine Times*, November 2002; in Rich, *The Barriers Come Down*.

32 Nick Griffin, "Back to the Future," *Identity*, no. 26 (November 2002); in Rich, *The Barriers Come Down*.

33 British National Party website, http://www.bnp.org.uk/news/2003_march/news_mar15.htm, 19 March 2003; in Rich, *The Barriers Come Down*.

34 Muslim Council of Britain website, http://www.mcb.org.uk/presstext.php?ann_id=33, 20 March 2003; in Rich, *The Barriers Come Down*.

35 BBC TV *Newsnight*, 14 July 2005.

36 Anas al-Tikriti, *Guardian*, 23 March 2004.

37 Azzam Tammimi, *Guardian*, 7 January 2005.

38 Osama Saeed, *Guardian*, 23 July 2005.

39 Sohaib Saeed, *Guardian*, 9 July 2004.

40 Max Hastings, *Guardian*, 20 September 2004.

41 Interview with military historian, 2005.

42 Ted Honderich, *After the Terror*, expanded and revised ed. (Edinburgh University Press, 2003).

43 Ben Hall, *Financial Times*, 24 January 2004.

44 Nigel Morris, *Independent*, 21 June 2002.

45 David Clark, *Guardian*, 20 June 2002.

46 Nigel Morris, *Independent*, 21 June 2002.

47 Canon Paul Oestreicher, letter to *Guardian*, 21 May 2004.

48 Melanie Phillips, *Jewish Chronicle*, 14 April 2005.

49 Correspondence with author, June 2005.

50 Melanie Phillips, *Observer*, 22 February 2004.

51 Interview with editor, 2005.

52 Interview with member of House of Lords, 2005.

53 *Sun*, 15 April 2002.

CHAPTER 8: ON THEIR KNEES BEFORE TERROR

1 Maev Kennedy, *Guardian*, 11 July 2005.
2 Christopher Morgan, *Sunday Times*, 4 September 2005.
3 Peter Mullen, "Farewell, Church of England?" *New Criterion*, September 2005.
4 Interview with bishop, 2005.
5 Mullen, "Farewell, Church of England?"
6 Lord Carey, interview with author, 2005.
7 Ruth Gledhill, *The Times*, 1 November 2005.
8 Steve Doughty, *Daily Mail*, 23 November 2005.
9 Lord Carey, Canon Andrew White, interviews with author, 2005.
10 Rowan Williams, *The Times*, 8 December 2005.
11 "Christianity and Islam: Collision or Convergence?" address by Lord Carey, Gregorian University, Rome, 25 March 2004.
12 Ibid.
13 Lord Carey interview.
14 Ibid.
15 Rowan Williams, *Writing in the Dust: Reflections on 11th September and Its Aftermath* (Hodder & Stoughton, 2002).
16 Ibid.
17 Archbishop of Canterbury's sermon, service of remembrance for soldiers killed in Iraq, 10 October 2003.
18 Archbishop of Canterbury's lecture to Royal Institute of International Affairs, 14 October 2003.
19 Archbishop of Canterbury's address at Al-Azhar Al-Sharif, Cairo, 11 September 2004.
20 Canon Andrew White, interview with author, 2005.
21 *Countering Terrorism: Power, Violence and Democracy Post 9/11*, a report by a working group of the Church of England's House of Bishops, September 2005.
22 Ibid.
23 Ibid.
24 Stephen Bates, *Guardian*, 1 July 2004.
25 Canon Andrew White interview.
26 See successive issues of *Christian Aid News*; also *Facts on the Ground: The End of the Two-State Solution?* October 2004.
27 Canon Andrew White interview.
28 Archbishop of Wales, "Religion and Conflict in Recent International Events," UNA (United Nations Association) Lecture, 20 November 2003; at www.churchinwales.org/uk/archbishop/b0002e.html
29 Press release, Church in Wales, 11 November 2004.
30 Anglican Peace and Justice Network, *A Report of Its Deliberations in Jerusalem, September 14–22, 2004*.
31 Ruth Gledhill, *Times*, 7 February 2006.

32 *Jewish Chronicle*, 17 February 2006.

33 Interview by Julia Fisher with Bishop Riah Abu el-Assal, 26 January 2002, St. George's Cathedral, Jerusalem.

34 Naim Ateek, *Justice and Only Justice: A Palestinian Theology of Liberation* (Orbis, 1989).

35 Robert Everett and Dexter Van Zile, *Jerusalem Post*, 24 June 2005.

36 Colin Chapman, *Whose Promised Land?* revised ed. (Lion, 1989).

37 Canon Andrew White and Lord Carey interviews.

38 Melanie Phillips, *Spectator*, 16 February 2002; Canon Andrew White interview.

39 Phillips, *Spectator*; interview with Dr. John Gladwyn, 2005.

40 Phillips, *Spectator*; interview with Dr. Stephen Sizer, 2005.

41 Canon Andrew White, Terence Prittie Lecture, 2001.

42 Canon Andrew White interview.

43 Lord Carey interview.

CHAPTER 9: THE APPEASEMENT OF CLERICAL FASCISM

1 Tony Blair speech, 16 July 2005.

2 Anne Perkins, *Guardian*, 28 September 2001.

3 Robert Winnett, *Sunday Times*, 18 September 2005.

4 Tania Brannigan, *Guardian*, 22 August 2005.

5 Downing Street press conference, 5 August 2005.

6 Marie Woolf, *Independent*, 11 August 2005.

7 George Jones, *Daily Telegraph*, 17 February 2006

8 Richard Ford, *The Times*, 20 December 2005.

9 *Three Month Pre-Charge Detention*, Home Office, 5 October 2005.

10 Faisal Bodi, *Guardian*, 5 May 2005.

11 Dr. Michael Nazir-Ali, interview with author, 2005.

12 Anton la Guardia, *Daily Telegraph*, 15 November 2002.

13 *BBC News Online*, 17 September 2005.

14 *Guardian*/ICM poll, March 2004.

15 *Hansard*, 4 July 2001, cols. 91–111.

16 *Manchester Evening News*, 19 April 2005.

17 *Hansard*, as above.

18 Ibid.

19 Greg Hurst, *The Times*, 22 November 2003.

20 Ibid.

21 Mike O'Brien, "Labour and British Muslims: Can We Dream the Same Dream?" *Muslim Weekly*, no. 61 (7–13 January 2005).

22 Ibid.

23 Ibid.

24 Hani Mohammad, *Islam Online*, 28 December 2004.

25 Interviews with British officials, 2005.

26 Osama bin Laden, "Letter to the American People," transcript published

in *Observer*, 24 November 2002.

27 Simon Walters, *Mail on Sunday*, 8 January 2006.

28 Letter from Sir Andrew Turnbull to John Gieve, 6 April 2004; *Observer*, 4 September 2005.

29 Letter from Sir Andrew Turnbull to John Gieve.

430 Letter from John Gieve to Sir Andrew Turnbull, 10 May 2004.

31 *Draft Report on Young Muslims and Extremism*, Foreign and Commonwealth Office/Home Office, April 2004.

32 Ibid.

33 Ibid.

34 Ibid.

35 Memo by Mockbul Ali, Foreign Office, 14 July 2005.

36 Ibid.

37 *Guardian Unlimited*, 19 July 2005.

38 Michael White, *Guardian*, 27 July 2005.

39 Jason Lewis, *Mail on Sunday*, 11 September 2005.

40 Padraic Flanagan, *Daily Express*, 12 September 2005.

41 Alasdair Palmer, *Sunday Telegraph*, 21 August 2005.

42 *Islam in Britain*, Institute for the Study of Islam and Christianity, 2005.

43 Inayat Bunglawala, in *Trends*, vol. 4, no. 4.

44 Ibid.

45 Inayat Bunglawala, in *Trends*, vol. 3, no. 7.

46 Ian Evans, *The Times*, 12 July 2005.

47 Olivier Guitta, "Tariq Ramadan Is Not a Victim," *American Thinker*, 22 December 2004.

48 Caroline Fourest, *Wall Street Journal*, 2 February 2005.

49 Guitta, "Tariq Ramadan Is Not a Victim."

50 Padraic Flanagan, *Daily Express*, 12 September 2005.

51 *"Preventing Extremism Together" Working Groups*, August–October 2005, Home Office.

52 Ibid.

53 Charles Clarke, interview with author, 2005.

54 Ibid.

55 Ibid.

56 Letter from William Ehrman to Sir David Omand, 23 April 2004; *Observer*, 4 September 2005.

57 Colin McColl, *Intelligence, Politics and the War on Terror*; Sir Robert Southey Winter Conversazione, 2004.

58 Ibid.

59 Ibid.

60 Peter Oborne, *Spectator*, 23 September 2005.

61 Ibid.

62 Ibid.

63 Jamie Doward, *Observer*, 11 December 2005.

64 Ibid.

65 Ibid.
66 *BBC News Online*, 30 December 2005.
67 Caroline Gammell and Aislinn Simpson, Press Association, 30 December 2005.

CONCLUSION

 1 Jason Burke, *Observer*, 13 November 2005.
 2 Rod Liddle, *Spectator*, 12 November 2005.
 3 Ibid.
 4 Colin Nickerson, *Boston Globe*, 6 November 2005.
 5 Charles Bremner, *The Times*, 8 November 2005.
 6 Tim Priest, "The Rise of Middle Eastern Crime in Australia," *Quadrant*, vol. 48, no. 1 (January–February 2004).
 7 Abd al-Hamid al-Ansari, *Al-Hayat*, 2 August 2004.
 8 Aisha Siddiqa Qureshi, *Muslim World Today*, 27 August 2004.
 9 Mansoor Ijaz, *Financial Times*, 11 July 2005.
10 Anthony Glees and Chris Pope, *When Students Turn to Terror: Terrorist and Extremist Activity on British Campuses* (Social Affairs Unit, 2005).
11 Dr. Ghayasuddin Siddiqui, interview with author, 2005.
12 Paul Sperry, "The Pentagon Breaks the Islam Taboo," *FrontPageMagazine.com*, 14 December 2005.

INDEX

The factions

intellectuals   entertainment
political   movies   writers : movies
judicial   Books   TV shows
                       magazines   newspapers
                       plays   satire shows
                       articles   shock jocks
                       television:
                         drama   news talk shows
xii - ummah   news   morning TV shows — the 'view', etc.
                         talk shows celebrities
the culprits p.23   education   Hollywood ~~circles~~ circles
                       primary
Human Rights Law   university

The Anglican   A society that has lost
Church   its way p. 51
  a state church   Salafi & Wahhabi
  Lost its moral compass
          p. 148   Islam vs other religions
                                                    p 142
                                      British public opinion p118

Labor Party   Antonio Gramsci p.118

July 2005 - Subway attack   secularism   ⎰ destruction
— Current political status - post 2006? radical Islamism ⎱   of
                                            p141   Christian-
British loss of national self-belief ~~...~~   ity
        p. XIX

Establishment
    &   social liberalism
Politicians   trans - national (nation-states)
                                      organizations: communism
Britain and streak   Islam
  of appeasement?
i.e. '1936', this volume. p.124,48   motive for Islamic extremism —
                                      tyranny of the Jewish state
periods of appeasement?   or
response to a shock - WWI ?   ~~...~~ expansionist nature of
or loss of empire and status ?   Islam